Production Planning and Repro Mechanicals for Offset Printing

Production Planning and Repro Mechanicals for Offset Printing

The First Updated User's Manual Including Phototypsetting and New Press Production Planning

Henry C. Latimer

McGraw-Hill Book Company

New York St. Louis San Francisco
Auckland Bogotá Hamburg Johannesburg
London Madrid Mexico Montreal
New Delhi Panama Paris São Paulo
Singapore Sydney Toyko Toronto

Library of Congress Cataloging in Publication Data

Latimer, Henry C
    Production planning and repro mechanicals for offset
printing.

    Previous editions published under title: Advertising pro-
duction planning and copy preparation for offset printing.
    Includes index.
    1. ˋOffset printing.   2. Advertising layout and
typography.   I. Title.
Z252.5.05L35   1980   686.2'315   79-15293
ISBN 0-07-036621-7

1234567890   HDHD   89876543210

The editors for this book were W. Hodson Mogan and
Beatrice E. Eckes, the designer was Edward J. Fox, and the
production supervisor was Teresa F. Leaden. It was set in
Palatino by University Graphics.

Printed and bound by Halliday Lithograph Corporation.

Contents

Foreword

PREVIOUS EDITIONS OF THIS USER'S MANUAL were titled *Advertising Production Planning and Copy Preparation for Offset Printing*. Because this book is now entering its tenth year of use by working professionals in the art departments of advertisers and their agencies as well as in publication editorial departments, the extent of the new procedures resulting from new technology—photocomposition methods and new applications of minicomputers and electronics for full-color illustrations, together with new cost factors in determining the most efficient press size for a job— called for a new manual and title rather than an attempt to update the material in previous editions.

Printing is said to be in its third revolution because of the introduction of automated phototypesetting and composition systems. Following the development of very sophisticated systems for typographers and large-volume producers, the trend now is to simple, direct-entry typesetters operated by a typist in an art or advertising department. Also, when the volume is sufficient, there are computerized typesetting systems costing less than $16,000 that produce galley repro proofs for repro mechanicals prepared in the art department.

A recent development is the use of the keyboard product of word-processing systems (the various types of magnetic media) for phototypesetting to avoid duplication of work. Art studios and agencies are installing complete phototype systems to take advantage of the economies available.

Not generally known outside the trade is the fact that most commercial art departments have taken over the desired production personnel because time and cost factors are now controlled in the creative planning stage. By the time that rough layouts have been approved, all production details have been decided.

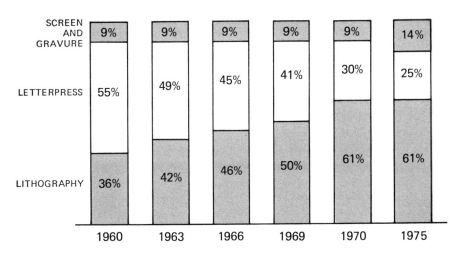

Use of printing processes for commercial printing. [Source: U.S. Bureau of the Census]

The Technical Association of the Pulp and Paper Industry (TAPPI) noted the change. A survey of 2400 art departments revealed that besides buying paper and composition, art was buying or specifying plates and color separations and that 66 percent of the departments were buying or specifying the printer.

In drawing up a bid list for suitable printers for a particular printing job it is important to determine the efficient press size and model for the quantity wanted. Formerly, when the quantity of pieces (the size of the order) increased, a larger press size was found to be more efficient. The number of pieces at which this change occurred was the "breaking point" in press efficiency. Five charts in earlier editions of this manual helped to determine which offset press size was most efficient for a particular job. The cost factors were the preparatory cost, the hourly press time cost, and the number of hours during which the press ran. Press speeds and the number of sheets printed in a 7-hour shift were about the same for all press sizes. This has changed.

The reason was the introduction of smaller and faster offset presses, both single-color and multicolor, with personnel schedules that permit two operators instead of three to handle quite a range of press sizes for both single- and two-color printing. Production speeds of the smaller and faster presses have increased by about 50 percent. Sheet-fed offset presses larger than 60 inches (1524 millimeters) have become obsolete. The large eight-unit (17- by 22-inch, or 432- by 559-millimeter, unit) multicolor sheet-fed offset presses are now used mainly for die-cut packaging. Advertising color printing has shifted to offset web (roll) presses because of their much higher press speeds and the economy of the in-line binding and folding operations.

This offset manual gives the user the how-to steps of offset production from the creative planning stage to the finished printed product, taking advantage of the freedom of time plate estimating, of the use of intermediate photo steps between original artwork and that for the camera (art production), and of the extra capabilities of the offset process.

This manual also provides the needed educational material for graduates of art courses whose instruction has not been relevant to the requirements of graphic arts reproduction. TAPPI's survey of 2400 art directors rated art graduates' training as follows:

	Adequate	Inadequate
Elementary production knowledge	117	414
Preparing mechanicals	121	414
Typeface selection	106	431
Type specification	52	484
Rough and comprehensive layouts	289	248

Credit is due both to the Printing Industry of Metropolitan New York and the National Association of Printers and Lithographers for contemporary data on offset press production and also to George C. Adams for assistance in updating.

HENRY C. LATIMER

Production Planning and Repro Mechanicals for Offset Printing

1

THE PRINTING PROCESSES

Offset Printing (Commercial Lithography) and letterpress are the two processes that are used for the great bulk of commercial printing, while rotogravure and silk-screen printing are responsible for only a relatively small volume. Flexographic (rubber-plate) printing is a form of letterpress used for some types of packaging and for book printing. Infrequent use is made of sheet-fed gravure because of its high cost and of commercial collotype (gelatin) printing because of limited production from one set of plates. Rotogravure is particularly well suited to long press-runs of photographic reproduction.

To present offset printing in its proper perspective for production planning and copy preparation, it is desirable to make a comparison with the methods and cost factors of the other major processes, particularly letterpress, since this process is so well known. All the processes use copy prepared for the camera and work with photographic negatives and positives for the combining and positioning of copy elements, and all employ photomechanical platemaking techniques. Letterpress, however, is the only one which prints from an assembly of metal type and plates or of plates (electrotypes, or electros, or stereotypes) alone. All the other processes print from a one-piece plate of the printing form or its equivalent. Offset, sheet-fed gravure, and commercial collotype use a thin sheet of metal which is clamped around the press plate cylinder. Rotogravure uses a copper-surfaced press cylinder. Silk-screen printing uses a stencil of the printing form.

PAGE AND FORM MAKEUP

For everything except type and rules, letterpress requires plates. Type, rules, and plates are assembled and positioned to make up each page. Except for short-run work, printing is usually done from duplicates (electros) of the made-up pages, which are positioned according to the binder's imposition to make up the printing form. Final positioning for register (lockup) and adjustment of pressures on plate areas (makeready) are accomplished on the press before printing can start.

In offset, gravure, and the other processes using the principle of the one-piece printing form, on the other hand, pages are made up on the drawing board with clean proofs or film of type matter instead of the actual metal type and with scaled photographs or art instead of engravings. (Or an outline may be used to indicate the position and size of photos or art.) This is called copy in paste-up form. Photographic negatives or positives of these page paste-ups are positioned on a large sheet of special goldenrod paper to make up the flat, the equivalent of a letterpress form. After the paper under all image areas has been cut and removed, contact (photographic) printing of this flat on the light-sensitized coating of the offset press plate, followed by developing operations, produces a press plate of the whole form in one piece. Both gravure and silk-screen printing employ a flat made with photographic positives, but the principle of the one-piece form is used: a printing cylinder is etched in gravure, and a stencil

Fig. 1-1 An offset press plate being clamped around the press cylinder. This is equivalent to a letterpress form.

is made photographically for silk-screen printing.

In letterpress, a photoengraver's flat is an assembly of individual halftone negatives on a large piece of glass ready to be contact-printed to the light-sensitized plate metal prior to the etching of the metal. The large metal engraving is subsequently cut apart to create the individual engravings. However, the one-piece form is now being used in letterpress with the new plastic relief plates.

SIMILARITY OF INITIAL PLATEMAKING PROCEDURES

In platemaking, the term "copy" refers to copy for the camera; it includes everything to be reproduced: type proofs, photolettering,

rules done with a drawing pen, photostat reverses, photos, and all forms of art. Copy for the camera is of two kinds, line and tone. For all three major processes line copy is photographed without the halftone screen on high-contrast film. The resulting negative is clear in the image parts and black elsewhere. Tone copy involves shades of gray or color as in photos, wash drawings, watercolor and oil paintings, and photo color prints and transparencies. To reproduce tone copy, both letterpress and offset use the halftone method and high-contrast film. The copy is photographed through a halftone screen in the camera.

The screen breaks the continuous-tone copy into a series of dots. A 133-line screen, for example, creates 17,689 dots in a square inch. The dots vary in size depending on the intensity of the light reflected from the spot on the copy to which they correspond. Light areas reflect strong light waves and expose large dots on the negative. Darker areas reflect less intense light and expose smaller dots to the negative film. The same number of dots per square inch is produced in shadow and highlight areas. The size of the dots and the clean film space between them determine the strength of the tone on the negative. When printed in positive form, large dots with little space between them create dark tones. Small black dots with much white paper between them cause the human eye to mix much white with little black and see light gray.

Gravure uses a system of ink "wells" of varying depth etched into the copper printing cylinder. The deeper wells hold more translucent ink and reproduce the darker tones of the subjects. The shallow wells deposit less translucent ink and produce the lighter tones. The paper employed for gravure permits the ink to spread. Gravure requires continuous-tone positives, contact-printed from the continuous-tone negatives of the camera, just like snapshot negatives. The light-sensitive emulsion used for preparing the printing image to be etched on the cylinder is exposed to light through a grid screen and the flat of positives. The grid forms the sides of the ink wells, and the tones of the positives determine the depth of the wells for both tone and line copy.

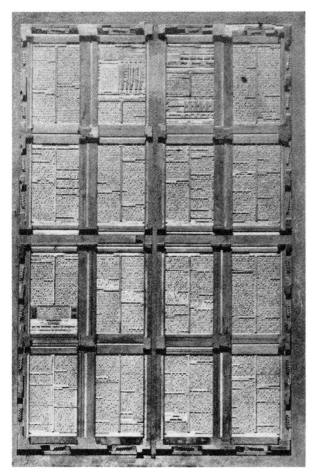

Fig. 1-2 A letterpress form of type and plates in a chase. It is used for shorter pressruns on a flatbed type of press.

Fig. 1-4 An offset flat, or printing form, made with photographic negatives positioned on special goldenrod paper or red plastic film. From this the press plate is made. The equivalent of letterpress imposition and lockup is handled in the platemaking operation. [*Courtesy Du Pont Photo Products*]

Fig. 1-3 A large book form of type and cuts positioned on the bed of the press.

Fig. 1-5 The plate cylinder with a nest of ink rollers above and the offset cylinder below. Not visible below is the impression cylinder, which presses the paper against the offset cylinder. [*Courtesy Dayton Rubber Co.*]

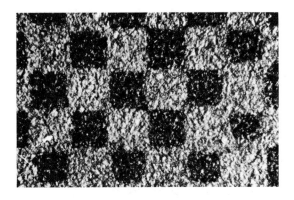

Fig. 1-6   *Offset:* The formation of a printing image which is developed to make it ink-receptive and to make the nonprinting areas ink-repellent. This is a planographic (single-plane) type of press plate, which resembles a black print on a large sheet of thin gray metal.

Fig. 1-7   *Photoengraving:* The formation of the printing image in an acid-resist coating which permits the subsequent etching operations to eat away the nonprinting areas of the metal, leaving the image in relief on the surface. On the press only the plate surface accepts ink.

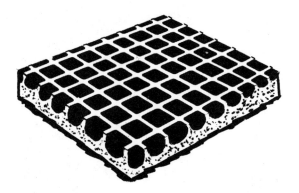

Fig. 1-8   *Gravure:* A resist image on gelatin of varying thickness which governs the depth of the etching operation in the ink wells. The thicker the gelatin resist layer, the less acid penetration and etching on the cylinder, the shallower the well, and the lighter the tone printed. The lighter areas of the copy reflect intense light to the camera and ultimately create a thick, hardened layer of gelatin. In the shadow areas, less intense light creates thinner hard-gelatin resist areas, permits greater acid penetration in etching, and creates deep wells which hold more translucent ink and produce darker tones. This is a form of intaglio plate with the printing image below the surface on the press; a scraper blade removes the ink from the cylinder surface.

Action of Light on Plate Coatings

For the plates of the three major printing processes the assembly of negatives or positives to be contact-printed by the action of light on the plate coatings results in the images shown in Figs. 1-6, 1-7, and 1-8.

Offset and Letterpress Tone Control

Although both offset and photoengraving use the halftone method, the engraver's negative is made with a preliminary halftone dot structure which permits a lateral reduction in size when the metal is etched by the acid. This procedure, which is called "reetching," lightens tones by reducing dot size. Thus much letterpress plate tone control is done on the metal plate.

For offset, the halftone negative is made with the final tones for reproduction. Tone correction is accomplished on film, as described in Chapters 7 and 10. This difference is very important because it is responsible for some of the unique capabilities and techniques of the offset process.

HOW OFFSET PLATE COSTS
ARE ESTIMATED

The general practice with offset producers is to have a *base plate charge* for each press size in their shops. This charge includes the unit line negatives, the stripping of these negatives to make the flat, and the exposure and development of the press plate. The procedure is equivalent to letterpress form imposition and lockup. Offset makeready consists of adjusting the press for the job and the paper.

Each shop develops the base plate cost by averaging the time required to strip the number of 8½- by 11-inch (216- by 279-millimeter) negatives that will go on the plate: four units on a 17- by 22-inch (432- by 559-millimeter) plate, eight units on a 23- by 36-inch (584- by 914-millimeter) plate, and so on. If units are small or large, the base plate cost is adjusted for time required. An adjustment is also made for multiple imposition: an eight-unit flat, two up on the plate, takes less time than stripping sixteen separate negatives.

An exception to this base plate charge is made when a step-and-repeat machine is used instead of a flat to put multiple images on a press plate. In this case the cost is a setup charge plus the time required to put the number of images on the press plate. The cost per image is nominal and varies little with size.

Unlike the price for letterpress, the price quoted for an offset printing job includes the cost equivalent of halftone and line engravings and electros. The price is not usually broken down to show plate costs as a separate item. For process color or a large number of halftones, a quotation is usually made "subject to seeing copy" even though an estimate has been made from a dummy or a description of copy.

For routine single-color work the price quoted is for "copy ready for the camera." This means camera copy supplied as units (mechanicals) with any separate copy elements as specified when the bid was requested.

With all processes except letterpress, plate costs are estimated on the basis of time, the time required for camera work, stripping, opaquing, exposure, and developing the press plate or cylinder. For this reason copy is supplied in paste-up form, usually as a unit of the complete page or layout including text and other type matter. Copy for the camera is prepared so as to save platemaking time and thus keep plate costs to a minimum. Size is a minor factor in plate costs.

With the time estimating method there are no economic restrictions on same-focus economies, and tone copy such as photos and artwork is planned for photographing in groups or in position on a mechanical paste-up regardless of the number of subjects or the reproduction size. There are no automatic premium charges for special types of halftones or forms of art; additional costs are incurred only for the extra time which may be required.

How do offset halftones compare in cost with photoengravings? For a single square halftone the cost is apt to be about the same except for large sizes, for which offset is usually less expensive. Special types of halftones (silhouette, highlight dropout, combination line-and-tone, and so on), which incur double- or triple-scale charges in photoengraving, usually cost less in offset. The economy in offset halftone costs is due to planning for group handling of tone elements. For example, if six tone elements are proportioned or are scaled and positioned on a paste-up, one camera exposure handles all of them, and the time is spread over the group. If the elements are positioned, stripping time is avoided. This also holds true for process color in offset. Instead of using electro duplicates, offset puts multiple images on the press plate by multiple exposure of the unit negative. Multiple imposition is handled by repositioning the flat and exposing it on the press plate as many times as are necessary. The time required for the additional exposure of the unit or flat, not the size of the unit or flat, is the cost factor.

REPRODUCTION QUALITIES OF COPY
FOR THE CAMERA THE SAME FOR
ALL PROCESSES

Copy for the camera—material suitable for reproduction and the copy preparation techniques—is the same for all the major processes. If a photoengraver can get a good negative from the copy supplied, so can the other processes; all the processes use "keylining" techniques to simplify copy preparation and

Fig. 1-9

to indicate work to be completed by the platemaker. They all work with film to position elements, combine line and tone work, surprint, and provide for color register when it is indicated or necessary.

The form in which copy is supplied, however, usually differs for offset and gravure because of plate costs. For letterpress, because of these costs copy ordinarily is not prepared for a combination line-and-tone engraving except for magazine color plates. For offset and gravure, in contrast, practically all copy is prepared for combination plates, and copy elements including process color are proportioned for group handling since there are no economic restrictions on plate economies with such copy. An exception with letterpress is the Dycril type of engravings; these are estimated on a time basis and not by the Photoengravers' Standard Scale.

COLOR CORRECTION

As is generally known, all the printing processes have the problem of color correction because of the limitations of ink pigments to three process colors and black, as compared with the wider color range of the artist's palette and of color photography. In photoengraving color correction is done on the metal of the plates by etching and burnishing to change dot size, whereas in offset and gravure color correction is handled on the photographic color separation films. The latter method permits step-and-repeat multiple images of process color work and multiple plate sizes from one set of separations, thus affording an important economy in plate costs. Photographic masking and electronic scanning methods have eliminated most of the handwork (dot etching) in color correction.

DUPLICATE PLATES; MULTIPLE IMPOSITION

In letterpress, the original engravings are not generally used for the actual printing. Electros (duplicates) are made of the whole plate to avoid damage or wear to originals and to permit the use of a patent base for fastening the plates on the press and avoiding work-ups with type in a chase. The cost of electros increases with their size.

For all but short-run work printing is usu-

ally done in multiples: several copies (not just one) will be printed on a sheet.

Duplicates for Offset

For offset the equivalent of original engravings consists of photographic negatives and positives. Contact prints can provide duplicates when needed, but since these are not used for the actual printing, duplicates are put on the press plates by one of two methods:

1. *Multiple images.* When the same piece (label, coupon, magazine insert, or the like) is to be printed in multiples, such as ninety-six labels on a sheet, a step-and-repeat machine is used to expose the same negative on the press plate over and over again in register to 1/1000 inch (0.0254 millimeter). The cost per image is nominal and varies little with size.

2. *Multiple imposition.* When a job involves several pages or other copy units, the flat is exposed several times on a large press plate. In the case of an eight-page booklet printed two on, the time cost for exposing the eight-page flat a second time is not as high as the cost of electros and the additional lockup and makeready in letterpress.

FORM LOCKUP AND MAKEREADY

Although users are not printers, they are vitally concerned with printing costs in their planning with letterpress. They must consider the number of hours during which a press is held standing while it is made ready to run, for they must pay for the time. The major preparatory cost in letterpress is the time required for form imposition and lockup and for makeready: the positioning of type and plates for layout of the form and for register with two or more colors and the adjustment of pressures for plate areas (overlay and underlay) for proper impression on the paper. Whether for 5000 or 50,000 sheets, this press preparatory time is the same.

One printing efficiency engineer[1] who has

[1]J. W. Rockefeller, Jr., *Report to the Printing Industry* (New York, 1949).

performed time-study work on letterpress preparatory operations states that lockup and form makeready take more than 90 percent of the preparatory time and that only 8 percent is required for press adjustments.

OFFSET PRESS MAKEREADY

With offset and the other one-piece–plate processes, the equivalent of form lockup (positioning for layout and register) is handled when the flat is stripped. In offset there is no form makeready in the usual sense: the rubber-surfaced offset cylinder compensates for any slight difference in the pressures of the plate.

In offset the term "makeready" applies to press adjustments: the 8 percent of letterpress preparatory time. Roughly, this amounts to about 1 hour per cylinder except for large presses and 2 hours per cylinder for multicolor presses. Not more than 10 hours of makeready usually is required for a large four-color offset press on process work.

PRESS IMPRESSIONS PER HOUR

Most letterpress commercial printing is done on sheet-fed cylinder presses. These operate on the reciprocating flatbed principle, printing every other revolution: the first revolution inks the form, and the second presses the paper against the form. Actual running speeds are governed by the size of the form, the number and type of halftones, and the quality required. One industry production standard gives 2500 impressions per hour (iph) for a 17- by 22-inch (432- by 559-millimeter) size for average commercial work and 900 iph for high-grade work on a 46¼- by 61½-inch (1175- by 1562-millimeter) two-color cylinder press. Large forms sacrifice press speeds with flatbed presses.

Rotary letterpresses are much faster, for they print every revolution. Because of high preparatory and plate costs (curved electros

are required), they are used only for long-run work. One producer specified 75,000 sheets as the minimum practical run for a two-color rotary. The smallest conventional rotary press is listed as 36 by 48 inches (914 by 1219 millimeters).

Offset Press Speeds

All offset presses are rotary in principle, printing every revolution. The new small presses, both single-color and multicolor, are capable of speeds up to 8000 and 10,000 sheets per hour (sph), but for a variety of reasons, they will not average more than 5000 sph on a 7-hour shift, particularly for process color printing.

Offset web (roll-fed) presses have replaced the large sheet-fed multicolor presses, particularly if folding is involved, for these presses do the folding. The web offset have speeds of 25,000 or 30,000 iph, printing both sides of the paper, and are available for from two to ten colors.

PAPER SURFACE AND TONE REPRODUCTION

The usual restrictions on the fineness of halftone screens suitable for different types of printing paper apply only to letterpress. Offset has the ability to print the finest halftones and process color on uncoated as well as on coated papers. Halftone screens coarser than 133-line are not used except for posters by projection; a 150-line screen is now standard for single-color work with many shops, and 175-line screens are used by offset for commercial process color work.

Because offset can reproduce fine halftone work on rough-textured papers, a wide variety of text, antique-finish, cover, and bristol papers are now available in addition to uncoated and coated offset papers. The various bonds, vellums, and ledgers have always been suitable for offset because of their surface sizing.

CHANGED PICTURE IN THE PRINTING INDUSTRY

Large users of printing and manufacturers of printing equipment have done much research to develop faster methods and lower costs. The results can best be applied to photochemical platemaking methods and to photocom-

position. Process color reproduction in all the major printing processes was greatly changed by the use of photographic masking to replace handwork in preliminary color correction and of electronic scanning machines to make color separations. The development of reproduction-quality color photoprints and transparencies was also an important factor in the new procedures used. As the all-purpose photomechanical process, offset printing benefited the most from these developments.

PHOTOTYPESETTING

Recent years have brought a variety of phototypesetting equipment, including many types computerized for typeface, type size, measure, spacing, and hyphenation. A typist operates a keyboard that perforates a paper tape. This tape is fed into the computer unit, which produces a second tape that is fed into the phototypesetting machine to produce type proofs on paper or film. Instead of tapes, magnetic disks which can be read by computers are also produced. The most recent development in phototype is optical character recognition (OCR), which avoids manual keyboard operation.

CREATIVE USE OF KNOWLEDGE OF PRINTING PRODUCTION

A knowledge of the printing process being used is helpful in choosing art media and in production planning. Both are governed to a large extent by the capabilities of the process and the method of estimating costs. Good planning, including the selection of the printing process, takes advantage of the procedures and techniques of the process and the equipment available.

Offset printing is also known as offset lithography, photo-offset lithography, photo-offset, photolithography, and planography. Whatever the term used, the basic process is lithography, invented by Aloys Senefelder in 1798 and based on the fact that grease and water repel each other.

EARLY LITHOGRAPHY

In the early form of lithography, an artist worked with a greasy lithographic crayon or ink directly on a slab of limestone. To get an impression, the artist sponged the stone off with an aqueous solution of gum arabic and acid etch and then rolled it up with a greasy litho ink. With the paper in position, the stone was passed under a scraper bar to apply pressure, and an inked impression of the design was produced on the paper. The greasy design on the stone refused the aqueous solution, but the nonprinting areas retained a wet film. The ink from the roller stuck to the image but did not adhere to the wet nonprinting areas.

Thus there developed a planographic type of printing plate that depended on a chemical rather than a mechanical means of inking the printing image. By repeating the operation, as many copies of the image could be made as desired.

Senefelder also invented a special transfer paper with soluble coating. With this paper, proofs of type matter or proofs from a small litho designer's stone could be transferred to the large printing stone. Thus illustrations finer than woodcuts could be included with text, or designs could be printed in multiples.

Fig. 1-10 The back of a large color camera with a circular halftone screen in place, located in the darkroom. Photography and photomechanical equipment are the essence of the producer's preparatory operations.

LINE COPY

TYPE   clean proofs used

PEN

BRUSH

CRAYON

WOLFF PENCIL

ROSS BOARD

SCRATCH BOARD

TONE SHEETS

REPRINTS   y no cost for line
at the printing is

TONE COPY

THE TWO KINDS
OF CAMERA COPY

Fig. 1-11 *Left:* Line copy, any copy which can be reproduced without the halftone screen. The entire copy is solid, lacking intermediate tones, as in a pen-and-ink drawing. *Right:* Tone copy, any copy requiring the halftone screen. It consists of intermediate gray tones, as in a photographic print.

Individual transfer proofs, positioned on a large sheet of paper, corresponded to a printer's form, and the whole assembly of pages or multiple designs could be transferred to the printing stone by means of a transfer press.

Much later came the development of fine color lithography, in which a separate stone was used for each color. Keys were traced from original paintings and transferred to the printing stones. A litho artist, a copyist, then worked each required color with opaque inks on a separate stone. This was the original form of mechanical color separation, a technique still used today in making preseparated color art for the camera.

The flatbed stone litho press (44 by 64 inches, or 1118 by 1626 millimeters, was a standard size) became power-driven and then was superseded by the direct rotary litho press, which used a zinc sheet clamped around the printing cylinder in place of the

stone. The direct rotary, in turn, was replaced by the offset press (invented in 1904), which has an intermediate rubber-covered offset cylinder between the plate cylinder and the paper. This cylinder is the origin of the term "offset lithography," or "offset printing." The offset cylinder doubled and tripled press production. Later, when the halftone method came into general use, it was found that the offset cylinder with its rubber surface removed all restrictions on the reproduction of fine halftones on rough-textured papers. Offset printing is now done commercially with 300-line halftones on either coated or rough-textured papers.

THE OFFSET PRINTING PROCESS TODAY

Photographic platemaking methods are now used almost entirely instead of the old direct hand and transfer methods. Pages or other copy units are made up on the drawing board in paste-up form, generally by the user or the

THE PRINCIPLE OF THE OFFSET PROCESS

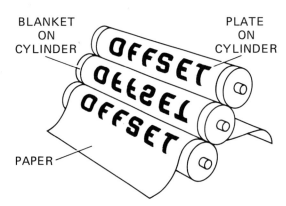

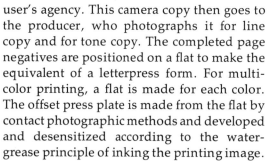

Fig. 1-12 Using the principle that grease and water do not mix in order to ink the printing image, the revolving plate cylinder first touches the dampening rollers and then the ink rollers. Water adheres only to the nongreasy, nonimage area. It repels ink, which adheres only to the greasy image, which is transferred to the offset cylinder and from there to the paper.

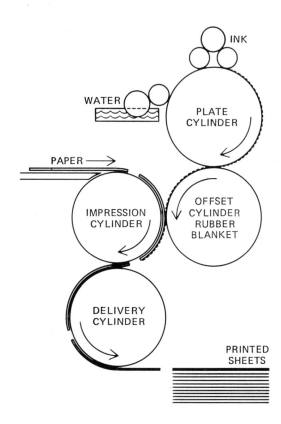

Fig. 1-13 The principle of the offset press.

user's agency. This camera copy then goes to the producer, who photographs it for line copy and for tone copy. The completed page negatives are positioned on a flat to make the equivalent of a letterpress form. For multi-color printing, a flat is made for each color. The offset press plate is made from the flat by contact photographic methods and developed and desensitized according to the water-grease principle of inking the printing image.

In contrast to letterpress production, offset producers make their own plates, giving them the control and responsibility of an integrated process.

LARGE CAMERAS, EXTRA-LARGE PROCESS PLATES

Offset uses large darkroom process cameras and cut film of different types and thicknesses. Popular camera sizes range from 24- to 48-inch-square (610- to 1219-millimeter-square) halftone screens, and circular-screen color cameras as large as 58 inches (1473 millimeters) are in use. Offset does not have the technical limitations of photoengraving in

etching large process plates and even uses projection to exceed camera sizes for posters and the like.

ELECTRONIC SCANNING MACHINES

In the search for faster methods electronic scanners were developed to make color separations of process color copy. A transparency or an assembly on film is wrapped around a glass cylinder that has a light beam which projects the colors. As the cylinder revolves, the colors are separated for the four-color process negatives. At present some models of the laser-beam scanner with computer make *screened* halftone color separations for offset in sizes up to 24 by 24 inches (610 by 610 millimeters). For larger sizes color cameras are used.

IMPORTANCE OF THE OFFSET HALFTONE NEGATIVE

The offset halftone negative differs from the photoengraver's negative, and this fact is important because it is responsible for some of the extra capabilities of the offset process. What a printing process can do, of course, is

A Process Camera

Figure 1-14 The 31-inch (787-millimeter) darkroom camera of Consolidated International Equipment Co. The back of the camera (left) is in the darkroom. Process cameras usually are capable of enlarging 5 times size and reducing 3 times.

How Tone Copy Is Reproduced by the Halftone Method

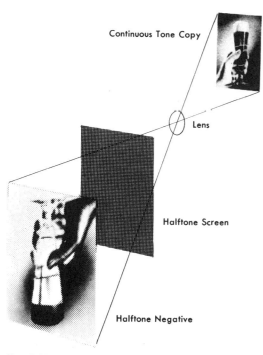

Continuous Tone Copy

Lens

Halftone Screen

Halftone Negative

Fig. 1-15 The glass halftone screen is positioned close to the film in the camera back, which becomes the halftone negative. The contact halftone screen, now standard with offset, is composed of minute vignette dots on a sheet of film. The light burns out the dot formation on the halftone negative, thus producing small and large halftone dots of tone copy.

important to a user who is planning production with it.

The offset camera operator works to get the *final* tones wanted in the halftone negative, whereas the photoengraver purposely only approaches the final tones in the halftone negative, for allowance must be made for the lateral reduction of the dots when the metal of the plate is etched with acid. If a photoengraver's halftone negative were used for offset, the halftone reproduction would be too dark because all the halftone dots would be too large.

Because the offset halftone negative or positive contains the final tones, enlargement or reduction is practical even for process color work, and multiple images can be put on the press plate by a step-and-repeat machine. Much of the handwork is also avoided in making special types of halftones (highlight dropout, vignette, outline) because the final tones are in the negatives. Camera copy can be masked for silhouette halftones.

CONTACT HALFTONE SCREEN

For single-color halftones, the magenta contact halftone screen is now widely used because of its tonal range. With this screen it is simple to drop out the background of pencil sketches and wash drawings; by manipulating the filter used and the exposure, much flat copy can be improved by adding contrast. For

Fig. 1-16 Halftone enlarged to show gradation of dots.

Enlarged Area of a Contact Screen

Fig. 1-17 The 150-line magenta contact halftone screen is standard in offset for black-and-white printing, and the 175-line gray screen is widely used for process color work. It is particularly good for highlight dropout printing, such as graphite pencil sketches.

Fig. 1-18 The invention of the process camera. [*Courtesy Pioneer-Moss Engraving Co.*]

process color, the gray contact screen can be used in addition to the conventional crossline glass screen. Here the 175-line contact screen is standard with many producers.

Electronic scanners are also widely used for simultaneous color separation and correction, the laser models producing *screened* color separations.

UNIT NEGATIVES FROM PASTE-UP COPY

Since copy for offset is supplied in paste-up form, either as a complete unit of text and illustrations or as a line copy unit with tone copy supplied as separate elements, there are many opportunities for composition and plate economies (covered in later chapters). A unit of line and tone copy can be photographed on the same film when a glass halftone screen is used. With the contact screen, separate line and halftone negatives are combined. When tone copy is supplied as separate elements, the individual halftone negatives are mortised into the base-line negative to complete the unit negative. This method produces the best quality.

Copy units may be single pages, (imposition) paired pages for booklets, or a whole broadside, poster, or the like.

OFFSET FLAT OR FORM

Imposition in offset is handled by positioning (stripping) the unit negatives on the goldenrod paper or plastic layout sheet of the printing form, a separate one being produced for each color. The same flat can be exposed on different areas of a larger press plate to provide multiple imposition, or two flats can be exposed on the same area to double-print (combine line and halftones) or expose all halftones separately from line copy, which is

Fig. 1-19 This Kodak magenta contact halftone screen is widely used for black-and-white work because of its wide tonal range.

Fig. 1-20 A transparent flat made with photographic positives for making a deep-etch plate, widely used for process color work and long pressruns. [*Courtesy Du Pont Photo Products*]

frequently done for catalogs.

For deep-etch plates, which are made from positives, the material of the flat must be transparent, and vinyl sheets are substituted for the goldenrod paper except with small forms. "Staging" (protecting) nonimage areas is required.

Color register for stripping is provided by a key layout guide made from the flat of the black plate, fastened on the glass stripping table, and illuminated from below.

OFFSET COLOR CORRECTION

In offset printing, screened color-corrected separations are generally made by the indirect method. First, a continuous-tone negative is made, and then from it a screened positive. Photographic masking is used for the negatives to handle most of the color correction, and the screened positives are dot-etched by hand for any additional correction. Dot etching consists of reducing the size of the dots on the film. It can be done in a tray or by applying a brush to specific areas. The dot or the film is denser at its core than at its perimeter, or halo. Chemical washing first removes the less dense outer portions of the dots. Because its dots are of uniform density from core to rim, the plate image is a precise record of the film image. Masking alone is sufficient for much process copy and saves time and cost.

MASKING METHODS

The use of photographic masks and filters has largely replaced the dot etching of positives for much color work. Some subjects can be handled well by masking methods alone, while others require dot etching for further color correction; this is a matter of color combinations and blending. For color at a low price, no handwork is used: the Eastman three-color automatic process designed for short-run (pleasing-picture) color work is based on masking and the use of the gray contact halftone screen.

After the four continuous-tone negatives (yellow, blue, red, and black) are completed by any method, each is placed in the transparency holder of the camera copyboard and photographed through the halftone screen to produce screened positives in reproduction size. Any further color correction is done by dot-etching the screened positives. When completed, each positive is positioned on the proper color flat by a stripper, guided by register marks on each copy element.

MULTIPLE PLATE SIZES

The same art is often required in many plate sizes for pieces entirely different in layout and copy. Any number of different-size positives can be made while the continuous-tone negative is mounted in the copyboard. All the required plate sizes of a subject are made from a single set of separation negatives. Color correction of this one set of negatives precludes dot-etching the multiple positives. Sizes needed may range from one smaller than a postcard to a twenty-four-sheet poster; all are made from one set of color separations.

ENLARGEMENT AND REDUCTION

In advertising production jobs frequently are needed in two or more sizes, for calendars, magazine inserts or cover ads, window strips, dealer material, and so on. For such needs offset can place the completed unit negatives or positives in the transparency holder and photograph up or down for size. Color separations can be made with heads or text in a particular color, and the whole job handled instead of just the artwork. In enlargement or reduction, the fineness of the halftone screen changes, but the tones of the illustrations do not.

THE PRESS PLATE

An offset press plate is a thin sheet of zinc or aluminum coated with a light-sensitive emulsion. A flat is positioned on the light-sensitive coated side, and the two are then positioned in a vacuum frame for exposure to arc lights. When the light goes through the clear portions of the films, the light-sensitive coating is hardened. The unexposed coating, which is water-soluble, is scrubbed off later, leaving the printing images. After developing and desensitizing operations, the result is an ink-receptive printing plate of the whole form ready to be clamped around the plate cylinder.

MULTIPLE IMAGES

In offset printing duplicates of units such as labels, stamps, coupons, postcards, box

Fig. 1-21 A vacuum frame is used to expose an offset flat for burning in the unit images on the light-sensitive coating of the press plate. [*Courtesy Strong Electric Co.*]

wraps, and folding cartons are called multiple images (equivalent to electros). Instead of stripping up a flat of duplicate negatives, one or more negatives or positives for the same color are positioned in the holder (chase) of a photocomposing machine called a step-and-repeat machine, which is operated automatically by a punched tape. The negatives are positioned and exposed across a large press plate for the number of images wanted. Different subjects can be inserted in the chase for a gang run. The machines register colors to $\frac{1}{1000}$ inch. For very small subjects, such as stamps, a multiple unit is made in a step-and-repeat camera back. This unit, to be stepped across a large press plate, may contain eighty stamps. A label, for example, may be four up to the unit. (See Fig. 1-22*B*.)

PROJECTION FOR LARGE PROCESS COLOR

Extra-large photographic subjects beyond the range of the large color cameras, such as truck and twenty-four-sheet posters, are handled by projecting a fine screen negative to the sensitized press plates. The resulting halftone screen is coarse, but since the posters are viewed at a distance, this is not important. Details of large posters are frequently accentuated by hand plate methods.

PRINT PROOFS

In offset, proofs for checking work done are photographic prints of various types, the most common being a vandyke or a blueprint made from the negatives. Blueprints of copy units should always be ordered for checking, and a blueprint of the form should also be checked.

Simple color breakup is checked on the same blueprint by varying the exposure of the flats: black shows as darkest, while red or other colors show lighter. An approximation of halftone quality is given by a silver print. All proving of this sort is done to catch errors before plates are made.

Process color can be checked to some extent by various types of transparent print proofs in color. When they are superimposed in register, the result of the four colors is approximated. For some work this test is sufficient and avoids the cost of regular ink proofs made from proof plates.

TYPES OF OFFSET PLATES

Plates made from negatives are called "surface plates," the light action hardening the emulsion. Examples of this type are albumin, presensitized, and wipe-on plates. Various kinds of plates used for offset duplicating machines are of this type. New types of surface plates have replaced the deep-etch plate for longer runs.

Small duplicating offset presses now use a variety of nonphotographic plates which generally are good for only a few thousand impressions but which are less expensive.

For deep-etch plates, which are made from positives, the light action on a different kind of plate coating produces a temporary resist over the nonprinting areas. The plate images are scrubbed off with warm water to expose the metal for a very slight etching with acid preliminary to a lacquer base and development of the image. The temporary resist over the rest of the plate is then removed.

Long-Life Polymetal Plates

For extra-long pressruns, there are several types of long-life offset plates, generally termed "bimetal plates." The principle of these plates is a copper image base and a nonimage area of chromium or stainless steel. These metals resist ink, permitting the dampening film to be cut to a minimum, and they also resist wear. They are good for more than 1 million impressions. Both surface and deep-

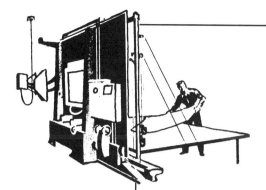

EQUIPMENT USED FOR MULTIPLE IMAGES

Fig. 1-22A This Rutherford step-and-repeat machine gives an idea of the equipment used for large press plates. Unit positives or negatives in a chase are exposed and repositioned the necessary number of times. Register is to 1/1000 inch (0.0254 millimeter) by perforated paper tape.

TAKE
THIS

AND
MAKE

Fig. 1-22B This drawing shows the principle of step-and-repeat work with photomechanical equipment, which is widely used for process color work.

etch platemaking techniques are used to make these plates, depending on the metal (plated) surface to be removed. Obviously, they are the most expensive type of offset plate, but they have opened up new fields of production to offset printing.

ADVANTAGES OF THE OFFSET PRESS PLATE

Because of the economic importance of the offset press plate to the user, it is important that production people realize that its cost includes the equivalent of letterpress form imposition, lockup, and makeready. The elimination of this major cost factor is very important in planning for press production. Offset makeready involves only press adjustments.

There is also the matter of reprints. The negative, positive, or offset flat can be stored and reused later. This avoids the expense of breaking up a letterpress form, storing the type or plates, and then repeating the cost of form imposition, lockup, and makeready.

THE OFFSET PRESS

Commercial offset presses range in size from 17½ by 22½ inches (445 by 572 millimeters) to 54 by 77 inches (1372 by 1956 millimeters) for single-color presses, but new faster presses have largely replaced those more than 60 inches (1524 millimeters) wide. The two- and four-color presses commonly available range from 18 by 25 inches (457 by 635 millimeters) to 44 by 60 inches (1118 by 1524 millimeters).

The multicolor web perfecting offset presses, printing on both sides of the paper, have made the larger two- and four-color presses obsolete because of faster speeds and bindery economies.

The switch to the smaller fast presses is due mainly to smaller manning requirements; frequently only two operators are needed instead of three. Some two-color presses can be converted in minutes to the perfecting type of press, printing one color on each side of sheet, once through the press.

Offset web presses have taken over the newspaper industry and many periodicals of less than 50,000 circulation. This means that right-reading negatives, emulsion side down, must be supplied instead of electros or mats.

Offset presses smaller than 17 by 22 inches (432 by 559 millimeters) are generally classed as duplicating presses.

Because all offset presses are rotary, with no sacrifice in speed when a larger form is used, and because there is no press standby time expense for form lockup and makeready, more printing is done in multiples, and shorter runs of process color are practical.

For advertising production, the important feature is the intermediate rubber-covered offset cylinder which transfers the inked image from the press plate to the paper. This feature permits the finest halftone reproduction on both coated and uncoated, rough-textured papers.

OFFSET INKS AND OFFSET PAPER

All the usual types of ink are available with offset: transparent and opaque, metallic, high-gloss and semigloss, fluorescent and rub-resistant inks, and inks meeting food-packaging regulations. Multicolor presses use the wet printing method, with inks adjusted to trap when overprinted. Press varnishing and bronzing are done regularly.

Offset offers an almost unlimited choice of paper for fine monochrome and process color reproduction, for in addition to coated and uncoated grades of offset paper, various antique and fancy finishes, text papers, vellums, cover papers, bristols, and other papers preferred for advertising material are now surface-sized for offset. Production planning frequently takes advantage of the offset process to use an inexpensive uncoated sheet in place of coated paper for long runs of color printing. Standard book paper sizes are now the same for offset and letterpress.

ADVANTAGES OF THE OFFSET PROCESS

It is generally acknowledged that each printing process has its own field, determined by the capabilities and economic advantages of its methods and equipment. No one is the best process under all conditions. The process selected for a printing job should be the one which best solves the problems of the particular job. One is preferred to the others because of its special qualifications. No process of itself assures quality; that depends on the standards of the producer and the skill of the producer's craft people.

Offset is usually employed for much advertising production because it offers the best solution to one or more of seven basic types of production problems. Proper analysis of the printing job, recognition of the basic problems involved, and an adequate knowledge of what offset can do frequently leads to the selection of this printing process. A good knowledge of production for offset will help keep costs to a minimum, facilitate delivery dates, and obtain the quality of reproduction desired.

The basic advantages of the offset process include:

- Removal of all restrictions on the choice of art media
- Fine halftones on any paper
- Cost of printing plates
- Absence of usual press lockup and makeready costs
- Composition economies
- For process color, multiple plate sizes, a range in quality and cost, and large reproduction sizes
- Early delivery

2

OFFSET PRODUCTION PLANNING

Offset Production Planning Is Now handled in the creative planning stage. The offset printing process is an integrated process: the printer makes the printing plates as well as doing the printing. The offset printing user's production role is to take full advantage of *time* plate estimating and the printer's *base plate charge,* described in Chapter 1. All line elements, including galley proofs of metal or phototype for text and photolettering for headlines, should be scaled and positioned on the mechanical. Same-focus economies should be planned for *tone* elements including process color art, the latter in the form of prepared copy for the camera (see Chapter 8). Efficient press size is discussed in Chapter 12.

ADDITIONAL AREAS OF
PRODUCTION PLANNING

Not only because of the economies of time plate estimating with its freedom from economic restrictions but also because of the extra capabilities of the offset process (described below), we can see that the user's production planning for offset is broader than that for letterpress. For example, offset's ability to print fine halftones even on uncoated papers such as the antique, text, and fabric finishes, opens the door to effects or economy. Substituting an inexpensive uncoated paper for a coated stock for long runs of process color can save a lot of money.

Chapters 4 and 5 show that there is a choice in composition methods even with metal type: galley repro type proofs are pasted on the mechanical for text, and display type is prepared on photolettering machines right in the art department.

Page makeup is handled on the drawing board. Direct-entry phototypesetting machines operated by typists are being installed by the printing user, or a special keyboard may be used to produce a diskette or cassette which can send the input over a telephone wire to a compatible phototype system. For the composition of small printing orders of a routine nature various economical cold-type methods are used.

With the freedom of time plate estimating, frequently coupled with the extra capabilities of offset, production planning starts in the creative planning stage because one eye must watch costs and the other available time. Here again the user can choose from a range of quality, cost, and time alternatives. For full-color production, planning is directed toward transferring the equivalent of some platemaking and typesetting operations to the copy preparation stage by intermediate photo steps between the original art and art prepared for the printer's camera. For single-color and simple color printing, projection prints are ordered from the original photographer and then are scaled and positioned on the mechanical to form a combination plate and thus avoid stripping time.

With process color copy, mixed-art media are reduced to a single medium in the form of transparencies or reproduction-quality color photoprints. If an assembly is to be color-separated by an electronic scanning machine, the "prepared" transparencies are color-balanced, scaled, and positioned (emulsion-floated) on clear film by a color photo laboratory or studio (see Fig. 2-1). Color prints are positioned on a tone mechanical (no black copy) so that all can be positioned on one set of color separations. For a 25- by 38-inch (635- by 965-millimeter) broadside this procedure avoids having the printer strip each individual subject to register on each of the four-color press forms (see Fig. 10-3).

COLLATERAL PRINTED MATERIAL

In national advertising there is always collateral printed material (window displays and other dealer aids, posters, calendars, broadsides, and the like), much of which involves large process halftones. To avoid duplicating color plate costs, publication color plates can be "converted" for the offset production of much of the collateral material (see Figs. 10-15 to 10-18). Or all the different plate sizes needed can be made from one set of offset color separations. Figures 10-12 to 10-14 show examples of such multiple plate sizes.

EXTRA CAPABILITIES OF OFFSET

It is important to understand that offset printing makes all the adjustments of tonal qualities on the photographic films to produce the final halftone negatives from which the press plates are made. No etching is done on metal as with photoengraving. This fact is responsible for some of the extra capabilities of the offset process:

Phototypesetting

The initial step in this form of composition is the input for the typesetting machine. The form varies for different machines: it may be a perforated paper tape or a magnetic diskette, cassette, or magnetic card (mag card) for systems that use a computer to activate the typesetter.

An editorial room is apt to use an optical character recognition (OCR) system which accepts manuscript typed by an IBM Selectric typewriter or its equivalent. An advertising agency or an art studio frequently uses a direct-entry phototype machine operated by a typist; such equipment is available at from $4000 to $16,000. A recent development is the use of word-processing magnetic media, such as the diskette, cassette, or mag card, all of which can be converted to the input suitable for a particular phototype system. By avoiding repetition of the original keyboarding this system offers a sizable economy. Such input goes to a video display and editing terminal (VDT) for the wanted type specifications, in a step termed "formating."

Fine Halftones on Uncoated Papers

Offset regularly uses a 175-line contact halftone screen for process color on antique-finish and other textured papers for advertising. This capability removes all restrictions on the choice of art media and offers cost economies for paper stock.

Modern Typefaces on Textured Papers

Modern typefaces with their fine hairlines and serifs were developed for coated papers and are not suited to antique or text finishes with letterpress. Offset, with its resilient rubber-surfaced offset cylinder applying the ink, can use any type of paper for these typefaces.

Printed Halftones Afforded by Good Copy

A printed photoengraving is good line copy for offset printing and can be reduced or enlarged within reasonable limits. Such printed halftones have been used as copy for some illustrations in this book. Letterpress cannot do this because the size of the halftone dots is reduced laterally when the copper plate is etched and any reproduction would look washed out.

Use of the Same Phototype Input for Different Layouts

Most phototype systems can be reset for different typefaces, type sizes, measures, and so on, and a tape or a diskette be rerun. The resulting second set of galley phototype prints costs about half as much as the first set.

Multiple Images

Another form of multiple is the multiple image: labels, magazine inserts, coupons, and so on. For these, whether process color

2A. Fly front bow blouse in polyester crepe by Gregory & Goldberg. Off white, seafoam or pink. 10-16. **17.00**
2B. White dotted Arnel® triacetate shirt in dusty green or pink by Sybil. 10-18. **15.00**
2C. Fur collared sweater. Natural or black dyed American lamb on basket weave 100% Wintuck® Orlon® acrylic. By Herald House in black or natural. S,M,L. **50.00**
2D. Tweed turtleneck by Jane Irwill. Camel, rust or green polyester-acrylic. S,M,L, **13.00**

Fig. 2-1 An assembly of process color elements: a spread in full color from a department store booklet. The multiple components of a process copy page are termed an "assembly." Art production sends the original art with the layout to a color laboratory, where all process elements are reduced to a single art medium (usually transparencies, but color prints can be used), scaled, positioned, and color-balanced. This method includes all process copy on one set of separations.

or not, the step-and-repeat machine is used. A negative for each color is placed in a chase for multiple exposure on an offset press plate. A perforated paper tape then activates the movement of the chase across the plate as it stops briefly for each exposure. There are a setup charge and a charge for the time needed for the number of multiples required (a few window displays or, say, ninety-six labels). All colors are in register to 1/1000 inch (0.0254 millimeter).

Multiple Plate Sizes

Collateral printed materials call for different plate sizes for the different layouts, such as dealer displays, car cards, window strips, and dealer literature. From a set of continuous-tone color separations of a key illustration all the needed plate sizes can be produced in the same halftone screen. Some pieces can be blowups (see Figs. 10-1 to 10-14).

No Restrictions on the Size of Process Color Plates

The restrictions on size of process color photoengravings do not apply to offset process plates. A poster can be one large full-color illustration.

Conversions

When an advertising campaign budget has had to be cut before the client would approve it, much of the plate cost for collateral material can be reduced by converting the magazine process photoengravings for offset production. This conversion is accomplished by several methods, the simplest being clean black proofs of each of the four process engravings. Usually just the artwork or part of it is wanted to integrate the collateral pieces with the current magazine schedule. Since the halftone screen is apt to be 120-line, reduction or enlargement is practical. Conversions cost about 25 cents on the dollar compared with original process engravings. (See Fig. 10-15.)

Prepress Process Proofs

The expense of proof plates can be avoided for much process printing by a known producer. From the screened separation negatives or positives a lamination of each color on very thin acetate will give a good idea of the quality. Such color proofs cost only 10 cents on the

dollar. Blueprints are used for black-and-white copy.

Range of Process Quality

New technology eliminated manual tonal adjustment for color correction by developing photographic masking for tonal adjustment. Such masking is sufficient for pleasing-picture quality, and process color separations can be obtained for less than $100. If necessary, further correction can be done. So the cost of full color ranges from less than $100 to more than $1000. (See Fig. 10-2.)

Laser Scanner Separations

Time-Life research developed the electronic scanning machine, which could produce continuous-tone separation negatives in minutes. Now the laser-beam scanner with a computer produces *screened* separations in minutes for the final tones for offset. Of the four process color methods, technicians rate the laser method the best.

Elimination of Press Lockup Cost

The equivalent of letterpress lockup cost is included in the base plate charge; the only makeready is for press adjustments, amounting to 8 percent of the relief makeready cost.[1] For book printing there is no need to break up forms and then make them up again for a second printing. Offset flats are saved in case a job must be rerun.

OFFSET COSTS

Inclusion of Other Cost Factors in Plate Costs

Copy in paste-up form offers the opportunity for page makeup on the drawing board, the cost of which can be much less than on the printer's stone. Since an offset press plate is equivalent to a letterpress form locked up and made ready, the usual cost for typographic press preparatory time is avoided. In a comparison of plate costs, this saving should be credited to offset plate costs.

Avoidance of Cost of Line Engravings

Since the base plate cost includes all line copy on unit paste-ups (illustrations and reverses

[1]J. W. Rockefeller, Jr., *Report to the Printing Industry* (New York, 1949).

as well as text repro proofs, all line copy elements should be scaled and positioned. The resulting unit negatives are the base negatives on which any separate halftone negatives are stripped to complete the unit. In offset, benday and pattern tints applied by the artist are considered line copy; screened Velox prints are also considered line copy. Line copy not on the paste-up costs extra for the camera time.

Key to Offset Halftone Costs

The cost of any halftone camera work is in addition to the base plate cost. With time estimating, either photos and tone copy should be scaled and positioned on the unit paste-up, or if separate tone elements are to be reduced in size for better detail, planning should provide for proportioned elements to be photographed in one or more groups in order to spread the time cost over the group or groups. The large halftone negative is then cut apart, and each subject is stripped to position on the unit line negatives. Requiring the camera operator to scale each subject separately is the most expensive way to supply copy. The cost of separate line negatives is about half that of halftones. Some small price-list shops, however, charge for black-and-white halftones according to bracketed size groups, disregarding proportioned copy and levying extra charges for the special types of halftones.

It is difficult to compare the cost of offset halftones with that of photoengravings. The engraver wants to know the size, and the offset producer wants to know the number of subjects and how many focuses will be required. The cost of a single square offset halftone is apt to be about the same as a photoengraving unless it is large or is a special type of halftone, in which case the cost is likely to be lower.

TRANSFER OF PRODUCTION PLANNING TO THE ART DEPARTMENT

The work of copy preparation has always been done in the user's art department or that of the user's agency, but in the early use of offset the approved rough layouts first went to the production department for its recommendations in order to keep costs within the limitations of a proposed budget and publication closing dates. It was not long, however, before art directors and their assistants learned production. Now when rough layouts have been approved, the decisions on paper, printing process, colors, and art medium have already been made.

With the realization of the importance of art directors' use of illustrative treatment of full-color advertisements to attract the desired audience they became important members of creative planning teams. Since they were held responsible for the quality of reproduction, they took on equal authority. Instead of working through the production department to reach suppliers, the art department started working directly with graphic arts suppliers. A production person who knew printing time and cost factors was transferred to the art department to give the answers on such questions in the creative stage.

Art Directors Revealed as Key Buyer Specifiers

The Technical Association of the Pulp and Paper Industry (TAPPI) made a survey[2] of 2400 art directors to learn their influence as buyers. The findings revealed that 76 percent worked directly with suppliers and that 85 percent used offset printing regularly. Some 84 percent of these art directors bought or specified typography, 86 percent bought or specified paper, 62 percent plates and separations, and 66 percent printing and binding.

About 25 percent of the advertising agencies, the smaller ones, have always operated with one person serving as both art director and production manager. In the largest agencies, the sheer volume of plates, mats, and negatives going to publications (traffic) requires a production department, but the production related to printing requires people to operate in teams: a team of generalists, who know all processes, handle two or three national accounts. With this method an account executive need go to only one person to learn the status of a job.

In the largest agencies a vice president of art and production is usually in charge and coordinates both departments.

[2]CA Report 16, Technical Association of the Pulp and Paper Industry, One Dunwoody Park, Chamblee, Ga. 30338.

FORM IN WHICH COPY FOR THE CAMERA IS PREPARED DETERMINED BY PRODUCTION PLANNING

Production planning starts in the creative planning stage because time and money are usually limited. Such restrictions frequently call for compromise. The art director would like to integrate the collateral material to the publication advertising through the key illustrations, some of the material being executed in a different art medium, or at least to work from the original camera copy to achieve better quality. The production department, in contrast, points to the budget and closing dates. Quite often the solution is conversion of the publication plates to get the separations for the different layouts and plate sizes.

Relatively little advertising or promotional material is planned for maximum quality because the cost is about double that of commercial-grade work. Award-winning specimens of printing in national exhibits usually involve no more than a 10,000-print order.

Production knowledge is important in the creative planning stage because of the limitations of time and money. Compromise is usual. By the time that rough layouts have been approved by the client, the decisions for colors, paper, printing process, art medium (determined by the budget), and composition will usually have been made.

Persons who handle production planning in a large organization do not do the actual paste-up work, but ultimate responsibility is theirs. For this reason coverage of copy preparation and related art production is comprehensive. For process work, a wrong procedure in planning for camera copy can cost both money and time. If a mechanical for flat-color work does not provide for color register or is not accurate, extra charges will result.

PRODUCTION OF COLLATERAL MATERIAL

Collateral material must be integrated with the advertising theme and current publication ads. The standard method is the use of one or two of the key illustrations in the publication ads (see Fig. 10-14). This procedure requires the same artwork in many different plate sizes for the various layouts. The offset process can handle all the sizes, up to billboards, from a single set of color separations. If the budget is tight, the full-color publica-

tion engravings can be converted to offset halftone positives for 25 cents on the dollar. Rotogravure positives can also be converted for offset production. Blowups are suitable for some collateral, such as window strips in several sizes, as well as for wall charts and calendars. The screened positives can be enlarged or reduced to the desired sizes by offset, which sets no technical restrictions on multiple and maximum plate sizes.

A company that sells mainly through dealers often handles its own collateral materials in conjunction with sales promotion.

NEW TECHNOLOGY AND NEW METHODS

With the printing industry using manual methods and labor costs increasing steadily, the need for faster methods and lower costs resulted in much research. The positive results of this research could best be applied to the photomechanical printing processes, particularly to offset, the all-purpose process, which became the dominant printing process in 1965.

The Big Break with Process Copy

The major development in process copy came in the late 1940s with the availability of reproduction-quality color photoprints, soon to be followed by Type C color prints. With these prints mixed-art media could be reduced to a single medium, with all elements in tonal balance, scaled or proportioned and positioned if an assembly was used in a full-color advertisement. Color change or correction was simple and fast; inserts and combinations could be prepared in hours to produce an illustration. Moreover, duplicates as large as 16 by 20 inches (406 by 508 millimeters) could be made for about 10 cents on the dollar, permitting multiple sets of the artwork needed in national advertising.

Shortly after the development of these dye-transfer color prints, large color transparencies became available. A magazine art director was the first to use transparencies for inserts and combinations. Later, color photo laboratories perfected techniques with transparencies and offered them at a lower cost than color prints. Transparencies usually are also required for electronic scanning machines. In recent years various types of reproduction-quality color prints have been developed for overnight delivery at a cost lower than that of dye-transfer prints.

Prepared Color Copy

No longer does the printing user require the printer to color-adjust, scale, and position color copy elements for an assembly. The user now submits the original artwork with a layout to a color photo laboratory or studio. The studio does the indicated work, reducing mixed-art media to a single medium, either transparencies or reproduction-quality color photoprints, scaled and positioned. Any color adjusting is handled in hours. It is common for work submitted by 4:00 P.M. to be ready by 9:00 A.M. the next day. Both time and money are sav

An importa
plate econo
color plate
positives
printed n
artwork i
ent in si
range fro.
supplied to the offse.
graphing to patented methods su. as Ludlow's Brightype, Du Pont's Cronapress, and Minnesota Mining and Manufacturing's Scotchprint. The latter two use a proof method. The cost of process plates by conversion of the original engraving is about 25 cents on the dollar as compared with working from the original art. Dealer material has been produced between the time of shipment of the publication plates and the publication issue.

PLACING OF RELATED JOBS WITH THE SAME PRODUCER

The usual practice is to place all jobs requiring the same artwork with the offset producer making the color separations, from which the different plate sizes are obtained. The offset producer will job out any forms of production which the producer does not handle, such as twenty-four-sheet posters.

By trade custom, negatives and plates are the property of the producer unless there is a written agreement to the contrary. If color separations made by one producer will be needed by another producer, arrangements should be made with the first producer. For example, catalog illustrations may be needed for showroom posters. The blowup method will be used for large sizes.

PRINT PROOFS

For single- and two-color work, blueprints should be ordered for checking. These are made from the producer's negatives before are made. For process color, proof tine work inexpensive are made from the

IENT PRESS SIZE

 nents now specify or ould be aware of two press production: the faster sheet-fed offset press perators; and the shift of multicolor printing from large, eight-unit presses to web-fed (roll-fed) offset perfecting presses. A press of this type not only prints both sides of the paper web as it goes through the press but also handles the folding and much of the binding (for example, of thirty-two pages with a cover of different stock). What a web offset press can do depends on the auxiliary equipment attached to it. Many such presses can print two on two or three on one; some can produce as many as five colors on both sides of the web. The details are covered in Chapter 12.

3

OFFSET PAPER

REFERENCES TO THE FINENESS OF halftone screens suitable for uncoated papers and to the fact that only line illustrations can be used with rough-textured papers apply only to letterpress. Such limitations on illustrative treatment do not apply to offset: even 300-line halftones can be used on antique-finish papers, and folding cartons are prepared with 200-line screens.

This ability of the offset process is a major reason for its use in advertising production. Art directors and designers are free of all restrictions on the type of paper they want to use for effect with tone reproduction. Cost-minded production people can save several thousand dollars on long-run color work by selecting an inexpensive uncoated stock, for paper is figured roughly as 23 percent of the cost of printed material.

In addition to antique- and fancy-finish uncoated offset papers, various other types of paper suitable for offset are in demand. There is a wide variety of such papers for advertising material, including text, vellum, cover, printing bristol, and index paper.

CHARACTERISTICS OF OFFSET PAPER

Paper suitable for the offset process is given a special treatment during manufacture. The uncoated grades are surface-sized to bond the surface fibers to the sheet, and the coated grades are "waterproofed" when coating with a proper pH content is applied. This treatment prevents the coating, a white pigment, from working back into the ink.

Coated offset is made in several grades and hues of white and in a variety of finishes, including a hard finish for gloss and metallic inks and a softer finish for process color. Coated-one-side (C1S) paper is used for labels and displays. The extra-smooth, glossy cast-coated papers were developed originally for offset label work. This type of coated paper is now also available in a coated-two-sides (C2S) type. Coated offset is used for fine detail, extra brilliance, and spirit varnishing. Dull-coated paper is now preferred for much advertising material. Coated offset is also classed as a book paper and comes in the same sizes as letterpress coated paper.

Both offset and letterpress uncoated and coated text papers now come in the same standard sizes and are classed as book papers. The standard sizes of book and other types of printing papers are shown in the tables of sizes and weights presented on following pages. Practically all types of printing papers are now suitable for offset printing. Bond and ledger papers have always been surface-sized to take pen and ink.

In recent years, pigmentation has been added to various types of uncoated paper suitable for offset. In addition to extra-opaque papers, there are now the whiter-than-white papers to give extra sparkle to halftones and extra contrast between printed

Fig. 3-1 The importance of illustrative treatment and color to the effectiveness of printed material is enhanced by papers of distinction, tone, and texture. The reproduction of halftones and process color on such papers is one of the advantages of offset printing.

and nonimage areas, as well as brilliants to intensify contrast. The fancy embossed finishes make black inks darker and colors brighter and truer. The unusual qualities of colored stocks and special textures and finishes have won them a place in advertising.

COST ADVANTAGES OF UNCOATED OFFSET

Very important in production planning is the fact that offset paper is generally figured as equal to a letterpress coated stock 10 pounds (4.5 kilograms) heavier in strength, bulk, and stiffness. Surface sizing gives stiffness and strength, and extra bulk is a characteristic of uncalendered paper.

For the longer runs of color work this factor presents a chance to save about 25 percent on the cost of stock. On a weight basis, 14 percent is saved when a 60-pound (27.2-kilogram) offset is used instead of a 70-pound (31.8-kilogram) letterpress coated paper; on

cost per pound, the economy of uncoated offset ranges from about 12 to 18 percent depending on whether expensive or cheaper grades of both types of paper are compared.

BULK-TO-WEIGHT ADVANTAGE

For much day-to-day advertising production requiring halftones and color it is unnecessary to use expensive papers in the heavier uncoated weights. In addition to uncoated offset, there are sulfate bristols, index papers, and tag stocks which take fine tone reproduction by offset. An uncoated offset can be bulked to .0085 caliper to substitute for cover paper. The bristols are now of such quality and cost that they can be substituted for heavy, more costly papers.

For example, two papers reasonably similar in appearance and characteristics were compared for a stock to be used by publishers for return postcards. Both had a caliper of .0085, sufficient to meet postal regulations. Stock A weighed 116 pounds, or 52.6 kilograms (23 by 30 inches, or 584 by 762 millimeters), and Stock B weighed 144 pounds (65.3 kilograms), for a difference of 28 pounds (12.7 kilograms) per 1000 press sheets; 1000 sheets of the first cost $21 as against $23.33 for the second, for a difference of $2.33. With Stock A there was a saving of 19 percent in weight and also a 10 percent advantage in price per pound—a very worthwhile saving.

Not all mill brands of offset or other types of paper have the same physical qualities. Each mill brand has its own characteristics: some bulk more than others, and some are stiffer than others. Frequently, brands are referred to as "hard" or "soft" papers. Folding qualities also differ with grades and brands.

OPACITY-TO-WEIGHT ADVANTAGE

When titanium pigment became commercially available, its first use with paper occurred in the manufacture of lightweight opaque bonds. The added opacity permitted printing and halftones by offset on both sides of thin paper with the tone of a bond, and the stock was widely used for statement enclosures and other forms of mailings.

Opaque offset papers appeared next. They permitted the use of a lighter-weight paper without loss of opacity. Now other types of paper, such as vellums, are opaqued. Frequently, a more suitable, more expensive paper can be used for a job without increasing the cost materially because a lighter weight can be employed.

The opacity-to-weight advantage is also used to solve bindery and mailing problems. A larger signature can be folded, or the thickness of a booklet or directory may come within the limitations of automatic mail-inserting machines. Avoiding hand operations in mailing can save thousands of dollars.

USE OF STANDARD PAPER SIZES

The sizes of printed pieces should cut efficiently from a standard paper size with a minimum of waste, and any departure from this rule should be made for a good reason. An inch of each dimension of the press sheet is usually required for a gripper margin on one long edge and for various trim margins.

Special paper sizes can be ordered in lots of 2000 to 5000 pounds (907 to 2268 kilograms)

for an extra 10 percent in cost; 20 percent over or under the order in pounds constitutes delivery. In many cases this differential makes a special-size order cost more than the same number of sheets in the next larger standard size. In fact, it frequently is cheaper to order the next larger standard size. For example, a special size between 36 by 48 inches (914 by 1219 millimeters) and 38 by 50 inches (965 by 1270 millimeters), say, 36½ by 48 inches (927 by 1219 millimeters), with the 10 percent differential added will cost more than the 38- by 50-inch size.

It is customary for printers to select the paper size and mill brand, for they know how a job is to be run and the production they can get with the paper used. Users should not order paper without first consulting their printers for such details.

STANDARD SIZES AND WEIGHTS OF PAPER[1]

The accompanying tables show standard paper sizes and weights per 1000 sheets for the different kinds of printing papers. No longer is there a difference between offset and letterpress paper sizes. Because offset does not require a coated paper for fine halftones, frequently it is possible to substitute one kind of paper for another to get a desirable standard size or character of surface for economy. Paper sales representatives or the printer can be of help here.

DETAILS OF PAPER AND SELECTION OF MILL BRAND HANDLED BY THE PRODUCER

Although the user selects the type of paper he or she wants, the producer chooses the mill brand and orders the paper more than 80 percent of the time. The producer must consider the formulation of inks for a particular brand, color of stock, workability, and printability, as well as the sheet size required for the way in which the job is to be run and bound and the quantity which will allow for both press and bindery spoilage. The form in Fig. 3-3 for processing orders for paper in sheets will give an idea of details to be considered when ordering.

[1]Data on standard paper sizes and weights courtesy of *Walden's Paper Catalog*, 1976. To convert from inches to millimeters, multiply by 25.4; to convert from pounds to kilograms, multiply by 0.4536.

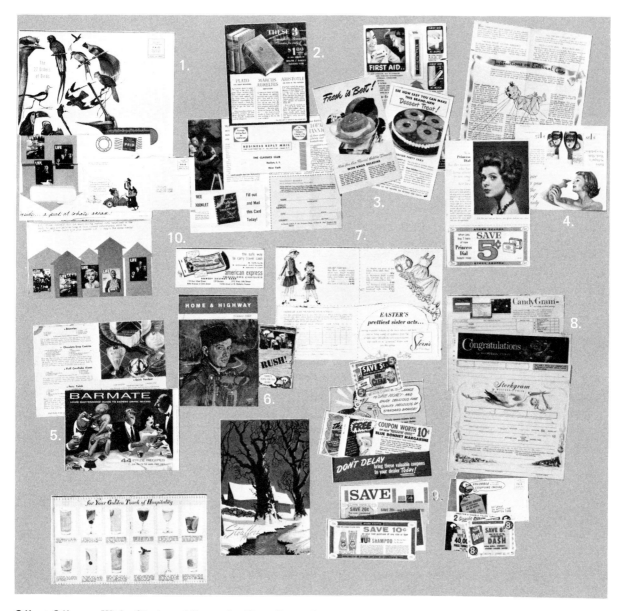

Offset Offers a Wide Choice of Paper for Tone Reproduction and Process Color

Fig. 3-2

1. Envelopes have a display as well as a utility value. Illustrative treatment is unlimited.
2. Return coupons and postcards should take pen and ink; postcards must meet postal regulations for thickness.
3. Package enclosures, shelf talkers, and the like are printed in such quantities that the cost of paper is an important factor. The thin opaque papers take tone work on both sides and reduce tonnage.
4. Softness is an important ingredient of literature for the infant market, and it is also desirable in cosmetic advertising.
5. Cookbooks and recipe booklets should be printed on uncoated paper because of the chance of wet hands' making pages stick.
6. A contrast of cover and text is frequently desirable, and it affords a change of pace with magazine inserts. A heavier antique stock is often used for process color.
7. With higher postal rates, the thin opaque bonds keep the weight of printed matter down. They can be printed on both sides.
8. Special-events telegram blanks require both process printing and the ability to take pen or pencil. An inexpensive stock for both requirements is handled by offset.
9. The various forms of merchandising coupons usually require tone reproduction and stiffness. Uncoated stock is frequently the choice.
10. Even uncoated blotting paper takes halftones by offset.

Comparison of Basis Weights of Book, Bond, Cover, and Bristol
Paper Based on Ream Weights

	Bond (17 by 22 inches)	Cover (20 by 26 inches)	Bristol (22½ by 28½ inches)	Book paper (25 by 38 inches)
Bond (basis weights in bold)	**13**	18	22	33
	16	22	27	41
	20	28	34	51
	24	33	41	61
	28	39	48	71
	32	45	55	81
	36	50	62	91
	40	56	69	102
	44	61	75	112
Cover (basis weights in bold)	18	**25**	31	46
	25	**35**	43	64
	29	**40**	49	73
	36	**50**	62	91
	43	**60**	74	110
	47	**65**	80	119
	58	**80**	99	146
	65	**90**	111	164
Book (basis weights in bold)	12	16	20	**30**
	16	21	27	**40**
	18	24	30	**45**
	20	27	34	**50**
	24	32	40	**60**
	28	38	47	**70**
	31	43	54	**80**
	35	48	60	**90**
	39	54	67	**100**
	47	65	80	**120**
	59	80	100	**150**
Mill bristols (basis weights in bold)	58	81	**100**	148
	70	97	**120**	176
	82	114	**140**	207
	93	130	**160**	237
	105	146	**180**	267
	117	162	**200**	296
Index (basis weights in bold)	53	74	**91**	135
	67	93	**115**	170
	82	114	**140**	207
	105	146	**180**	267
Postcard (basis weights in bold)	58	81	**100**	**148**
	76	105	**130**	193
	87	122	**150**	222

Standard Weights of Book Paper per 1000 Sheets, Both Letterpress and Offset (Basis, 25 × 38 Inches)

Basis (inches)	30	35	40	45	50	60	70	80	90	100	120	150
17½ by 22½	25	29	33	37	41	50	58	66	75	83	99	124
19 by 25	30	35	40	45	50	60	70	80	90	100	120	150
23 by 23	42	49	56	63	70	84	98	112	126	140	169	. . .
23 by 35	51	59	68	76	85	102	119	136	152	170	204	. . .
22½ by 35	50	58	66	75	83	99	116	133	149	166	199	249
24 by 36	54	64	72	82	90	110	128	146	164	182	218	272
25 by 38	60	70	80	90	100	120	140	160	180	200	240	300
26 by 40	66	76	88	98	110	132	154	176	198	218	262	328
28 by 42	74	86	100	112	124	148	174	198	222	248	298	372
28 by 44	78	90	104	116	130	156	182	208	234	260	312	390
30½ by 41	78	92	106	118	132	158	184	210	236	264	316	396
32 by 44	88	104	118	134	148	178	208	238	266	296	356	444
33 by 44	92	106	122	138	152	184	214	244	276	306	366	460
35 by 45	100	116	132	150	166	198	232	266	298	332	398	498
36 by 48	108	128	144	164	180	220	254	292	328	364	436	544
38 by 50	120	140	160	180	200	240	280	320	360	400	480	600
41 by 54	140	164	186	210	234	280	326	372	420	466	560	700
44 by 64	178	208	238	266	296	356	414	474	534	592	712	888
35 by 46	102	118	136	152	170	204	238	272	306	338	406	. . .
38 by 52	124	146	166	188	208	250	292	332	374	416	500	. . .
41 by 61	156	184	212	236	264	316	368	420	472	528	632	. . .
42 by 58	154	180	206	230	256	308	358	410	462	512	615	. . .
44 by 66	178	208	238	266	296	356	414	474	534	592	712	. . .
46 by 69	201	234	267	301	334	400	468	534	602	668	802	. . .
52 by 76	250	292	332	374	416	500	582	666	748	832	998	. . .

Cut Sizes (Weights per 1000 Sheets; Basis, 17 by 22 Inches)

Size	Substance								
	13	16	20	24	28	32	36	40	44
8½ by 11	6.50	8.00	10.00	12.00	14.00	16.00	18.00	20.00	22.00
8½ by 13	7.68	9.44	11.81	14.18	16.54	18.90	21.27	23.63	26.00
3½ by 14	8.26	10.18	12.72	15.26	17.81	20.36	22.90	25.45	28.00
11 by 17	13.00	16.00	20.00	24.00	28.00	32.00	36.00	40.00	44.00

Standard Weights of Tag Paper per 1000 Sheets (Basis, 24 by 36 Inches)

Basis	90	100	125	150	175	200
22½ by 28½	134	148	186	223	260	297
24 by 36	180	200	250	300	350	400
28½ by 45	268	296	372	446	520	594

Sheet Areas of Basic Paper Sizes

Size (inches)	Area (square inches)	Type of paper
17 by 22	374	Bond, ledger, writing, vellum
19 by 24	456	Blotting
20 by 26	520	Cover
22 by 28	616	Blank
23 by 35	805	Bristol
25 by 38	950	Book
24 by 36	864	Kraft, newsprint, tag
25½ by 30½	778	Index

Standard Weights of Index Bristol per 1000 Sheets (Basis, 20½ by 24¾ Inches)

Basis	90	110	140	170
20½ by 24¾	117	144	182	222
22½ by 28½	148	182	230	280
22½ by 35	182	223	284	344
25½ by 30½	180	220	280	340
28½ by 45	296	364	460	560

Standard Weights of Bond, Ledger, Safety, Writing, Translucent, Xerographic, and Micr Bond, Papers per 1000 Sheets

Size (inches)	Substance								
	13	16	20	24	28	32	36	40	44
16 by 21	23½	29	36	43	50½	57½	65	72	79
16 by 42	47	58	72	86	101	115	130	144	158
17 by 22	26	32	40	48	56	64	72	80	88
17½ by 22½	27	34	42	51	59	67	76	84	93
17 by 26	31	38	47	57	66	76	85	95	104
17 by 28	33	41	51	61	71½	81½	92	102	112
18 by 23	29	35½	44½	53	62	71	80	89	97½
18 by 46	58	71	89	106	124	142	160	178	195
19 by 24	32	39	49	58½	68½	78	88	98	107
20 by 28	39	48	60	72	84	96	108	120	132
21 by 32	47	58	72	86	101	115	130	144	158
22 by 25½	39	48	60	62	84	96	108	120	132
22 by 34	52	64	80	96	112	128	144	160	176
22½ by 22½	35	43	54	65	76	87	97	108	119
22½ by 34½	54	66	83	99	116	133	149	166	183
22½ by 35	56	67	84	101	118	134	152	168	186
23 by 36	58	71	89	106	124	142	160	178	195
24 by 38	64	78	98	117	137	156	176	196	214
24½ by 24½	42	51½	64	77	90	103	116	128½	141
24½ by 28½	49	60	75	90	105	119½	134½	149½	164½
24½ by 29	49½	61	76	91	106½	122	137	152	167
24½ by 38½	66	81	101	121	141½	161½	182	202	222
24½ by 39	66	82	102	122	144	164	184	204	225
25½ by 44	78	96	120	144	168	192	216	240	264
26 by 34	62	76	94	114	132	152	170	189	208
28 by 34	66	82	102	122	143	163	184	204	224
34 by 44	104	128	160	192	224	256	288	320	352
35 by 45	109	135	168	202	236	270	303	337	371

Standard Weights of Printing Bristol per 1000 Sheets (Basis, 22½ by 28½ Inches)

Basis	80	90	100	120	140	160	180	200	220
22½ by 28½	160	180	200	240	280	320	360	400	440
27½ by 35	. . .	. . .	250	300	350	400	. . .	. . .	. . .
26 by 40	. . .	. . .	330	396	. . .	. . .	. . .	. . .	. . .

Standard Weights of Cover Paper per 1000 Sheets (Basis, 20 by 26 Inches)

Basis	50	60	65	80	90	100
20 by 26	100	120	130	160	180	200
22½ by 28½	123	148	160	197	222	246
23 by 29	128	154	167	205	231	256
23 by 35	155	186	201	248	279	310
26 by 40	200	240	260	320	360	400
35 by 46	310	372	402	496	558	620

Some mills and many paper merchants stock special sizes when there is sufficient demand; for example, the standard size of 35 by 45 inches (889 by 1143 millimeters) is also usually available in 35 by 46 inches (889 by 1168 millimeters) to allow trim margins for bleed design and frequently in 36 by 46 inches (914 by 1168 millimeters) to provide for gripper margins on both long sides of sheet for a work-and-tumble pressrun.

The larger offset producers tend to standardize on several brands, which they buy in carload lots. The technical details of paper, inks, dot structure, and moisture content have all been worked out, and press production can be estimated accurately. Usually, a better price is possible for long runs of color work if one of these standard brands is used.

PAPER PRICE BRACKETS

Printing paper is sold by the pound or hundredweight; the greater the quantity bought, the lower the price. These are the price brackets:

	Cartons	Skids
Number	Weight (pounds)*	Weight (pounds)*
1	150	5,000
4	500	10,000
16	2000	20,000
		36,000

*Weights approximate; 1 pound equals 0.4536 kilogram.

With the better grades of uncoated offset paper the price differential between 2000 and 36,000 pounds (between 907 and 16,330 kilograms) is 10 to 12 cents a pound, and less with the cheaper grades.

A knowledge of the packing count of different paper mills is another reason why the producer usually selects mill brand. One brand may be packed in 1000-sheet cartons, and another in 1250-sheet cartons; yet the four-carton price bracket will apply to both.

PAPER THICKNESS

The average offset press can handle any thickness from a thin onionskin to an 8-ply (30-point) board. Stock for car cards is the heaviest usually run.

Window displays on heavier board are lith-

Form for Processing Inquiries, Orders

Paper In Sheets

Salesman .... Date ....
Customer .... Purchasing Agent ....
Address ....
Ship to .... Purchase # ....
Address .... Deliver ....
GRADE ....
QUANTITY .... (Sheets) .... (Pounds)
SIZE & WEIGHT .... M; .... basis weight
COLOR .... FINISH .... DESIGN ....
CALIPER THICKNESS .... 1-sheet .... 4-sheets .... pages-to-inch
☐ WATERMARKED ☐ UNWATERMARKED
GRAIN DIRECTION ☐ long ☐ short ☐ optional (one dimension)
DESIGN OR PATTERN NUMBER ☐ long ☐ short ☐ optional (one dimension)
TRIMMING ☐ machine ☐ trimmed-2-sides
TO ONE SIZE ☐ trimmed-2-ends
☐ trimmed-4-sides
PRESS SHEET ☐ Sheetwise ☐ Work-and-Turn ☐ Work-and-Tumble
REPRODUCTION METHOD (indicate which)
☐ Letterpress ☐ 1-color ☐ 2-colors ☐ 3-colors ☐ 4-colors
☐ wet ☐ dry
☐ Lithography ☐ 1-color ☐ 2-colors ☐ 3-colors ☐ 4-colors
☐ wet ☐ dry
☐ Gravure
☐ Photogelatine
☐ High-gloss inks ☐ metallic inks
☐ Finishing ☐ varnishing ☐ lacquering
☐ acetate laminating ☐ liquid laminating
☐ polyethylene laminating
☐ embossing
PLANT HUMIDITY REQUIREMENTS ....
PURPOSE FOR WHICH THIS PAPER IS INTENDED ....
PACKING ☐ Ream-marked in cartons ☐ Ream-marked in bundles
☐ Ream-sealed in cartons
☐ Ream-marked on single-tier skids
☐ Ream-marked on double-tier skids
☐ Ream-marked on 4-tier skids
☐ Felt-side-UP ☐ Felt-side-DOWN
SKID SPECIFICATIONS ☐ 4-way-entry ☐ 2-way-entry
runners ☐ short-way ☐ long-way
minimum distance between runners ..... inches
maximum height ..... inches
maximum weight ..... pounds
Note — MARK SKID NUMBER AND ORDER NUMBER ON RUNNERS
SHIPPING siding on .... RR
plant can accommodate trailers up to ..... feet long
☐ sidewalk delivery by winch-truck
Most satisfactory delivery hours
AM to ..... AM
PM to ..... PM
Receiving platform closed ..... to .....
SPECIAL MARKINGS ON SKID-WRAPPERS ....
SPECIAL INSTRUCTIONS NOT IDENTIFIED ABOVE ....
SAMPLE FOR MATCHING ACCOMPANYING ....
NOTE: Be sure to send out-turned samples in advance of shipment

Fig. 3-3 This paper merchant's form gives an idea of the details which may have to be considered in ordering paper.

GRIPPER MARGIN

WORK AREA
OF PRESS SHEET

Fig. 3-4 The dotted lines indicate the maximum work area on the press sheet. At least a ½-inch (12.7-millimeter) gripper margin on one long side and ⅛-inch (3.175-millimeter) trim on the other sides are required.

ographed on paper which is later mounted (pasted) on cardboard of any thickness and then die-cut, scored, and so on. Display material on corrugated board is handled similarly: the outer sheet is printed on a roll-fed offset press, and later the printed roll is fed into the corrugated-board machinery.

PAPER IN ROLLS

Web-fed offset presses use paper in rolls. A few sheet-fed presses feed from rolls with sheeting equipment attached. There is a 25 percent price differential for paper in rolls instead of sheets, but for various reasons spoilage is higher, and the user does not get the full benefit of the lower price. The use of regular newsprint for periodicals is common, and letterpress machine-coated papers are also used in web-fed offset presses because of the special inks and drying equipment attached.

OTHER MATERIALS

Cellophane and wax paper are not suitable for offset because of their wax content. Wax works back on the press plate, and scumming results when the wax picks up the ink.

Offset does much production on thin plastic films and sheets. The color transparencies in illuminated window displays are process color printed on plastics by offset. Many of the banners and pennants used in merchandising are lithographed on cloth.

Metal decorators who print tin signs and metal displays use offset; tin cans and other metal packaging are also printed with this process. Drying ovens and special presses are required for lithographed metal.

4

COMPOSITION IN THE ART DEPARTMENT

WITH THE OFFSET PROCESS DOMINANT in commercial printing since 1965 (it is now used for 75 percent of all advertising and book printing), it was natural for the art department to take over planning for type matter because it prepared the paste-up mechanical for the camera. Since the layout must provide for the copywriter's text, the mechanical artist must know *copy fitting* better than the designer making the original rough layout for approval by the client. The designer is more deeply concerned with selecting a suitable typeface for the product or service.

PRODUCTION TAKEN OVER BY ART

A survey of art directors by the Technical Association of the Pulp and Paper Industry (TAPPI) revealed that 83 percent of the art departments deal directly with suppliers. Besides specifying or buying typography and paper, they handle plates and color separations and even 66 percent of the printing and binding.

Today the creative planning of an advertising campaign is a team operation, and the art director is an important member of the team. Production planning—solving the problems of time and cost—is now the art department's responsibility. Advertising agencies and art studios are installing phototypesetting equipment, and organizations using word-processing systems are converting their mag-

netic media (diskettes, magnetic tapes, and mag cards) for use in typesetting. This development avoids repetition of the keyboarding operation, and type specifications can be changed for different jobs.

SHIFT TO PHOTOCOMPOSITION

Working with Type

Since the graphic arts are being adjusted to the photomechanical printing processes, which can use any form of composition that can be photographed, even typewriter copy, we shall emphasize the nonmetal methods, particularly phototypesetting. However, a general knowledge of typefaces, type sizes, measure (length of line), spacing between lines of type, and the like is pertinent to all methods of preparing composition for camera copy.

Composition for the Camera

The forms of composition used for camera copy can be grouped in three categories:

1. Metal, either hand-set or machine-set. Only good proofs are needed.

2. Photographic, ranging from desk-top lettering appliances to commercial phototypesetting machines operated by phototypesetters used by typographic services that also provide metal composition.

3. Cold-type, with methods ranging from transfer paper letters for large type and mechanical lettering aids to special electric typewriters with book typefaces. Such composition is used for small orders that cannot bear the cost of metal type or photocomposition.

Regardless of the kind of composition, the typefaces are essentially the same. The diagram of the metal letter *M* in Fig. 4-1 shows the details of a piece of foundry, or hand-set, type used for the larger sizes. Note that the point size (lines per inch) includes a shoulder to provide space for descenders (*j*'s, *p*'s, *y*'s, and so on); the type body allows space for capitals and ascenders (*b*'s, *d*'s, *f*'s, and so on).

TERMINOLOGY

The design of a style of type, called the "face," is identified by name: Cheltenham, Bodoni, Futura. Machine-set text type, such as 8-point and 10-point type, is usually available in two styles of the same face, such as roman and bold or roman and italic, from the same Linotype magazine.

Type larger than 14 points, used for headlines, is apt to be individual foundry type for hand setting, but it may be machine-set; it comes in normal, condensed, or extended form and frequently in italic or boldface. Some styles are available in light or medium weights as well as in boldface.

The International Typographic Composition Association (ITCA) classifies typefaces as Old Style, modern, square serif, sans serif, and special, or miscellaneous (see Fig. 4-3).

Since faces can fall into two groups, classification is not rigid.

The term "leading" refers to extra space between lines of type. The longer the line, the more space is desirable for readability. With hand-set type, leading is provided by thin strips of type metal. With machine-set type the mold for the type slug can be made thicker for leading, for example, 10-point typeface on a 12-point slug, like this line of type.

HAND-SET TYPE

Today hand-set type is used principally for display headlines. It generally comes in sizes from 18 to 48 points, but there are both larger and smaller sizes. New typefaces initially are hand-set; later, if the demand warrants, they are put on the machines.

Hand-set type is foundry type, purchased by the printer from a type founder. A typographic service also buys this type but does not release it when supplying metal composition to a printer. Instead, an electro of any hand-set type is supplied and positioned with machine type for a locked-up page. The original type is used for a repro proof and electros, but in either case hand-set type is returned to the typecases for reuse.

LUDLOW TYPE

A variation of hand-set type is Ludlow type. An assembly of Ludlow matrices of characters is positioned manually and locked in a special type stick, which serves as a mold for molten type metal to form a type slug of a headline. The matrices are put back in a typecase, and the slug is eventually remelted. The advantage to the printer is that the inventory of regularly used faces is reduced and the foundry type need not be redistributed into the typecases. Newspaper headlines are usually set by this method.

MACHINE-SET METAL TYPE

Practically all body or text type is set by machine: Linotype, Intertype, or Monotype. An operator at a keyboard assembles automatically little brass matrices of the characters to form the desired line of type. A lever is then pressed to let the molten type metal flow into the mold to form the type slug of the line.

The typefaces come in several forms: *roman,* the commonly used form with vertical

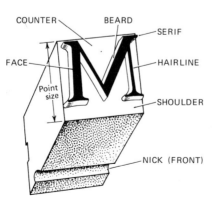

The Anatomy of Type

COUNTER BEARD SERIF FACE HAIRLINE Point size SHOULDER NICK (FRONT)

Fig. 4-1 A piece of foundry, or hand-set, type.

stems; *italic,* which is slanted; *bold,* which is a heavier version of the roman; and *bold italic,* a heavier version of italic. Some faces are also available in small capitals.

The matrices are carried in a magazine; most type machines are equipped to handle two magazines. A magazine for body type usually carries roman and one other form, either italic or bold but rarely both. The Intertype catalog form of listings is shown in Fig. 4-2.

In general, machine-set body type is available in sizes from 6 to 14 points, but there are a few faces with smaller sizes. Display type sizes range from 18 to 42 points, with a few faces available in 48 and 60 points. Since machine-set type is cheaper than hand-set type, it is best to check and see if the face and size you want for display type are available in machine-set type.

The average printer carries only a limited selection of typefaces and sizes. The printer or the customer goes to a typographic service for a larger selection. Advertising typographers have the largest and most nearly current selections. With their local association they publish a directory of typefaces and sizes and the names of the firms that have them.

MONOTYPE

Monotype machines cast individual type characters instead of line slugs. Many faces come in sizes as small as 6 points, but some come only in sizes of 14 points or larger. All tend to run as large as 36 or even 48 points, with some ranging to 72 points. Their selection avoids the use of hand-set type for some display faces. When machine-set type is no longer needed, it is remelted, as are any electros of hand-set type, which generally is not released.

Type founders publish catalogs of their faces and sizes, and typographic services that set type but do no printing publish lists of their faces and sizes. Printers supply customers with type sheets of what they have on hand.

CLASSIFICATION OF TYPEFACES

Typefaces were developed from the hand script of monks copying manuscripts in the Middle Ages, which produced a type style similar to that which we call Old English,

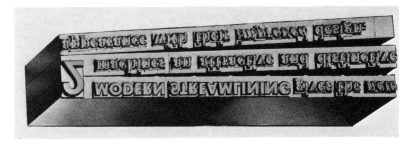

Fig. 4-2A Machine-set type slug.

11 Pt. Baskerville with Italic and Small Caps. Font 854   Code WIOYJ

INTERTYPE matrices excel in type 123123
INTERTYPE matrices excel in type VBCVBC

Alphabet 130 pts. Figures .076. Characters to 1 pica 2.63
Special characters available. See alphabet section

11 Pt. Baskerville with Bold. Font 857   Code WJEUP

INTERTYPE matrices excel in type 123123
INTERTYPE matrices excel in type 123123

Alphabet 133 pts. Figures .0761. Characters to 1 pica 2.58

Fig. 4-2B Machine-set body type: two magazines.

used for decorative purposes at Christmastime. German script printing was an offshoot of this style. Finally, the less cluttered Italian lettering on Roman temples was adopted, resulting in the roman style of today's typefaces.

Typographers today generally group typefaces in five classifications as mentioned previously: Old Style, modern, square serif, sans serif, and special, or miscellaneous. However, some typographers consider that certain typefaces fall within two classifications.

COST OF METAL COMPOSITION

The basic cost of text composition is calculated for "straight matter," type set in a single typeface and size, flush left and right. Display type, whether hand- or machine-set, usually involves time charges for positioning. For advertising layouts this positioning and form lockup can amount to half the composition cost (the page makeup).

Premium-cost composition reflects extra time required, as when changing magazines on the Linotype machine or when breaking away from straight matter. You should always remember that machine-set type is less costly

Old Style: Such faces as Garamond Old Style, Caslon 540, and Baskerville have moderately heavy and thin designer's strokes, with the inside curve of the serif originating from the curved pen or chisel stroke. They are popular book faces well suited to soft uncoated book papers. In advertising they are best suited to formal or dignified layouts.

ABCDEFGHIJKLMN
abcdefghijklmnopqrst
Baskerville

Modern: These faces represent a transition from Old Style, with greater contrast between the thick and thin strokes of the letters and a slight difference in the serifs of many letters, which are more mechanical in design. The development of these faces with finer serifs and hairlines was due to the invention of smooth coated paper. Bodoni, Caledonia, and Craw Modern are examples of modern faces. For letterpress, these faces are not suited to the soft uncoated printing papers such as antique and text papers.

HSMANOETRGUYKJW
hsmanoetrguykjwbfpcv
Craw Modern

Square Serif: Typefaces in this classification tend to be heavier than those of the first two groups. They were developed to obtain bolder headlines for commercial printing, particularly texts in large sizes. Such faces include Craw Clarendon, Cairo Extra Bold, and Beton Extra Bold.

HSMANOETRGUYKJW
hsmanoetrguykjwbfpcv
Craw Clarendon

Sans Serif: This style of face without serifs came into use with the development of modern art and layout, in which details are eliminated. Examples are the Gothics; Futura, which is very popular in all weights; Univers; and Lydian.

ABCDEFGHIJKLMN
abcdefghijklmnop
News Gothic Bold

Miscellaneous: This is a catchall classification of typefaces not included in the first four groups. They are used by designers for moods or special effects. Special faces are often employed by fashionable retail shops to capture a distinctive appeal.[1]

HSMA hsmanoetrguykjw
ABCDEFGHIJKL ABCDEFGH
HSM hsmanoetrguykj
AN hsmanoetr ANO anoet

Fig. 4-3 Classification of typefaces.

[1]Baskerville, Craw Modern, Craw Clarendon, News Gothic Bold, and many other typefaces are available in ATF Spectype transfer letters at art supply stores.

than hand-set type. It is wise to consult a type catalog for a suitable machine-set face and size.

Apparently there are no official premium charges with photocomposition, but such charges seem to be applied to some extent. Almost all phototype fonts contain roman, italic, and boldface of a particular typeface. Some phototype fonts have sizes up to 36 points in text type; usually the line measures up to 45 picas wide.

Fig. 4-4 To lock up type slugs with mounted plates, slugs usually must be sawed. Paste-up proofs do not require this cutting of metal.

Premium-Cost Metal Composition

Metal text composition is set by machines (Linotype, Intertype, or Monotype) and priced per 1000 ems or by the line set. The basic rate is for straight matter (one size and one face in same width) in galley form. The maximum slug width is usually 30 picas (5 inches, or 127 millimeters), and the size not over 14 points.

When you depart from straight matter—mix sizes or faces, vary idention, center, use all caps, use type in columns or in widths greater than 30 picas, and so on—you incur premium charges. With machine-set type in slug lines (unless combination fonts or mixers are used) the premium scales are:

25 percent premium. Lines containing roman and italic or roman and boldface, tabular matter with single justification, and leaders (lines of small dots).

50 percent premium. Matter requiring varying indention, tabular matter leadered out to columns, lines containing all caps, centered lines, rectangular runarounds (counted lines), and straight matter more than 30 picas wide.

100 percent premium. Program matter with periods or hyphens interspaced, lines set in roman small caps or caps and small caps, matter requiring the numbering of each line, running headings with folios on one line, and tabulated matter more than 30 picas wide.

More intricate composition such as technical formulas, boxed headings, roman, italic, and boldface mixed in one line, and two- or three-line initials or figures cast on Linotype are priced as time work. Most display type larger than 14 points is charged on a time basis because it either is hand-set foundry type or, if machine-set, requires hand operations. Typographers supply specification sheets giving details of extra-cost composition.

Premium costs, of course, are greatly responsible for the use of cold composition when this offers an economical solution. Desk-top photolettering machines have come into wide use because they eliminate the high cost of resetting just three or four words in a headline, not to mention saving time.

6 pt. Helvetica

8 pt. Helvetica

10 pt. Helvetica

12 pt. Helvetica

14 pt. Helvetica

18 pt. Helvetica

24 pt. Helvetica

30 pt. Helvetica

36 pt. Helvetica

Fig. 4-5   A type series.

Avant Garde Bold

Avant Garde Bold CONDENSED

Avant Garde Book

Avant Garde Book CONDENSED

Avant Garde DEMI BOLD

Avant Garde DEMI BOLD CONDENSED

Avant Garde X-Light

Avant Garde GOTHIC BOLD

Avant Garde Gothic Bold CONDENSED

Fig. 4-6   A family of type.

SPACING OF TYPE

Measure and Spacing for Body Type

A suitable column width (measure) for readability depends on the type size and the spacing between the lines (leading). A widely accepted rule is that the line be 1½ to 2 times the length of the lowercase alphabet of the selected type size. This measurement is given in type catalogs. Another theory is that the measure should not exceed the width of fifty characters of the type used.

To illustrate, part of the preceding paragraph is shown in three different measures, each with different leadings, in Fig. 4-7.

Spacing Capital Letters in Headlines

A common problem in typography with metal capital letters involves spacing certain adjacent letters for appearance, particularly capitals 30 points or larger. For example, a word containing *A* followed by *V* or *A* and *T* next to each other may require adjustment (see

8/9 by 12 picas

A suitable column width (measure) for readability depends on the type size and the spacing between the lines (leading).

8/10 by 20 picas

A suitable column width (measure) for readability depends on the type size and the spacing between the lines (leading). A widely accepted rule is that the line be 1½ to 2 times the length of the low-

8/11 by 23 picas

A suitable column width (measure) for readability depends on the type size and the spacing between the lines (leading). A widely accepted rule is that the line be 1½ to 2 times the length of the lowercase alphabet of the selected

Fig. 4-7   The longer the line of type, the more space between lines.

TAVERN
AS SET — NO LETTERSPACING

TAVERN
LETTERSPACED TO EXTEND "ERN"

Fig. 4-8
TAVERN
LETTERSPACED TO CONDENSE "TAV"

Fig. 4-8). Your judgment will determine whether such letters should be brought closer together or whether other letters in the word should be spaced further apart. Such spacing is usually adjusted on the drawing board, but a Photo-Typositor photolettering machine may be used. With the machine you can see the position of the letter before it is exposed. The smaller the bold caps are in a headline, the greater the space between the lines must be to command attention.

Display sizes of many of the popular commercial typefaces are available in the form of transparent self-adhesive transfer sheet letters. Greeking sheets (simulated composition) in 8- and 10-point sizes are sold for the text of comprehensive layouts.

With the photomechanical processes chapter initials are usually handled by means of transfer letters, which are inserted on the mechanical with the repro proofs of text. The proper alignment of raised and sunken initials is as follows:

R AISED initial aligns.

T HE sunken initial should align at both top and bottom for best appearance.

Selecting the Typeface

Selecting a suitable typeface and type size calls for judgment under specific conditions. Usually some compromise is necessary because of limitations of space on the layout, local resources, and, with small print orders, frequently cost.

For the beginner it is usually best to know type styles rather than specific faces. In advertising both display and text faces are closely related to the product or service being advertised. Industrial equipment, for example, is apt to call for bold or extra-bold square-serif or sans-serif headlines and for a modern face for the text because of their extra weight. A woman's specialty shop is likely to use typefaces of a more delicate nature, such as one of the miscellaneous display faces for small ads or a light sans-serif display face for large ads. The text is apt to be set in an Old Style face because it is lighter than modern typefaces.

Type can suggest masculinity or femininity, dignity or the lack of it, exclusiveness, cheapness, modernity, or antiquity. Selection is a matter of judgment and taste, and rarely are one face and one size the best. The way type is handled in a layout does more for appearance than the face selected.

REPRO TYPE PROOFS

The most expensive form of composition is a repro proof of a made-up page of type. A semi-made-up page proof may position only the columns of text, perhaps with subheads, and display composition, widely scattered blocks of type, and running headings with folios, proofed without regard to position. A third form of repro proof consists of the galley proofs of the type as it comes from the machines: text, subheads, and display type, all in separate galleys. With these proofs the page can be made up on the drawing board by the production artist, and the cost of composition is cut in half. Today this form of composition is widely used even for letterpress when type matter is to be part of the engraving.

When repro proofs are delivered, they should be carefully checked for imperfections. The galley proofs should be of equal weight so that when they are pasted up, one column or page will not be darker than the next one. You should also make certain that

Lingerie Blouses

common sense

ANTIQUITY

Speed and Motion

ATTENTION

INVESTMENTS

Coal Mines

DIGNITY

SAVINGS ON A

SUITINGS

The shirtdress

On top of it all

A MAKE-UP SO RICH

Fig. 4-9 Two panels of typefaces, traditional and contemporary.

columns of type are not "cocked"; otherwise, they cannot be aligned. Hairline rules should not be used because of the danger of portions of the lines dropping out; hairline rules should always be inserted on a mechanical with a ruling pen.

With the use of a mechanical only a proof of foundry type is needed, and the cost of composition has been reduced. Foundry display faces are the newer hand-set faces not yet on typesetting machines. The typographer does not release this type as metal but supplies an electro, while retaining the original type. Since only repro proofs of the type are needed for the mechanical, the cost of electros is avoided.

Photostats are used for reversing type or any line element on the mechanical and also for enlarging or reducing type to get an exact fit of a headline.

MARKING COPY TO BE SET IN TYPE

Typewritten copy to be set in type should be on 8½- by 11-inch (216- by 279-millimeter) paper, with each page numbered and the last page marked "end." Your instructions for face, size, measure, and leading should be placed in the right-hand margin. The left-hand margin, which should measure 1½ inches (38 millimeters), is for the printer's instructions to the composing room: which copy is to be hand-set and machine-set, which machine is to be used, and so on. If there is considerable body type, as for a book, you should send two copies so that two typesetters can work on the job. Refer to the example in Fig. 4-11 for your form of markup.

If a made-up advertising page is wanted, a layout should accompany the typed copy and any separate blocks of type should be keyed (*A, B, C* or 1, 2, 3) for position. The makeup operator will position the metal. Markup instructions should not go on the layout but on the typed manuscript copy.

Words in the body type that should be set in boldface, italics, small caps, and so on are indicated by proper proofreader's marks, as shown in Fig. 4-11, and not by notation in the right-hand margin. Symbols and underlining are the typographer's language and should be used.

The standard proofreader's marks (Fig. 4-12) should always be used on the reader's type proof to indicate corrections. Their use avoids confusion as to what is wanted.

When ordering type, specify the printing process to be used and, if offset or gravure, the kind of repro proof wanted. The repro proof can consist of the made-up page, as for letterpress; the partially made-up page, to be completed on the drawing board by the paste-

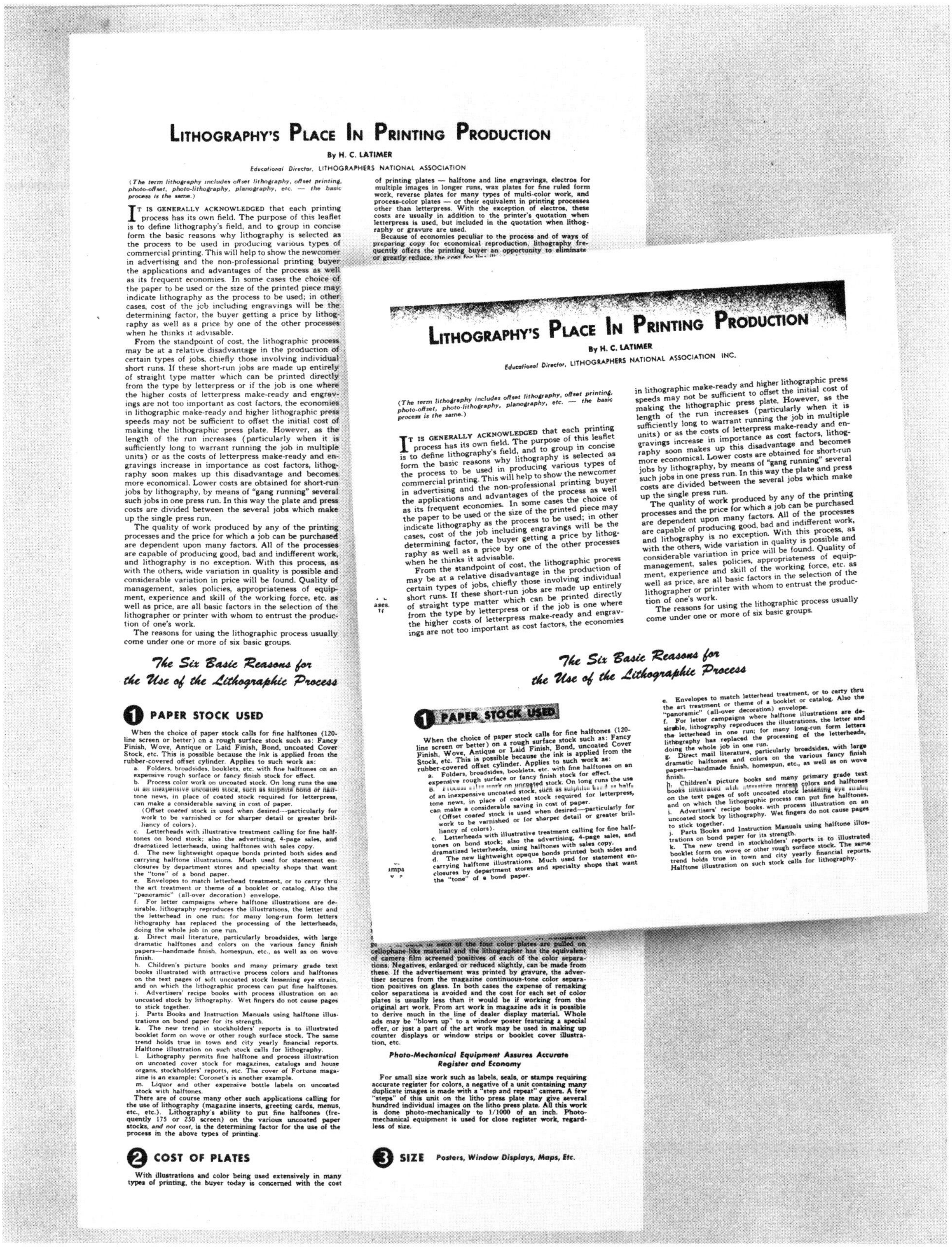

LITHOGRAPHY'S PLACE IN PRINTING PRODUCTION

By H. C. LATIMER

Educational Director, LITHOGRAPHERS NATIONAL ASSOCIATION

(The term lithography includes offset lithography, offset printing, photo-offset, photo-lithography, planography, etc. — the basic process is the same.)

IT IS GENERALLY ACKNOWLEDGED that each printing process has its own field. The purpose of this leaflet is to define lithography's field, and to group in concise form the basic reasons why lithography is selected as the process to be used in producing various types of commercial printing. This will help to show the newcomer in advertising and the non-professional printing buyer the applications and advantages of the process as well as its frequent economies. In some cases the choice of the paper to be used or the size of the printed piece may indicate lithography as the process to be used; in other cases, cost of the job including engravings will be the determining factor, the buyer getting a price by lithography as well as a price by one of the other processes when he thinks it advisable.

From the standpoint of cost, the lithographic process may be at a relative disadvantage in the production of certain types of jobs, chiefly those involving individual short runs. If these short-run jobs are made up entirely of straight type matter which can be printed directly from the type by letterpress or if the job is one where the higher costs of letterpress make-ready and engravings are not too important as cost factors, the economies in lithographic make-ready and higher lithographic press speeds may not be sufficient to offset the initial cost of making the lithographic press plate. However, as the length of the run increases (particularly when it is sufficiently long to warrant running the job in multiple units) or as the costs of letterpress make-ready and engravings increase in importance as cost factors, lithography soon makes up this disadvantage and becomes more economical. Lower costs are obtained for short-run jobs by lithography, by means of "gang running" several such jobs in one press run. In this way the plate and press costs are divided between the several jobs which make up the single press run.

The quality of work produced by any of the printing processes and the price for which a job can be purchased are dependent upon many factors. All of the processes are capable of producing good, bad and indifferent work, and lithography is no exception. With this process, as with the others, wide variation in quality is possible and considerable variation in price will be found. Quality of management, sales policies, appropriateness of equipment, experience and skill of the working force, etc. as well as price, are all basic factors in the selection of the lithographer or printer with whom to entrust the production of one's work.

The reasons for using the lithographic process usually come under one or more of six basic groups.

The Six Basic Reasons for the Use of the Lithographic Process

1 PAPER STOCK USED

When the choice of paper stock calls for fine halftones (120-line screen or better) on a rough surface stock such as: Fancy Finish, Wove, Antique or Laid Finish, Bond, uncoated Cover Stock, etc. This is possible because the ink is applied from the rubber-covered offset cylinder. Applies to such work as:

a. Folders, broadsides, booklets, etc. with fine halftones on an expensive rough surface or fancy finish stock for effect.

b. Process color work on uncoated stock. On long runs the use of an inexpensive uncoated stock, such as sulphite bond or halftone news, in place of coated stock required for letterpress, can make a considerable saving in cost of paper.

(Offset *coated* stock is used when desired—particularly for work to be varnished or for sharper detail or greater brilliancy of colors).

c. Letterheads with illustrative treatment calling for fine halftones on bond stock; also the advertising, 4-page sales, and dramatized letterheads, using halftones with sales copy.

d. The new lightweight opaque bonds printed both sides and carrying halftone illustrations. Much used for statement enclosures by department stores and specialty shops that want the "tone" of a bond paper.

e. Envelopes to match letterhead treatment, or to carry thru the art treatment or theme of a booklet or catalog. Also the "panoramic" (all-over decoration) envelope.

f. For letter campaigns where halftone illustrations are desirable, lithography reproduces the illustrations, the letter and the letterhead in one run; for many long-run form letters lithography has replaced the processing of the letterheads, doing the whole job in one run.

g. Direct mail literature, particularly broadsides, with large dramatic halftones and colors on the various fancy finish papers—handmade finish, homespun, etc., as well as on wove finish.

h. Children's picture books and many primary grade text books illustrated with attractive process colors and halftones on the text pages of soft uncoated stock lessening eye strain, and on which the lithographic process can put fine halftones.

i. Advertisers' recipe books with process illustration on an uncoated stock by lithography. Wet fingers do not cause pages to stick together.

j. Parts Books and Instruction Manuals using halftone illustrations on bond paper for its strength.

k. The new trend in stockholders' reports is to illustrated booklet form on wove or other rough surface stock. The same trend holds true in town and city yearly financial reports. Halftone illustration on such stock calls for lithography.

l. Lithography permits fine halftone and process illustration on uncoated cover stock for magazines, catalogs and house organs, stockholders' reports, etc. The cover of Fortune magazine is an example: Coronet's is another example.

m. Liquor and other expensive bottle labels on uncoated stock with halftones.

There are of course many other such applications calling for the use of lithography (magazine inserts, greeting cards, menus, etc., etc.). Lithography's ability to put fine halftones (frequently 175 or 250 screen) on the various uncoated paper stocks, *and not cost*, is the determining factor for the use of the process in the above types of printing.

2 COST OF PLATES

With illustrations and color being used extensively in many types of printing, the buyer today is concerned with the cost of printing plates — halftone and line engravings, electros for multiple images in longer runs, wax plates for fine ruled form work, reverse plates for many types of multi-color work, and process-color plates — or their equivalent in printing processes other than letterpress. With the exception of electros, these costs are usually in addition to the printer's quotation when letterpress is used, but included in the quotation when lithography or gravure are used.

Because of economies peculiar to the process and of ways of preparing copy for economical reproduction, lithography frequently offers the printing buyer an opportunity to eliminate or greatly reduce the cost for ...

... of each of the four color plates are pulled on cellophane-like material and the lithographer has the equivalent of camera film screened positives of each of the color separations. Negatives, enlarged or reduced slightly, can be made from these. If the advertisement was printed by gravure, the advertiser secures from the magazine continuous-tone color separation positives on glass. In both cases the expense of remaking color separations is avoided and the cost for each set of color plates is usually less than it would be if working from the original art work. From art work in magazine ads it is possible to derive much in the line of dealer display material. Whole ads may be "blown up" to a window poster featuring a special offer, or just a part of the art work may be used in making up counter displays or window strips or booklet cover illustration, etc.

Photo-Mechanical Equipment Assures Accurate Register and Economy

For small size work such as labels, seals, or stamps requiring accurate register for colors, a negative of a unit containing many duplicate images is made with a "step and repeat" camera. A few "steps" of this unit on the litho press plate may give several hundred individual images on the litho press plate. All this work is done photo-mechanically to 1/1000 of an inch. Photo-mechanical equipment is used for close register work, regardless of size.

3 SIZE *Posters, Window Displays, Maps, Etc.*

LITHOGRAPHY'S PLACE IN PRINTING PRODUCTION

By H. C. LATIMER

Educational Director, LITHOGRAPHERS NATIONAL ASSOCIATION INC.

(The term lithography includes offset lithography, offset printing, photo-offset, photo-lithography, planography, etc. — the basic process is the same.)

IT IS GENERALLY ACKNOWLEDGED that each printing process has its own field. The purpose of this leaflet is to define lithography's field, and to group in concise form the basic reasons why lithography is selected as the process to be used in producing various types of commercial printing. This will help to show the newcomer in advertising and the non-professional printing buyer the applications and advantages of the process as well as its frequent economies. In some cases the choice of the paper to be used or the size of the printed piece may indicate lithography as the process to be used; in other cases, cost of the job including engravings will be the determining factor, the buyer getting a price by lithography as well as a price by one of the other processes when he thinks it advisable.

From the standpoint of cost, the lithographic process may be at a relative disadvantage in the production of certain types of jobs, chiefly those involving individual short runs. If these short-run jobs are made up entirely of straight type matter which can be printed directly from the type by letterpress or if the job is one where the higher costs of letterpress make-ready and engravings are not too important as cost factors, the economies in lithographic make-ready and higher lithographic press speeds may not be sufficient to offset the initial cost of making the lithographic press plate. However, as the length of the run increases (particularly when it is sufficiently long to warrant running the job in multiple units) or as the costs of letterpress make-ready and engravings increase in importance as cost factors, lithography soon makes up this disadvantage and becomes more economical. Lower costs are obtained for short-run jobs by lithography, by means of "gang running" several such jobs in one press run. In this way the plate and press costs are divided between the several jobs which make up the single press run.

The quality of work produced by any of the printing processes and the price for which a job can be purchased are dependent upon many factors. All of the processes are capable of producing good, bad and indifferent work, and lithography is no exception. With this process, as with the others, wide variation in quality is possible and considerable variation in price will be found. Quality of equipment, management, sales policies, appropriateness of equipment, experience and skill of the working force, etc. as well as price, are all basic factors in the selection of the lithographer or printer with whom to entrust the production of one's work.

The reasons for using the lithographic process usually come under one or more of six basic groups.

The Six Basic Reasons for the Use of the Lithographic Process

1 PAPER STOCK USED

When the choice of paper stock calls for fine halftones (120-line screen or better) on a rough surface stock such as: Fancy Finish, Wove, Antique or Laid Finish, Bond, uncoated Cover Stock, etc. This is possible because the ink is applied from the rubber-covered offset cylinder. Applies to such work as:

a. Folders, broadsides, booklets, etc. with fine halftones on an expensive rough surface or fancy finish stock for effect.

b. Process color work on uncoated stock. On long runs the use of an inexpensive uncoated stock, such as sulphite bond or halftone news, in place of coated stock required for letterpress, can make a considerable saving in cost of paper.

(Offset coated stock is used when desired—particularly for work to be varnished or for sharper detail or greater brilliancy of colors).

c. Letterheads with illustrative treatment calling for fine halftones on bond stock; also the advertising, 4-page sales, and dramatized letterheads, using halftones with sales copy.

d. The new lightweight opaque bonds printed both sides and carrying halftone illustrations. Much used for statement enclosures by department stores and specialty shops that want the "tone" of a bond paper.

e. Envelopes to match letterhead treatment, or to carry thru the art treatment or theme of a booklet or catalog. Also the "panoramic" (all-over decoration) envelope.

f. For letter campaigns where halftone illustrations are desirable, lithography reproduces the illustrations, the letter and the letterhead in one run; for many long-run form letters lithography has replaced the processing of the letterheads, doing the whole job in one run.

g. Direct mail literature, particularly broadsides, with large dramatic halftones and colors on the various fancy finish papers—handmade finish, homespun, etc., as well as on wove finish.

h. Children's picture books and many primary grade text books illustrated with attractive process colors and halftones on the text pages of soft uncoated stock lessening eye strain, and on which the lithographic process can put fine halftones.

i. Advertisers' recipe books with process illustration on an uncoated stock by lithography. Wet fingers do not cause pages to stick together.

j. Parts Books and Instruction Manuals using halftone illustrations on bond paper for its strength.

k. The new trend in stockholders' reports is to illustrated booklet form on wove or other rough surface stock. The same trend holds true in town and city yearly financial reports. Halftone illustration on such stock calls for lithography.

Fig. 4-10 With semi-made-up page type proofs, pages of a folder made up on the drawing board.

MARKUP OF COPY TO BE SET IN TYPE

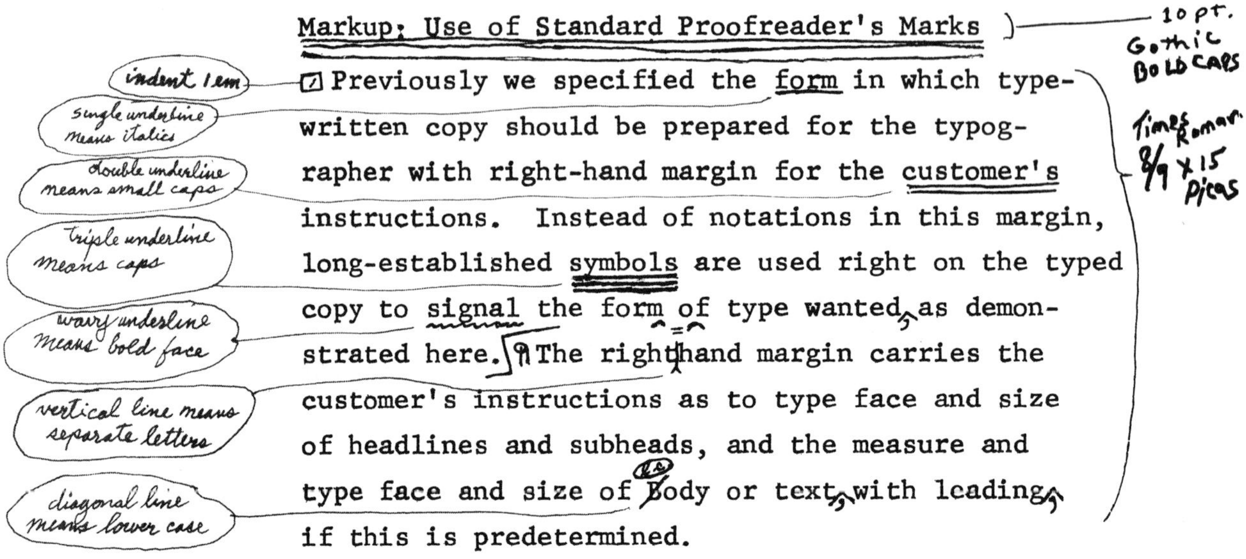

Markup: Use of Standard Proofreader's Marks) ———— 10 pt.
Gothic
Bold Caps

indent 1 em

single underline means italics

double underline means small caps

triple underline means caps

wavy underline means bold face

vertical line means separate letters

diagonal line means lower case

Previously we specified the form in which type-written copy should be prepared for the typographer with right-hand margin for the customer's instructions. Instead of notations in this margin, long-established symbols are used right on the typed copy to signal the form of type wanted, as demonstrated here. The righthand margin carries the customer's instructions as to type face and size of headlines and subheads, and the measure and type face and size of body or text, with leading, if this is predetermined.

Times Roman
8/9 x 15 picas

LEFT 1¼" MARGIN IS FOR TYPOGRAPHER'S MARKUP. CUSTOMER'S TYPE SPECIFICATIONS SHOULD GO ON TYPED COPY, NOT ON LAYOUT.

THE ABOVE COPY WITH MARKUP WOULD RESULT IN THIS TYPE SET:

Previously we specified the *form* in which type-written copy should be prepared for the typographer with right-hand margin for the CUSTOMER'S instructions. Instead of notations in this margin, long-established SYMBOLS are used right on the typed copy to **signal** the form of type wanted, as demonstrated here.

The right-hand margin carries the customer's instructions as to type face and size of headlines and subheads, and the measure and type face and size of body or text, with leading, if this is predetermined.

Fig. 4-11 The marked copy at the top would result in the typeset lines to the right below.

up artist; or galley repro proofs, to be used on the paste-up mechanical with photolettering for display type or with mechanical lettering aids or transfer letters.

Check all final or repro proofs carefully for broken letters, cocked lines, and so on before accepting them.

The end use of a printed job usually determines the choice of typeface, size, measure, and spacing. For books readability is very important, but for commercial printing, particularly advertising, the amount of space available for text or for blocks of type may outweigh considerations of readability.

COPY FITTING

Estimating Required Space

Since the art department now specifies and usually buys typography and the designer handles such details for magazines and books, commercial art instruction does not only include specifying typography. For a layout the artist must also be able to estimate the space required for the copywriter's typed text when set in suitable type.

Too often an art graduate has been led to believe that the character of the work of an art department is still as it used to be: a rough

Punctuation

⊙	Period
⌄	Comma
⊙:	Colon
⌄;	Semicolon
⌄	Apostrophe
"	Open quotes
"	Close quotes
=	Hyphen
1/N 1/M 2/M	Dash (show length)
( )	Parentheses

Delete and insert

ℱ	Delete
ℱ	Delete and close up
out see copy	Insert omitted matter
stet	Let it stand

Paragraphing

¶	Paragraph
fl ¶	Flush paragraph
① ②	Indent (show no. of ems)
run in	Run in

Spacing

#	Insert space
eq #	Equalize space
⌣	Close up

Style of type

wf	Wrong font
lc	Lower case
cap	Capitalize
ic lc	Initial cap, then lower case
sc	Small capitals
c sc	Initial cap, then small caps
rom	Set in roman
ital	Set in italics
lf	Set in light face
bf	Set in bold face
3	Superior character
3	Inferior character

Position

] [	Move right or left
⊓ ⊔	Raise, lower
ctr	Center
fl l fl r	Flush left, right
=	Align horizontally
‖	Align vertically
tr	Transpose
tr #	Transpose space

Miscellaneous

X	Broken type
⌇	Invert
↓	Push down
sp	Spell out
/	Shilling mark (slash)
⊙⊙⊙	Ellipsis
see l/o	See layout
? query	Query

STANDARD PROOFREADER'S MARKS

Fig. 4-12 When ordering composition, provide the printer with marked-up typed copy and layout if for a made-up page. Blocks of type on the layout should be keyed by letter or number to typed copy for positioning.

Multiple-line heads should be marked to be set flush left or right or centered.

Narrow-measure text (to pass an illustration) should be set flush right or left with one side left ragged to avoid awkward spacing or hyphens.

When clippings of printed matter are supplied as text, paste them on 8½- by 11-inch (216- by 279-millimeter) paper.

When proofreading typeset matter for corrections, always use standard proofreader's marks.

To reverse type (show white on black) use a Photostat negative on the paste-up.

To enlarge type beyond the available sizes, use a Photostat positive or the newer proof-positive print.

Repro proofs of metal or strike-on type are usually sprayed with fixative to prevent smearing, but check to be sure that this has been done. Do not approve repros until you are sure that there are no broken or gray-spot characters, cocked text lines, or smears and that all corrections have been made.

Curving a Headline

Fig. 4-13   The old method of cutting a type proof is now outdated.

Fig. 4-14   The simplest method is to draw the curve in blue and then use transfer letters (sold by art supply stores) on transport film. (See Chapter 5.)

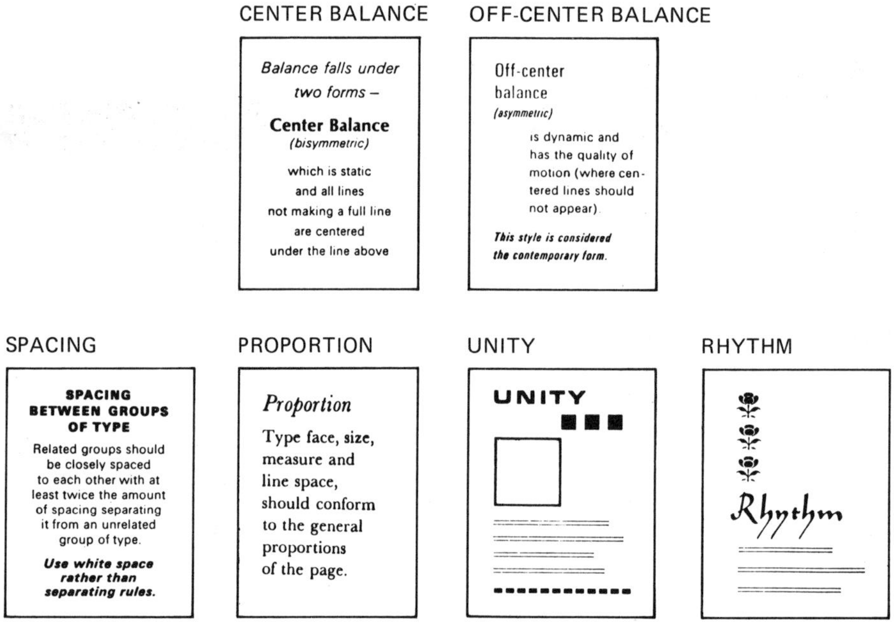

CENTER BALANCE

Balance falls under
two forms –

Center Balance
(bisymmetric)

which is static
and all lines
not making a full line
are centered
under the line above

OFF-CENTER BALANCE

Off-center
balance
(asymmetric)

is dynamic and
has the quality of
motion (where cen-
tered lines should
not appear).

*This style is considered
the contemporary form.*

SPACING

**SPACING
BETWEEN GROUPS
OF TYPE**

Related groups should
be closely spaced
to each other with at
least twice the amount
of spacing separating
it from an unrelated
group of type.

*Use white space
rather than
separating rules.*

PROPORTION

Proportion

Type face, size,
measure and
line space,
should conform
to the general
proportions
of the page.

UNITY

UNITY

RHYTHM

Rhythm

Fig. 4-15   Thumbnail illustrations of working with type courtesy of the International Typographic Composition Association, *Guide for Buyers of Typography*, Washington, D.C., 1966.

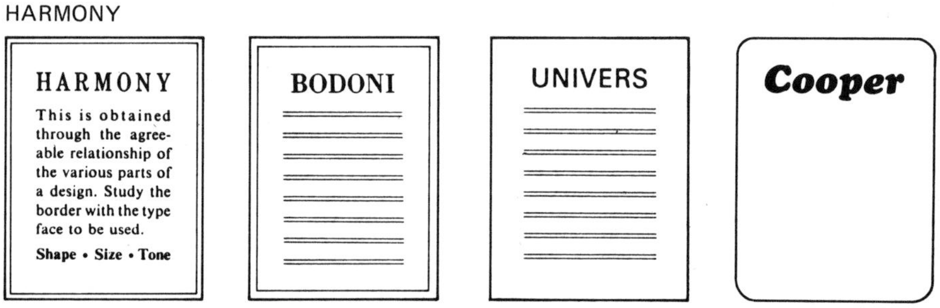

HARMONY

HARMONY

This is obtained
through the agree-
able relationship of
the various parts of
a design. Study the
border with the type
face to be used.

Shape • Size • Tone

BODONI

UNIVERS

Cooper

Fig. 4-16   Borders should reflect the typeface.

CHARACTER COUNT TO LINE INCH

Count the number of characters (letters), punctuation marks, and spaces between words in an average line. These are *Copy Units*. Then count *Lines of Copy* and multiply by the number of *Copy Units* in the average line. This indicates the *total number of Copy Units*.

Education-To prepare us for complete living is the function which education has to discharge. H. Spencer. Education is properly to draw forth, and implies not so much the communication of knowledge as the discipline of the intellect, the establishment of the principles and the regulation of the heart. Webster.

10 lines of copy

← copy units in average line →

10 × 30 = 300 or total number of copy units

☆ CASLON No. 540   Foundry

6²⁷ 8²⁰ 10¹⁷·⁵ 12¹³ 14¹¹ 18 24 30 36 42 48 60 72 84

ABCDEFGHIJKLMNOPQRSTUVWXYZ&
abcdefghijklmnopqrstuvwxyz

character count

layout or copy space

width of type space **2"** × **17.5** = **35** characters to the line

total number of copy units **300 ÷ 35 = 9** lines of type

Education-To prepare us for complete living is the function which education has to discharge. H. Spencer. Education is properly to draw forth, and implies not so much the communication of knowledge as the discipline of the intellect, the establishment of the principles and the regulation of the heart. Webster.

Typewritten copy is easy to figure since the number of CHARACTERS in a line can be measured with a ruler. Elite typewriter runs 12 CHARACTERS to the inch and Pica typewriter runs 10 CHARACTERS to the inch.

Fig. 4-17 [*Courtesy Monsen Typographers, Inc., Chicago*]

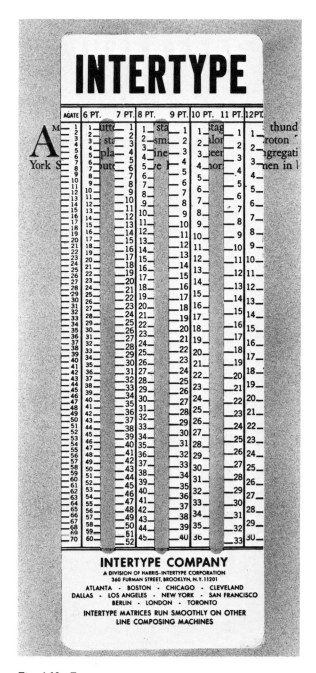

Fig. 4-18 Type gauge.

A. A rough layout such as this is not suitable for the typographer.

B. A more comprehensive layout such as this, with the copy fitting and sizes of type worked out, is needed. If the budget permits, the typographer can handle these details.

C. The finished makeup will be obtained without many delays and without resetting of type for size and fit.

Fig. 4-19

layout with finished artwork and the typed text of the copywriter to be turned over to the production department. Now, however, by the time that rough layouts have been approved all decisions have been made as to paper, colors, printing process, art medium and its preparation (governed by the budget), and usually the typeface. The rough layout should approximate the space for type matter, but the client will usually make some changes. The production or mechanical artist preparing the paste-up mechanical of the page or job should be capable of figuring closely the space he or she should allow for the text copy and the length of a headline. Too often beginners miss job opportunities be-

cause they do not know copy fitting, a relatively simple job.

Rough layouts are the result of planning. The copywriter receives instructions: the size of the space or job, what is to be emphasized, and the components to be included. Before writing the copy, he or she usually makes a preliminary rough to determine the space available for the copy. In a professional department the copywriter is rarely handed a layout and told to fill the indicated space with copy. Thus commercial art is concerned with copy fitting: how much space in a layout or dummy will be required for copy already written? Too often the layout artist does not know how to fit copy or specify type. Both are now the responsibility of the art department instead of production, as in the past.

Typed Manuscript Copy

Copy for text matter should be typewritten to provide word or character count, double-spaced, on 8½- by 11-inch (21- by 279-millimeter) paper, with a left-hand margin of 1½ inches (38 millimeters), a right-hand margin of 1 inch (25.4 millimeters), and a space of 1½ inches at the top and 1 inch at the bottom. The margins provide space for marking copy for type sizes, and with a pica typewriter (six lines to 1 inch) the page has room for 250 words, with a 60-character count, or about 10 words to the line.

Approximating Needed Space

Space for the type size can be approximated by ruling off several square inches of a specimen of printing that you feel would be suitable for the job and counting the words to obtain a count per square inch. From your typed copy you can estimate the total number of words and approximate the number of square inches of space needed for the type you like. If your calculations are close, send the typographer your type specimen and mark the copy and layout "Set to fill."

Use of Type Tables or Systems

Words per square inch	Point size						
	6	7	8	9	10	11	12
Set solid	45	37	30	26	20	16	13
Leaded 2 points	33	26	22	20	15	13	11

Lower Case ALPHABET LENGTHS

To DETERMINE the character count of the Linotype faces listed below (or any other face), find the alphabet length in points of the size you are interested in. Then refer to the *Characters By Picas* tabulation, where characters for measures from 1 to 42 are listed according to different alphabet lengths.

For computing faces not listed, you need only know the alphabet length of the point size desired. Then, by consulting the *Characters By Picas* table and taking the nearest alphabet length listed (the next longest if the exact length is not listed) you will have the figures for the measure-lengths needed.

(The names of the type faces marked † in the following listing are registered by Linotype in the U. S. Patent Office)

Face	5	5½	6	6½	7	7½	8	9	10	11	12	14	18	24	30	36
Antique No. 1 w. Italic	...	...	97	...	...	...	122	132	141	...	165	190	...	...	...	...
Antique No. 1	...	...	...	...	...	...	...	...	...	...	...	...	229	305	...	...
Antique No. 1 Italic	...	...	...	...	...	...	...	...	...	...	...	...	229	...	...	...
*Baskerville w. Italic & S. C.	...	...	90	...	95	...	106	116	129	139	149	170	...	...	...	...
Baskerville w. Baskerville Bold	...	...	...	...	95	...	107	116	130	139	149	171	...	...	...	...
Baskerville Bold w. Italic	...	...	...	...	96	...	107	118	131	141	150	173	...	...	...	...
Bell Gothic Two-Letter	...	...	75	...	88	...	98	...	...	...	...	...	...	...	...	...
Benedictine Book w. Italic & S. C.	...	...	84	...	95	...	109	120	135	148	161	184	...	...	...	...
Benedictine Book	...	...	...	...	...	...	...	...	...	...	...	...	224	...	...	...
Bodoni w. Italic & S. C.	...	...	82	...	96	...	109	...	132	...	145	163	208	272	...	...
*Bodoni	...	...	...	...	...	...	...	...	...	...	...	...	208	267	317	385
Bodoni Italic	...	...	...	...	...	...	...	...	...	...	...	...	207	267	328	...
Bodoni Condensed	...	...	...	...	...	...	...	...	...	...	...	...	...	233	288	...

CHARACTERS BY PICAS, continued

Alphabet Length	1	10	12	14	16	18	20	22	24	26	28	30	32	34	36	38	40	42
110	3.05	31	37	43	49	55	61	67	73	79	85	92	98	104	110	116	122	128
112	3.	30	36	42	48	54	60	66	72	78	84	90	96	102	108	114	120	126
114	2.95	30	35	41	47	53	59	65	71	77	83	89	94	100	106	112	118	124
116	2.9	29	35	41	46	52	58	64	70	75	81	87	93	99	104	110	116	122
118	2.85	29	34	40	46	51	57	63	68	74	80	86	91	97	103	108	114	120
120	2.8	28	34	39	45	50	56	62	67	73	78	84	90	95	101	106	112	118
122	2.75	28	33	39	44	50	55	61	66	72	77	83	88	94	99	105	110	116
124	2.7	27	32	38	43	49	54	59	65	70	76	81	86	92	97	103	108	113
127	2.65	27	32	37	42	48	53	58	64	69	74	80	85	90	95	101	106	111
129	2.6	26	31	36	42	47	52	57	62	68	73	78	83	88	94	99	104	109
132	2.55	26	31	36	41	46	51	56	61	66	71	77	82	87	92	97	102	107
135	2.5	25	30	35	40	45	50	55	60	65	70	75	80	85	90	95	100	105
138	2.45	25	29	34	39	44	49	54	59	64	69	74	78	83	88	93	98	103
142	2.4	24	29	34	38	43	43	53	58	62	67	72	77	82	86	91	96	101
146	2.35	24	28	33	38	42	47	52	56	61	66	71	75	80	85	89	94	99
150	2.3	23	28	32	37	41	46	51	55	60	64	69	74	78	83	87	92	97

Fig. 4-20 The above is a portion of the tables from Mergenthaler's *Copy-Fitting Method*, based on the character count for lowercase alphabet lengths. Intertype's *Ready Reckoner* gives characters per pica and alphabet lengths in a different form.

Frequently boldface and italics take a little more space than the regular type of a font and size.

There are also many forms of typefitting tables available. [*Courtesy Merganthaler Linotype Company*]

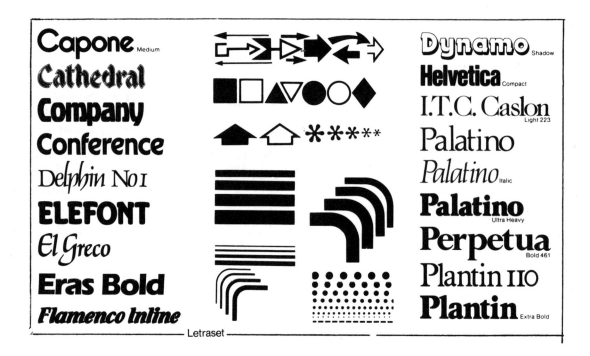

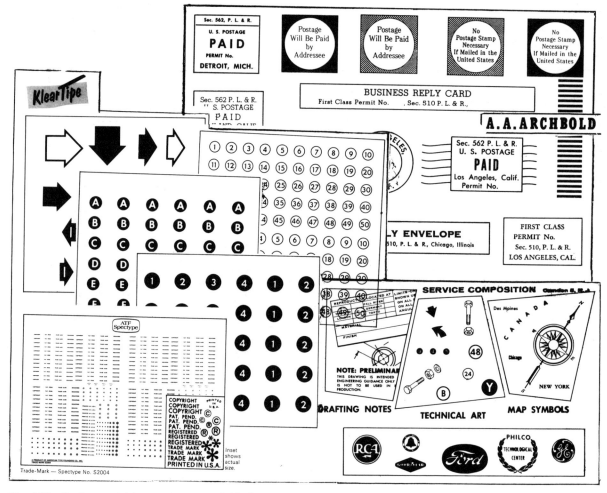

Fig. 4-21 Stock material for paste-ups, available from art stores and other sources. There are clip books, monthly services, and special proofs. The many new typefaces available with phototype are now offered in dry transfer form for comprehensive and packaging dummies, in any place where finished-quality lettering is required. Some are offered in colors, and some stock art and symbols are also available in colors.

From a type catalog giving alphabet (lower-case) length or characters per pica for each face and size you can make your own table.

When you specify leading between type lines, you reduce the number of lines per inch. With 10-point type leaded 2 points, for example, you get six lines per inch instead of seven plus.

Character Count, the Most Accurate Method

Character count is a more accurate copy-fit- ting method, to be used after author's alterations and changes have been made. Figure 4-2*B* shows two Intertype magazine face listings, each of which gives the number of characters per pica. Phototype catalogs and type sheets also usually show characters per pica. The Linotype catalog, however, uses the character count per line inch (6 picas). The Monsen explanation (Fig. 4-17) shows how to figure the number of characters in typed copy.

5

PHOTOTYPESETTING

AFTER WORLD WAR II MUCH research was done to reduce the cost and time required to produce printed material. One of the most successful developments occurred in typesetting, with the use of photography to get type characters on paper. Subsequently, photography was combined with electronics and computers to automate the equivalent of the manual methods of metal typesetting.

GENERATIONS OF PHOTOTYPESETTING

Intertype's Fotosetter (1947), a manual, all-mechanical machine, is termed the "first gen-

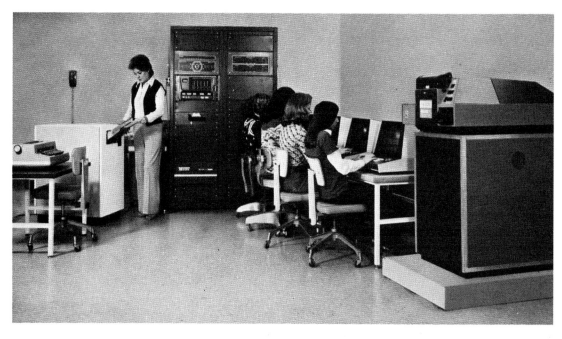

Fig. 5-1 This phototype composing room is typical of those of many new typographers who provide composition alone on a price basis. All that is needed is an average-size room for the equipment and a few typists.

eration" of phototype settings. Subsequently the use of keyboarding to produce a perforated paper or magnetic tape automated the movement of several different stencil forms of type fonts and greatly increased the speed of phototypesetting on paper or film in galley form. This development is referred to as the second generation of phototypesetting.

The third generation, used by the extremely fast commercial phototype systems, photographs individual characters on a cathode-ray tube (CRT). A computer's digital input is translated into light flashes on the tube, which places type character images on film at the rate of 1000 or more per second. It is this kind of system, equipped with memory banks, that is used to revise repetitive material such as parts lists, some catalogs, and telephone directories, dropping the deadwood and inserting the new listings in alphabetical order. It is anticipated that eventually blocks of type instead of individual letters will be photographed.

PERFORATED PAPER TAPES

In the early stage of phototypesetting the industry followed the newspaper industry's use of Teletypesetter perforated paper tapes for its specially adapted linecasters. A typist operating a keyboard which produced the perforated paper tape ignored the usual details of typesetting, such as typeface, type size, measure, and hyphenation, which the Linotype operator had to provide; naturally manual speed was much faster. The fantastic speed of phototype systems, however, is due to the use of computers and automation.

Perforated paper tapes, though still used to a limited extent, have largely been replaced by computerized magnetic diskettes or cassettes (magnetic tapes). These are produced by a keyboard, such as that of the EditWriter in Fig. 5-8 or the AlphaComp in Fig. 5-26. The latter has just a visual display line rather than a visual screen to aid the typist.

A diskette, or "floppy disk," as it is called in the trade (Fig.5-6), looks like a 45-rpm record but is a magnetic recording disk which records, files, indexes, and retrieves up to 300,000 type characters. This is claimed to be equivalent to half a mile of perforated tape. Diskettes index and retrieve by random access, the storage technique used by the com-

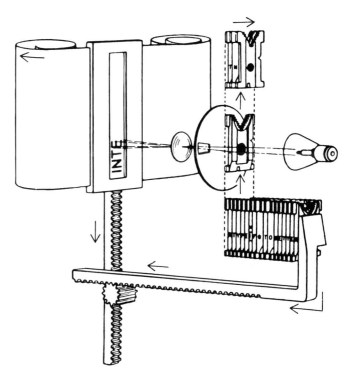

Fig. 5-2 Intertype's Fotosetter, a manually operated phototypesetting machine, was of the first-generation type. A light beam passes through a matrix stencil of letters to project their image on film to compose the line.

puter industry, which is organized for later correction and updating. The disks, which are very thin, can be filed like letterheads. Cassettes used in word processing and in phototypesetting are a different form of computerized magnetic medium, but they have the same capabilities for storing, indexing, retrieval, and so on as the diskettes.

Both the AlphaComp and Compugraphic's EditWriter 7500 systems, discussed below under "Direct-Entry Phototypesetters," produce a floppy disk for storage and retrieval. This is optional with Mergenthaler's Linoterm and VIP systems. The Dymo Graphic Systems phototypesetter, which is employed in conjunction with general-purpose computers, can use a Redactron cassette for input. The Redactron cassette does require an interface unit for most phototypesetters and goes directly to the VDT terminal for type specifications or additional copy.

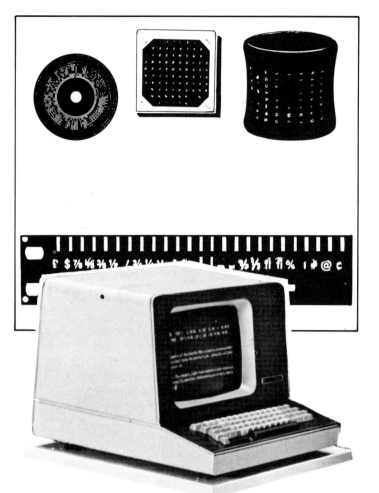

Fig. 5-3A A beam of light passing through some form of stencil used with a second-generation phototypesetter projects type images onto film.

Fig. 5-3B Type font in the form of a film strip.

Fig. 5-4 This AM Comp/Set unit is representative of the phototypesetting equipment used to code and format the various forms of keyboard input such as diskettes and magnetic and perforated paper tapes. Corrections, changes, and type specifications are handled here for the typesetter units.

A new development is the composition area management (CAM) terminal, which shows type in actual size, position, and weight on the VDT screen. The output stream from the CAM terminal is the input of commands and text for the phototypesetter to produce what the operator sees on the screen.

A Diskette

Fig. 5-5 This keyboard of Dymo Graphic Systems is representative of the earlier phototypesetting models with viewing screens for a few lines of the typist's work. These come in justifying and nonjustifying models and may be augmented with optional equipment and accessories.

Fig. 5-6 A computerized diskette or magnetic tape produced by a keyboarding unit provides storage of information with retrieval, editing, and correcting capabilities through the use of a video display terminal.

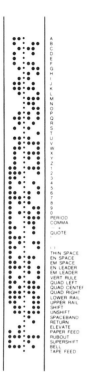

Fig. 5-8 The EditWriter 7500 keyboard is logically arranged and easy to operate, giving complete control over input, proofing and correcting, formating, and word management as well as the final output.

Fig. 5-9 The 7500 display is a true visual communicator, continually monitoring operational functions as well as serving as a guide to accurate composition. It is also a true editing screen, allowing the operator to work on as many as 6000 characters at a time.

Fig. 5-7 The standard six-level perforated paper tape used in the typesetting industry.

THE EDITWRITER KEYBOARD WITH FORMATING KEY PADS

Fig. 5-10

1. The *initializing key pad* controls the hyphenation logic and character fit. It also activates the automatic depth calculator, which allows formating of complete pages. An operator can specify the copy depth in picas and points. The system will rapidly scroll to the desired copy depth and stop for the insertion of base-line rules, footnotes, and page numbers.

2. The *typographic key pad* is used to select the line length, typeface, size, and leading.

3. The *editing key pad* provides full cursor control and virtual scrolling of up to 200 lines of copy of 6000 characters, or more than three pages of copy for the average 6- by 9-inch (152- by 229-millimeter) book.

4. The *file management key pad* has all controls for storage and retrieval, file indexing, and typesetting.

The above are details of Compugraphic's EditWriter phototypesetter (see Fig. 5-24).

PRODUCTION PLANNING FOR PHOTOTYPE

Each phototype system is different. The customer or user should obtain from the typographer a type-buying guide, which should include available type specimens together with the number of characters per pica, or the equivalent, for copy fitting. Very important is a job layout, which helps the typesetter determine the relationship of all elements in the job.

For phototype, all copy should be edited before it is sent to the typesetter, not on the galley proofs. Editing is intended to correct the spelling of proper names, assure uniform indention of paragraphs, regularize punctuation, and secure author's alterations, if possible. Changes on film are expensive. But when it comes to additional text, such as a new paragraph or a change in position, you should remember that the paste-up *mechanical* is the page makeup. You can handle such changes more efficiently than the typesetter.

**Three-Column
Advertisement in
*The New York Times***

Fig. 5-11 Printers are beginning to encourage customers to use available economies with phototypesetting. The VYDEC system produces a diskette form of phototype output suitable for conversion to any phototype system. The Burroughs Redactron keyboard produces a magnetic cassette tape.

WORD-PROCESSING SYSTEMS AND PHOTOTYPE

Most word-processing systems produce a magnetic tape cassette or a diskette to automate subsequent operations. For example, the Burroughs Redactron produces a cassette, and the VYDEC system produces a small diskette by means of a typist's keyboard work. Both provide a storage system for computerized indexing, retrieval, and editing or correcting.

The product of the initial word-processing keyboard operation can be used to avoid a second keyboarding of body type if the same text is needed for other forms of printed material. All that is required is that it be *coded* by a visual display and editing terminal (Fig. 5-4), a process that is the equivalent of type markup and formating for the job.

CONVERSION OF WORD-PROCESSING OUTPUT FOR PHOTOTYPESETTING

We suggest that printing users who have word-processing systems check with their systems' makers about what can be done with their form of magnetic medium or paper tape to convert it into a suitable input for one or more of the phototypesetting systems and so avoid repetition of the keyboard operation by the typographer. Or users can ask the phototypographers if they can employ the form of magnetic medium that the users' word-processing systems produce. A diskette or a cassette provides a computerized form of composition for storage, indexing, and retrieval for correction or additions.

Several makers of direct-entry phototypesetters have announced the availability of "interface" units to convert word-processing magnetic media into the form of input their systems require (see Fig. 5-12). Conversions can also be made for commercial phototypesetters, whether the required input is floppy disks, magnetic tape or card systems, or perforated paper tape. There are at least five makers of conversion units which are purchased by the phototypographers. In metropolitan areas many phototypographers have added interface units to convert word-processing media to suitable inputs for their systems. Small converters have also appeared.

**Word-Processing Typing
Converted for
Phototypesetting**

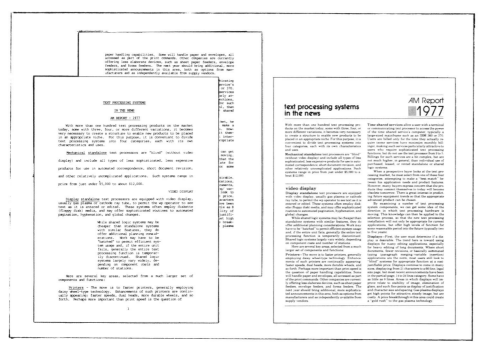

Fig. 5-12 The original keyboard typing of most word-processing systems also produces some form of magnetic medium (a diskette or a cassette) for which the system has further use. By means of an interface unit such a medium can also be used in most phototype systems to translate one form of magnetic medium into another form suitable for a particular system. The equivalent of type markup is performed by the typographer's video display terminal to get the wanted typeface and type size, measure, spacing, and so on. The layout with type proofs goes to the mechanical artist.

A form of magnetic medium may be compatible with a phototype system, and in such a case no interface is necessary. The illustration shows such an example. The diskette produced by the Addressograph Multigraph Corporation's AmText 425 text-processing system is suitable for its Comp/Set phototypesetter (Fig. 5-22) without the use of an interface unit by the typesetter, thus avoiding a second keyboard operation and effecting a sizable economy.

A Conversion Unit

Fig. 5-13 An interface unit translates the "language" of a phototype system to that of another system. WordCom, Compugraphic's word-processing interface unit, is intended particularly for its EditWriter typesetters, but the manufacturer claims that the unit operates with a variety of word-processing media to produce a diskette for later editing, storage, or additions.

FIRST CASE HISTORY

Company magazines, in-house publications, and newpapers are rapidly taking advantage of this new production-planning procedure. The first case history of a company publication switching from letterpress to web offset for lower costs appeared in the April 1978 issue of *Graphic Arts Monthly,* describing the conversion of the Burroughs Redactron word-processing cassettes for phototypography to avoid a second keyboarding of composition.

OPTICAL CHARACTER RECOGNITION (OCR)

A very important development in phototype is that of the OCR systems, some of which are very expensive. All appear to function by the difference between light paper and dark ink, as illustrated in Fig. 5-14.

Widely used by in-house publishers, printers, and typographers is the Context Model 201 optical page reader for which manuscript pages (8½ by 11 to 14 inches, or 216 by 279 to 356 millimeters) are typed with a single-element (ball) type font and single-use carbon ribbon. (The reader costs less than $15,000.) The specimen of typing in Fig. 5-17 gives details; the type font used (OCR B, size 1) distinguishes between the letter *l* and the number 1 to avoid confusion by the OCR page reader. The typist's font bears no relation to the type font and size used for the phototype.

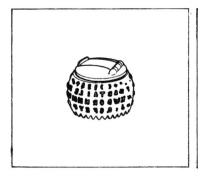 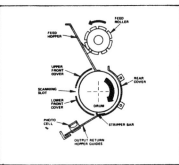 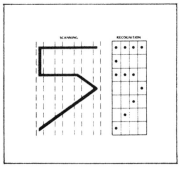

Fig. 5-14 [*Courtesy* TypeWorld] All OCR devices start with an electric typewriter with a known font and carbon film ribbon to get a good black. The scanner looks at the difference between light paper and dark ink and "draws" a picture of each character in its memory. The recognition logic compares each "picture" with another one in its memory and makes comparisons. Thus an OCR device "reads."

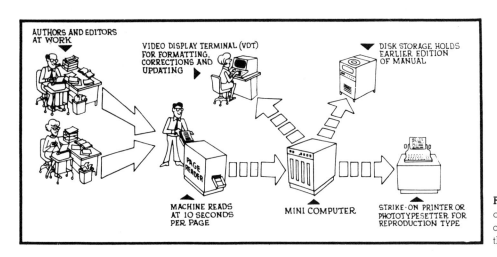

Fig. 5-15 An in-house publishing operation with a Context optical character recognition unit producing the text phototype input.

The Model 201 optical page reader (Figs. 5-16A and B), when interconnected to a direct-entry typesetter or text-editing system, lets you

- Capture the typing of the original manuscript.
- Free system keyboards for editing and markup.
- Expand capacity by adding typewriters.
- Interface with word-processing equipment.

Fig. 5-16A The Context 201 optical character reader is claimed to be an economical, high-speed peripheral OCR machine, designed to produce input for a wide range of microcomputer- and minicomputer-based systems for the graphic arts.

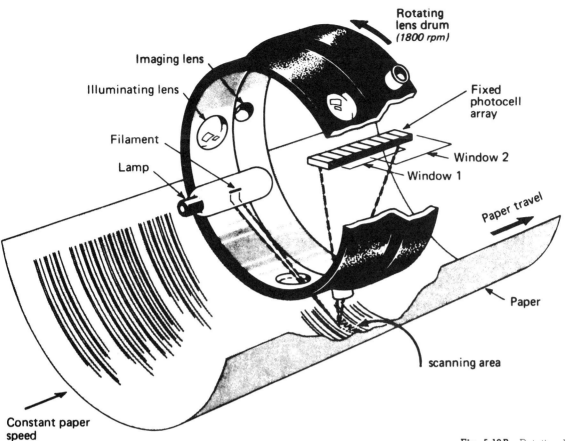

Fig. 5-16*B* Rotating lens drum assembly.

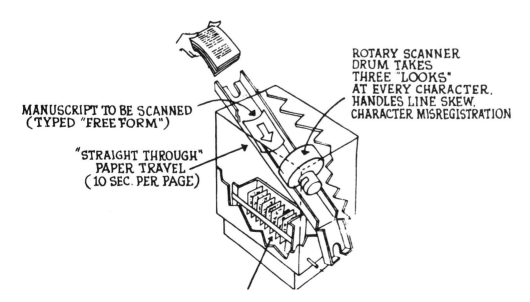

Fig. 5-16*C* The OCR reader scans a page in 10 seconds.

This is a sample of actual typewritten copy as it
is read by the CONTEXT Model 201. Copy can be prepared on any single element typewriter at ten-pitch,
without special modification or adjustment. Copy is
prepared at five or fewer lines per inch.
Copy may be deleted after typing by marking out with
a No. 2 pencil or black marker:
Single ~~words~~ or ~~groups of words~~ may be deleted.
~~Whole lines may be deleted also, if desired.~~
Editorial markup, corrections, and additions can be
shown directly on the copy with red or blue marker
or pencil.

Fig. 5-17 Standard character set, OCR B-86 (IBM type element part No. 1167210). Options are available.

Model B Dymo
Bar-Code Reader

Fig. 5-18 The Model B Dymo bar-code reader is an optical scanner that automatically converts typewritten and edited copy into phototypesetting input. It accepts copy typed on an IBM Selectric typewriter and can either produce clean, unjustified typesetter tape, complete with editing and typesetting formats, or be directly interfaced with many composition systems. No rekeyboarding is needed.

Practically all direct-entry phototype systems now have interface units to convert word-processing magnetic media into suitable input for the typesetter. The Context page reader's magnetic output, when interconnected through a word-processing interface, is also compatible with most direct-entry typesetters and with many editorial and typographic systems.

BAR-CODE PAGE READERS

In addition to the OCR page scanners there are bar-code scanners, or readers, which read the code marks under the typed characters of the typist. The typing appears like this:

method for setting type

Composition from a special IBM Selectric typewriter font is used by several OCR composing methods. The typist reads the letters, and the scanning machine reads the code symbols below them and produces a punched paper tape. Errors are corrected before the tape goes to the phototypesetter. Tapes can be reprogrammed for different type specifications.

AUTOMATION MOVES TYPOGRAPHY
INTO EDITORIAL OFFICES
AND ART DEPARTMENTS

Since this is an offset user's manual, we are not concerned with the details of commercial phototype systems. The typographer's bid will reveal whether the typographer has the right equipment for the job at hand. We are concerned with what the user can do to reduce composition costs either by installing simple, inexpensive phototype equipment which a typist can operate for the smaller typesetting jobs (equipment that costs less that $16,000) or by supplying text material in such a form that the phototypographer's input costs are reduced. At the Vision '77 communications typographics symposium held at the Rochester Institute of Technology, experts concluded that as photographic methods "become increasingly automated, the responsibility for quality and accuracy of copy moves back into the editorial office and art department."

```
This illustrates the editing features of the
⸀⸀⸀ ⸀⸀⸀ ⸀⸀⸀ ⸀⸀⸀ ⸀⸀ ⸀⸀ ⸀⸀⸀ ⸀⸀⸀ ⸀⸀⸀
Dymo optical page reader.
⸀⸀⸀ ⸀⸀⸀ ⸀⸀⸀ ⸀⸀⸀ ⸀⸀⸀ ⸀⸀⸀
1. Character Delete k← works like this.
⸀⸀⸀ ⸀⸀⸀ ⸀⸀⸀ ⸀⸀⸀ ⸀⸀⸀ ⸀⸀⸀
2. Word Delete mkes←← makes words disappear.
⸀⸀⸀ ⸀⸀⸀ ⸀⸀⸀ ⸀⸀⸀ ⸀⸀⸀ ⸀⸀⸀
3. Line Delete eliminates the entire line.←
⸀⸀⸀ ⸀⸀⸀ ⸀⸀⸀ ⸀⸀⸀ ⸀⸀⸀ ⸀⸀⸀
4. Marker Pen Delete makes this disappear.
⸀⸀⸀ ⸀⸀⸀ ⸀⸀⸀ ⸀⸀⸀ ⸀⸀⸀ ⸀⸀⸀
5. Interline Insert lets you replace or add.
⸀⸀⸀ ⸀⸀⸀ ⸀⸀⸀ ⸀⸀⸀ ⸀⸀⸀ ⸀⸀⸀
          ↑permits you to↑
6. Paragraph Insert lets you insert phrases,
⸀⸀⸀ ⸀⸀⸀ ⸀⸀⸀ ⸀⸀⸀ ⸀⸀⸀ ⸀⸀⸀
   sentences, or paragraphs anywhere in the
   ⸀⸀⸀ ⸀⸀⸀ ⸀⸀⸀ ⸀⸀⸀ ⸀⸀⸀ ⸀⸀⸀
   text, with 2-keystroke codes like *A or *4.
   ⸀⸀⸀ ⸀⸀⸀ ⸀⸀⸀ ⸀⸀⸀ ⸀⸀⸀ ⸀⸀⸀
```

Fig. 5-19 In this specimen of bar-code typing there are command characters for deletions (a letter or a whole line) and for insertions. When the typed copy is fed to the optical scanner unit, the changes and corrections are made. Bar-code scanning units are less expensive than optical character recognition machines.

Fig. 5-20 A bar-code type font. The font is the Context subminiature bar code. The typewriter is an IBM Selectric II or 71, 10-pitch.

PHOTOTYPE SYSTEMS SUITABLE FOR THE USER

Our approach to phototypesetting by the printing user has been to favor the use of the methods available with word-processing systems and the use of simple OCR equipment to supply forms of copy which reduce the phototypographer's cost for galley proofs to be employed on the paste-up mechanicals. Since the larger users of printed material, such as the advertising agencies and departments and the editorial departments of publications, are rapidly taking over typesetting, at least in part, we shall now consider the phototype systems specially designed for them.

DIRECT-ENTRY PHOTOTYPESETTERS

Initially, there was only one phototype system suitable for the small printer. The year 1974 saw the introduction of several tabletop photographic systems termed "direct-entry phototypesetters" because no perforated tapes were necessary. In addition to the keyboard, these machines usually have facilities for viewing two lines of composition on a small viewing opening. Keys are pressed to obtain type sizes of the fonts positioned in the unit. The library of typefaces is quite large.

With prices ranging from $4,000 to $16,000, it is natural that in art departments and studios these units are taking their place beside the desk-top photolettering machines such as the Photo-Typositor. A typist operates such a unit when its services are needed.

Direct-entry systems include the Compu-Writer IV (Fig. 5-21), which permits virtually unrestricted mixing of eight type styles and twelve sizes in a 45-pica line; and the Vari-Typer Comp/Set 500 (Fig.5-22), with a range

Fig. 5-21 The CompuWriter IV is a direct-entry phototypesetter operated by a typist. No punched paper tape is required; the manual operation permits mixing eight type styles and twelve sizes in a 45-pica line.

of on-line type sizes. If various keys are pressed, the Comp/Set 500 can handle some positioning. The Mergenthaler Linoterm typesetter (Fig. 5-23) has sizes ranging from 6 to 36 points.

Compugraphic's new EditWriter 7500 (Fig. 5-24) is a direct-entry photocomposition machine with editing, storage, and retrieval capabilities for small amounts of photocomposition. A computer-controlled diskette storage system captures all key strokes for recall, facilitating author's alterations and editing. The use of a diskette is optional with the Linoterm.

The AlphaComp (Fig. 5-25) is not a direct-entry machine, but the system is so greatly simplified that it gives the user the advantage of the computerized diskette for retrieval to edit, change, or enlarge. It costs less than $16,000.

Large-Volume Phototypesetters

Typographic services have supplemented their metal composition facilities with the more sophisticated phototypesetting equipment, and their type catalogs also show these faces and sizes.

This type of equipment can generally print

AM VariTyper
Corporation
Comp/Set Series
Direct-Entry
Phototypesetters

33 Sizes from 5½ to 36 point are available at one time and all sizes are mixed on line to 45 picas

Fig. 5-22 The Comp/Set 500 is a flexible typist-operated typesetter. The operator can move the cursor pointer to any point on the line of the video display screen to make corrections. Fonts and sizes are selected by command from the keyboard. The line width is 45 picas for all sizes. The mixing of fonts and sizes is unlimited, and four fonts may appear on a line with all type bases aligned. Lines may be justified manually or automatically. Lines appear on the reader screen in 14 points for easy reading.

VariTyper's type library has more than 100 popular typefaces.

The Comp/Set 500 system now is compatible with a new AM VariTyper word-processing system without the need for an interface between the word-processing magnetic medium and the typesetting system.

roman, italic, or boldface type in sizes from 6 to 18 points from a single type font, as illustrated by the VariTyper AM 747 system Palatino face (see Fig 5-28). The maximum measure is usually about 45 picas. Any desired letterspacing can be used. Part of a type sheet from a New York suburban phototype service using this VariTyper machine is shown in Fig 5-29.

Phototypesetting Costs

Our inquiries show that in a metropolitan area the cost of photo straight matter runs about 15 cents per line of 10 points on 12, 18 picas wide. When volume and time permit handling the material as a "filler," the cost is much less. Galley proofs on a filler basis are now offered at a price as low as 1 cent a word from price shops.

Mergenthaler's Linoterm
Typesetting System

Diskettes

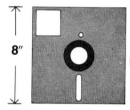

8″

290,000
keystrokes

● **A single, eight-inch-square diskette stores 290,000 keystrokes.** This is equivalent to almost one-half mile of paper tape.

Fig. 5-23 This is a versatile, low-cost direct-entry machine with a keyboard and video screen. Input is produced by a typist using the keyboard in an art, advertising, or editorial office or by a previously prepared, computerized magnetic diskette. There are manual, semiautomatic, and automatic justification models. The video screen has a capacity of twenty-four lines of up to eighty characters. Four faces and five sizes from 6 to 36 points may appear on a line. The line length is 45 picas; fourteen sizes are available, as is Mergenthaler's library of typefaces.

Display formats include a single column of twenty-three lines of eighty characters; a dual column of forty-six lines of forty characters; and a split screen of twenty-three lines of forty characters. One job can be typeset at the same time that another is being edited.

ABCDEFGHIJKLM abcdefghijklmnopqrstu
ABCDEFGHIJKLM abcdefghijklmnopqrstu
ABCDEFGHIJKLM abcdefghijklmnopqrstu
ABCDEFGHIJKLM abcdefghijklmnopqrstu
6-7-8-9 Times Roman

ABCDEFGHIJKLM abcdefghijklmnopqrstu
ABCDEFGHIJKLM abcdefghijklmnopqrstu
ABCDEFGHIJKLM abcdefghijklmnopqrstu
ABCDEFGHIJKLM abcdefghijklmnopqrstu
10-11-12-14 Times Roman

ABCDEFGHIJ abcdefghijklm
ABCDEFGHIJ abcdefghijklmn
ABCDEFGHIJ abcdefghijklmn
16-18-20 Times Roman

ABCDE abcdefgh
ABCDE abcdefgh
ABCDE abcdefgh
24-30-36 Times Roman

Video Screen
of Linoterm

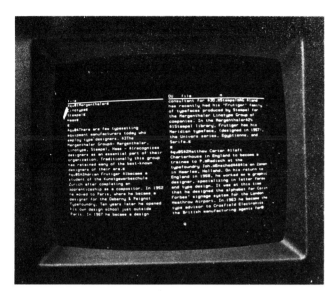

Fig. 5-23A The screen on Mergenthaler's Linoterm typesetting system delivers twenty-three working lines, each eighty characters wide, or, in double-column or split-screen modes, forty-six lines of forty-character width.

AlphaComp Keyboard and
Typesetter by Alphatype

Fig. 5-25 The AlphaComp is not a direct-entry phototypesetter, but its system is so greatly simplified that it is within the price range of an editorial or art department even though a minicomputer is required to handle the problems of formating. A visual display panel shows the operator what is being keyboarded, and corrections and changes can be made before a line is printed.

The AlphaComp keyboard, with the aid of its command keys, programs the job as well as the composition through a minicomputer by means of magnetic coding on a thin plastic floppy disk coated with ferric or chromium oxide. The disk is used to activate the separate phototype unit.

The phototype unit prints the type on photo paper, using a disk form of type font in actual sizes instead of lenses to change the type size. A type font carries three kinds of typefaces, all in the same size. The disk is retained for the storage and retrieval of wanted composition. Type lines can be justified or set flush left or flush right and centered. Command keys can give a length up to 45 picas, ½-point or 1-point rules, and leader lines; a word or a sentence can be underscored by the keyboard. Other type capabilities are available with the keyboard. Type sizes run from 5 to 24 points, with a maximum of 45 picas.

COMPUGRAPHIC'S
EDITWRITER 7500

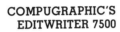

Fig. 5-24 The EditWriter 7500 is offered as a low-cost, all-in-one, direct-entry photocomposition machine with editing, storage, and retrieval capabilities for small amounts of photocomposition. Its simplified keyboard layout is designed for efficient copy input and job control. Typographic pads on the keyboard control automatic hyphenation logic, character fit, and copy depth for page formating and size, line length, font, and line spacing; they simplify the recall of stored information.

The video screen uses 12 inches (305 millimeters) of a 15-inch (381-millimeter) CRT tube and visually "talks" to the operator through two message lines. A computer-controlled floppy-disk storage system captures all key strokes for recall for proofing, editing, and author's alterations. This information can be changed, edited, or searched quickly. The photo unit produces fully mixed composition of eight styles in twelve sizes in either 8 to 72 points or 6 to 36 points (low range). There is a large type library.

Fig. 5-26 Keyboard with a visual display line at the top showing what is being keyboarded. The computerized diskette that is produced activates the type font in the typesetter for composition on paper.

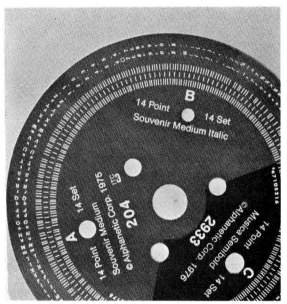

Fig. 5-27 Type font with three faces of AlphaComp.

MOST COMMERCIAL PHOTOTYPESETTERS PRODUCE REGULAR, ITALIC, OR BOLD FACES IN SIZES UP TO 18 POINTS

The state of the art of composition has taken great strides with the advent of phototypesetting. The average reader cannot readily identify the method used in setting the copy being read. With the need

The state of the art of setting type has taken great strides with the advent of phototypesetting. The average reader cannot readily identify the method used in setting the copy being read. With the need for speed and complete versa

The state of the art of composition has taken great strides with the advent of phototypesetting. The average reader cannot readily identify the method used in setting the copy being read. With the need

PT — 27 Palatino

	Reg.	Italic	Bold
6	4.0	5.0	4.0
7	3.4	4.2	3.4
8	3.0	3.7	3.0
9	2.6	3.2	2.6
10	2.3	2.9	2.3
11	2.0	2.6	2.0
12	1.9	2.4	1.9
14	1.6	2.0	1.6
18	1.2	1.0	1.2

CHARACTERS PER PICA

Fig. 5-28 This typical example from a type library shows a phototype face in regular, italic, and boldface, all on the same type font of a commercial typesetter. Characters per pica are shown for copy fitting and for information on the sizes which can be produced from the font. The material is drawn from type sheets of the VariTyper phototypesetting AM 747 system. The system can also handle intraline mixing of as many as twenty sizes.

Megaron	Typography is architecture, and the typographer is the architect. The building bricks he uses are the type faces, and the mortar is the spacing he selects for his composition. His blueprints are	Typography is architecture, and the typographer is the architect. The building bricks he uses are the type faces, and the mortar is the spacing he selects for his composition. His blueprints are called layouts	Times Roman
Medium			
Medium Italic	*Typography is architecture, and the typographer is the architect. The build-*	*Typography is architecture, and the typographer is the architect. The building*	Italic
Bold	**Typography is architecture, and the typographer is the architect. The build-**	**Typography is architecture, and the typographer is the architect. The building**	Bold
Univers	Typography is architecture, and the typographer is the architect. The building bricks he uses are the type faces, and the mortar is the spacing he selects for his composition. His blueprints are	Typography is architecture, and the typographer is the architect. The building bricks he uses are the type faces, and the mortar is the spacing he selects for his composition. His blueprints are	Bodoni
Medium			
Medium Italic	*Typography is architecture, and the typographer is the architect. The build-*	*Typography is architecture, and the typographer is the architect. The build-*	Italic
Bold	**Typography is architecture, and the typographer is the architect. The build-**	**Typography is architecture, and the typographer is the architect. The build-**	Bold
News Gothic Cond.	Typography is architecture, and the typographer is the architect. The building bricks he uses are the type faces, and the mortar is the spacing he selects for his composition. His blueprints are called layouts and his type rule	Typography is architecture, and the typographer is the architect. The building bricks he uses are the type faces, and the mortar is the spacing he selects for his composition. His blueprints are	School-book
Italic	*Typography is architecture, and the typographer is the architect. The building bricks*	*Typography is architecture, and the typographer is the architect. The build-*	Italic
Bold	**Typography is architecture, and the typographer is the architect. The building bricks**	**Typography is architecture, and the typographer is the architect.**	Bold

Fig. 5-29 Part of a type sheet of a small-town phototypesetter, available in 6-, 7-, 8-, 9-, 10-, 11-, 12-, 14-, and 18-point sizes. Employing galley prints of text matter, the user makes up pages on the drawing board to be ready for the camera. A phototype service of this kind will also make up a page in paste-up form (almost all typographers will do this).

In general, costs are lower for phototype than for metal composition, particularly for straight matter in volume, the equivalent of galley repro proofs used for the mechanical. Like metal typographers, phototype services will do page makeup (the mechanical).

A Fast-Developing Industry[1]

Today there are more than 100 models of phototypesetters, 60 keyboards, and 20 video editing terminals, as well as at least 10 OCR devices. Computerized systems can be programmed to position composition as specified in a layout. With the cathode-ray tube, the third generation of equipment, some sys-

tems can now show the made-up pages rather than just lines of type. Page makeup on a mechanical is thus avoided. You get what you see on the video display terminal.

Display phototype from desk-top photolettering machines is employed in art departments for economy in time and cost. A headline can be reset in a different size in minutes for use in a mechanical paste-up. The Photo-Typositor is widely used.

PHOTOGRAPHIC VARIATIONS WITH TYPE PROOFS

Since with offset only copy, rather than metal type, is necessary for the paste-up, headlines which do not fit can be photocopied up or down to avoid resetting type. Photolettering services with trick lenses can condense or ex-

[1]To keep abreast of developments, consult *TypeWorld,* a monthly trade journal, 15 Oakridge Circle, Wilmington, Mass., 01887.

Wordspacing Phototype

Unless you are familiar with a particular phototypesetting system, avoid specifying the exact number of units of wordspacing. There are just too many different phototypesetting systems, and each uses a different unit system. What may be a desirable number of units of wordspacing on one system may not be on another. Therefore the best way to specify wordspacing is to use the broad terms: *loose, normal, tight,* and *very tight.* As an aid we have set this paragraph in each of these styles: examine each carefully and decide which setting is the most legible or desirable for your purpose and use it as a guide for future jobs and to show your typographer the spacing you prefer.

LOOSE WORDSPACING

Unless you are familiar with a particular phototypsetting system, avoid specifying the exact number of units of word-spacing. There are just too many different phototypesetting systems, and each uses a different unit system. What may be a desirable number of units of wordspacing on one system may not be on another. Therefore the best way to specify wordspacing is to use the broad terms: *loose, normal, tight,* and *very tight.* As an aid we have set this paragraph in each of these styles: examine each carefully and decide which setting is the most legible or desirable for your purpose and use it as a guide for future jobs and to show your typographer the spacing you prefer.

NORMAL WORDSPACING

Unless you are familiar with a particular phototypesetting system, avoid specifying the exact number of units of word-spacing. There are just too many different phototypesetting systems, and each uses a different unit system. What may be a desirable number of units of wordspacing on one system may not be on another. Therefore the best way to specify wordspacing is to use the broad terms: *loose, normal, tight,* and *very tight.* As an aid we have set this paragraph in each of these styles: examine each carefully and decide which setting is the most legible or desirable for your purpose and use it as a guide for future jobs and to show your typographer the spacing you prefer.

TIGHT WORDSPACING

Unless you are familiar with a particular phototypesetting system, avoid specifying the exact number of units of word-spacing. There are just too many different phototypesetting systems, and each uses a different unit system. What may be a desirable number of units of wordspacing on one system may not be on another. Therefore the best way to specify word-spacing is to use the broad terms: *loose, normal, tight* and *very tight.* As an aid we have set this paragraph in each of these styles: examine each carefully and decide which setting is the most legible or desirable for your purpose and use it as a guide for future jobs and to show your typographer the spacing you prefer.

Fig. 5-30   Prepared by James Craig. [*Courtesy International Typeface Corp.*]

Fig. 5-31   The Photo-Typositor with lens handles sizes from 8 to 144 points. It is widely used for headlines since the operator can see the position of the letter before printing it.

pand type without changing its height. A whole page can be handled this way.

Photographic enlargement can frequently be used to produce type in an extra-wide measure and in sizes 18 points and larger to avoid hand-setting display lines. The applications of changes in size are endless.

When type or plates of previous jobs are not available, all that is necessary for a reprint is a clean specimen for camera copy. A widely used form of reprint consists of the original job in a different size. A field edition (pocket size) of an 8½- by 11-inch (216- by 279-millimeter) desk edition of a catalog can be reprinted without resetting the type. A page can be reprinted as a wall poster, and a magazine insert for two different page sizes is handled by the camera.

PHOTOTYPESETTING PROCESSOR WITH A BUILT-IN CAMERA SYSTEM

For a number of years art departments have been adding equipment to avoid the need for outside services and thus save time. Visual Graphics' POS ONE daylight camera (Fig 5-36) has come into wide use to produce a pos-

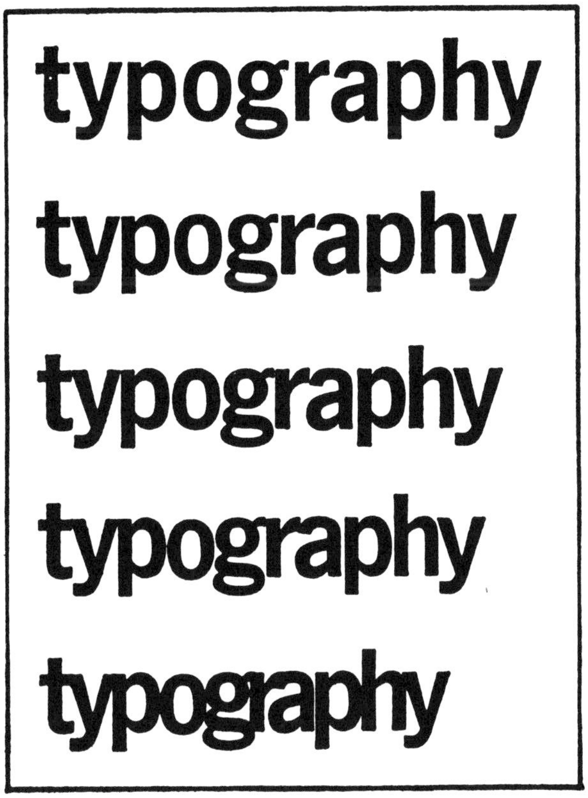

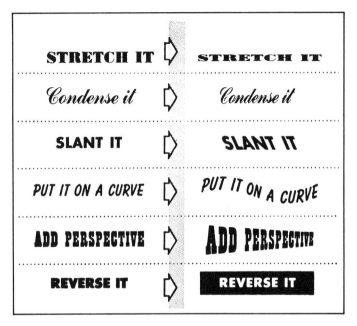

THE
WONDROUS
FLEXIBILITY
OF
PHOTOTYPOGRAPHY

Fig. 5-33 Many typographers who are equipped for composition on film or photographic paper not only handle conventional forms of setting type but also undertake trick composition with special lenses. [*Warwick, St. Louis*]

Fig. 5-32 These settings, from top to bottom, are called normal, tight, very tight, very, very tight, and too tight. [*Courtesy The New York Times*]

Fig. 5-34 To obtain type in perspective, a type proof and a rough pencil sketch showing the size and effect wanted are sent to a photolettering service. [*Warwick, St. Louis*]

itive copy of any type of print in one step, from a Photostat to a screened halftone negative or a Velox print. The POS ONE CPS 516 is converted with the flick of a switch, from a phototypesetting unit to a processor for RC (resin-coated) photo paper or film. The processor accepts RC paper from 4 to 10 inches (from 102 to 254 millimeters) wide by any length and delivers the dry proof of the photocomposition. Thus the user has a two-in-one unit for the price of a single unit. No plumbing is necessary.

Visual Graphics has also introduced an automatic four-bath deep-tank processor for volume work. This versatile processor enables owners of both phototypesetting and camera equipment to process the output of

DESIGNERS CAN USE PHOTOCOMPOSITION AS AN ART MEDIUM

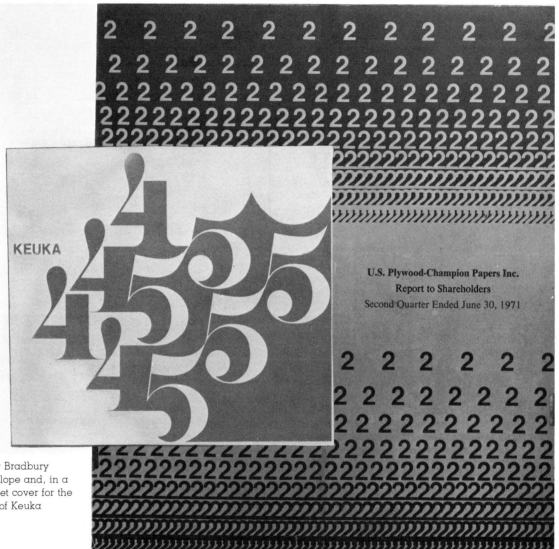

Fig. 5-35A Design by Bradbury Thompson for an envelope and, in a larger size, for a booklet cover for the forty-fifth anniversary of Keuka College.

Fig. 5-35B Cover of a stockholder's report in light blue (two-thirds size).

the two systems in a single automatic processor. One series of chemicals does the entire job, handling RC paper in widths from 4 to 10 inches by any length and producing dry proof in 90 seconds. The machine processes positive and negative working materials in the same system, using the same solutions. It can be used in a darkroom or in a normally lit room with a daylight cassette loader.

COLD-TYPE COMPOSITION

The day-to-day printing needs of both large and small organizations present the problem of small print orders of a utility nature—price lists, parts lists, instruction sheets or folders, and the like—for which the end use does not require quality work. The basic problem is the cost of composition: for 1000 copies of a Multilith job metal composition could run as

Fig. 5-36 With the flick of a switch this POS ONE ® print camera is converted to a photoprint processor that develops dry prints of phototype.

high as 80 percent of the total cost. In addition, tabular composition, spaced for columns, and algebraic formulas for textbooks are particularly expensive in metal.

This short-run composition cost problem and the advantages of small offset presses using any form of composition for the camera resulted in the development of photographic composition methods that do not involve hot metal. For text there are now special electric typewriters with proportional spacing and margin alignment that get the second typing automatically from a punched paper tape. Transfer letters on transparent paper are still used for display type, but mechanical lettering aids and templates are employed for larger headlines.

In a large user's production department with a large volume of small print orders, cold-type methods produced such composition for 25 cents on the dollar. Cold-type composition services estimate their selling price as 60 percent of that of metal.

Many ruled business forms, as well as tabular material, are prepared with cold-type composition. When small typefaces are not available, you should prepare a paste-up large enough to take the faces used, with vertical ruled lines in light blue, so that a negative may be prepared in the size wanted. The printer can scribe the fine vertical rules on the negative. (The large number of pieces of paper on the paste-up prevents vertical pen ruling in black on the paste-up.)

Because of the cost of metal composition, short-run offset printing developed a demand for alternative methods. Electric reproduction typewriters producing proportional spacing

DISPLAY COMPOSITION METHODS USED IN THE ART DEPARTMENT

Transfer Letters

**HOW IT WORKS:
RUB ON LETTER WITH PENCIL
AND LIFT AWAY SHEET**

Fig. 5-37 Art supply stores carry a large selection of various forms of typefaces on paper or self-adhesive clear sheets. Some are transferred to the paste-up by pressure, while others are positioned, cut with a needle, and rubbed down.

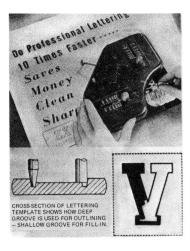

Fig. 5-38 Varigraph, a pantographic type of mechanical lettering aid widely used.

Fig. 5-39 A phototypesetter, one of a number of desk-top machines.

Fig. 5-40 Polaroid's MP-4 industrial view camera, used by many art studios and publications for odd scaling jobs and ordinary-quality halftones.

Fig. 5-41 Wrico, a stencil outline guide for drawing large letters.

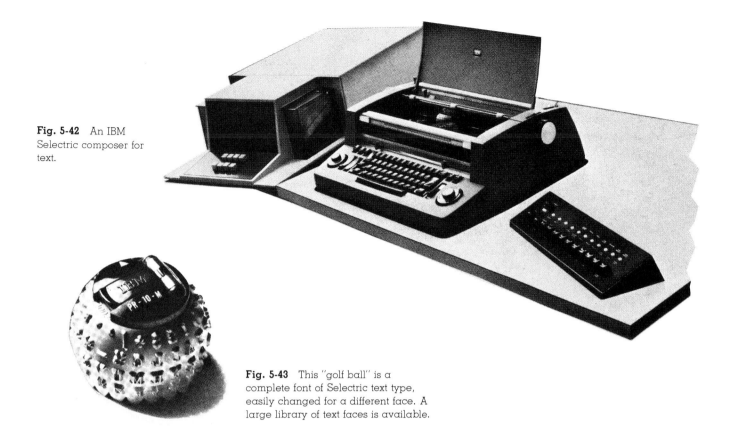

Fig. 5-42 An IBM Selectric composer for text.

Fig. 5-43 This "golf ball" is a complete font of Selectric text type, easily changed for a different face. A large library of text faces is available.

of book faces and right-hand margin alignment came into use for text matter with various forms of nonmetal display type, such as photolettering, for headlines.

IBM SELECTRIC COMPOSER UNIT

A byproduct of the IBM Selectric typewriter, which provides changeable type fonts, is the IBM Selectric composing unit, which produces a magnetic tape for an automatic second typing. The typist can make corrections by retyping over the error. Running the magnetic tape through the composing unit automatically produces corrected and justified composition for the paste-up.

The ability to type camera-ready copy at speeds up to 150 words a minute is one of the distinct advantages of the IBM magnetic-tape Selectric composer.

10 Pt. Medium

ABCDEFGHIJKLMNOPQRSTUVWXYZ
abcdefghijklmnopqrstuvwxyz
1234567890$.,-'`:;!?*½¼¾—()[ ]=†/+%&@

Bodoni Book is an upright, well-delineated type face. It is especially characterized by distinctly contrasting thick and thin strokes. Its serifs are also distinctive, with a perfectly flat line. The strong vertical accent in the construction of each letter marks it clearly as a modern type face. Because of its easy readability, it

Bodoni Book is an upright, well-delineated type face. It is especially characterized by distinctly contrasting thick and thin strokes.

Bodoni Book is an upright, well-delineated type face. It is especially characterized by distinctly contrasting thick and thin strokes.

Fig. 5-44 Examples of IBM Selectric typefaces.

There is a sizable library of text typefaces, including the popular Baskerville, Bodoni Book, Century, Copperplate Gothic, Press Roman, and Univers. Sizes range from 6 to 12 points, but most are available in 8 to 12 points in medium, italic, and bold. There are also some special newspaper faces.

IBM Electronic Selectric Composer

An offshoot of the IBM composer unit, this is an electronic typewriter using the same text faces but having a memory for composition in different formats. A typist does one draft, correcting errors by backspacing and retyping over mistakes; a few buttons are pushed, and the machine is coded in the wanted format. The automatic retyping is in this format. The machine can be rented. More than 125 interchangeable typefaces are available. Format examples are shown in Fig. 5-46.

Bibliography. *Glossary of Automated Typesetting and Related Computer Terms,* Composition Information Services, 1605 North Cahuenga Boulevard, Los Angeles, Calif. 90028; Frederic W. Goudy, *The Alphabet and Elements of Lettering,* reprint of 1922 work, Dover Publications, Inc., 180 Varick Street, New York, N.Y. 10014; *Guide for Buyers of Typography,* International Typographic Composition Association, 5223 River Road, Washington, D.C. 20016, 1966.

The catalog of the Dick Blick Company, P.O. Box 1287, Galesburg, Ill. 61401, is suggested for those who live far from art supply stores.

Fig. 5-45 IBM electronic Selectric composer.

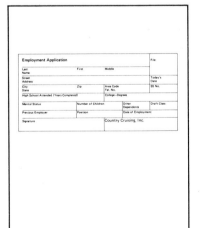

Fig. 5-46 Various formats, including vertical and horizontal ruling, produced from original typing by pressing keys.

6

OFFSET ART AND MECHANICAL PREPARATION

WHAT WE HAVE COVERED IN previous chapters—the printing process, production planning using the extra capabilities and advantages of the process, the wide choice of paper surface for tone reproduction, composition methods, and the advantages of *time* estimating for plate costs—now converges in art and repro-mechanical preparation for the camera.

Production planning was started in the creative stage by the art director as a member of the creative team. Decisions were made on publication advertising schedules and related collateral printed material. Layouts were made, and a budget was prepared for client approval.

With approval of a rough layout, decisions have been made on colors, paper, printing process, choice of art media, and, frequently, composition. The limitations of time and money available have been considered, together with the quality of printing planned. Details on camera copy in preparation have been noted on the rough layout along with any instructions.

THE REPRO MECHANICAL

At this point the rough layout with any photos or artwork and instructions is moved to the art department. A rubber stamp impression on the rough shows the delivery dates required for composition and other elements as well as date on which the material is due at the printer.

There are just two ways to make up a page or other copy unit for printing: assembling composition and engravings in metal form, as for letterpress, and getting a proof; or using proofs of text and headlines and photo copies or suitable original art, all scaled and positioned according to the rough layout. Offset uses the latter method, called a "repro mechanical."

BASIC ADVANTAGES

The mechanical, which is an assembly operation to provide copy for the printer's camera, permits the printing user to transfer to the art department the matter of page makeup, the scaling and positioning of both line and tone elements, and the matter of positioning type matter by pasting the proofs of type on the mechanical. Obviously, this method is ideally suited to the use of phototype as well as to the cold-type methods covered in previous chapters.

One of the advantages of time plate estimating is the fact that a base plate charge for each press size includes all line copy scaled and positioned; only the halftones carry an

A ROUGH LAYOUT IS THE STARTING POINT FOR THE MECHANICAL

Fig. 6-1 The approved rough layout goes to the production (mechanical) artist with instructions and related data. Colors, paper, size, process, and art media have already been selected. Composition may have been ordered, or the artist may specify it. A rubber stamp indicates the delivery dates for artwork, engravings or separations, composition, and so on and the delivery date to the printer. Everything must be within the limitations of the budget and the closing dates.

Top Half
of a
Two-Page
Spread,
10 by 7½ Inches (254
by 190½ Millimeters),
in Two Colors

Remodeling a smaller house

Here's enthusiastic proof of the theory that sometimes it's wiser to buy an older house and modernize, than it is to buy a newer one roofing and siding and aluminum-framed windows and window walls, complemented by an all-brick fireplace wall. A custom-designed panel The window wall in the end gable provides enough light for a finished attic without the necessity of adding a dormer out the rear. A small front strength and sliding glass doors installed. The resulting light and ventilation for the basement area allowed it to be finished off as part of the

Fig. 6-2 The preparation of the mechanical is shown in Chapter 9. Copy for the second color was produced on a clear film overlay in red with a Magic Marker. Red photographs as black and frequently is used to indicate that color will be employed.

extra cost. In Chapter 10, in which we discuss process color copy, we cover "prepared" color copy: the intermediate photo steps between the original artwork and that prepared for the camera. These steps include combining, inserting, and color-balancing color elements to make an illustration or to prepare them for same-focus process copy so that a group of color subjects can be positioned on the mechanical for a large subject, such as a 25- by 38-inch (635- by 965-millimeter) broadside. The result is that all such reproductions can be handled with one set of color separations, without the necessity to strip each reproduction to register on the four color press plates. For simple or flat-color printing, usually in black and one color, the mechanical gives the paste-up artist the opportunity to provide for the register of touching colors (a slight lap) by the use of "keylining," an old lithographic technique. This means that the printer need not perform the equivalent operation at about $20 per hour.

OVERLAY COPY MAY SUPPLEMENT THE MECHANICAL

Different kinds of camera copy and most multicolor copy often require the use of an overlay on the mechanical, usually a sheet of clear film on which copy is pasted; or the artist may use various techniques to work on the film. To keep plate costs to a minimum with multicolor printing color work can go on the overlay and black on the mechanical. The printer's camera operator places a sheet of white paper under the overlay for the color negative and then folds back the overlay to make the negative for the black. In practice, this method is risky if accurate lap color register is to be achieved. Producers believe that the overlay should be avoided for color work when possible; they prefer copy in one piece with the various forms of keylining. This procedure is covered in Chapter 8.

INDICATING SEPARATE ELEMENTS

Some forms of artwork are not suitable for positioning on the mechanical: a 35-millimeter transparency or a large watercolor, for example. Such elements are indicated for size and position by a red outline on the mechanical, and the keyed elements are supplied separately. If the mechanical is used as a comprehensive layout for an agency's client, Photostats or inexpensive color prints are employed on the mechanical instead of outlines.

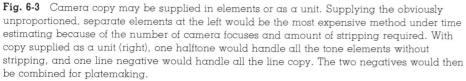

Fig. 6-3 Camera copy may be supplied in elements or as a unit. Supplying the obviously unproportioned, separate elements at the left would be the most expensive method under time estimating because of the number of camera focuses and amount of stripping required. With copy supplied as a unit (right), one halftone would handle all the tone elements without stripping, and one line negative would handle all the line copy. The two negatives would then be combined for platemaking.

A MECHANICAL PERMITS ANY FORM OF COMPOSITION

The use of the mechanical paste-up not only permits pages to be made up on the drawing board but also allows the use of any form of composition: paper letters, mechanical lettering aids, and display type produced by desktop photolettering machines. The text can be handled with galley proofs of metal type, photocomposition, or special reproduction typewriters for small printing orders that cannot bear the cost of metal type or phototype.

PREPARING THE MECHANICAL

Copy in paste-up form is usually prepared in the same size as a unit. It is equivalent to page makeup on the drawing board with pieces of paper (repro proofs, photos, scaled art, and so on) instead of on the printer's composing stone with metal type and plates. Whatever the form in which copy for the camera has been prepared (separate elements, overlay copy), the mechanical is the key copy. Various keylining techniques are used with multicolor copy to signal the platemaker to complete certain work: provide for color register, surprint on color, and the like. A tissue overlay in rough form indicates the desired results and carries any needed instructions.

When you have a line mechanical and the tone elements are supplied separately, the line negative provides the base film on which the halftone negatives are positioned to complete the unit negative. When an overlay is used for a second color with register marks, the mechanical provides the key for color register.

As a precaution in case of damage in handling, an extra set of repro proofs of type matter should accompany the mechanical. The producer can repair damage with these without holding up the job.

For all but simple jobs it is important to prepare a dummy or tissue overlay to indicate the final result wanted: color breakup, reversed elements, halftone tints, surprinting on color, lines to be held or dropped. The dummy should be sent to the producer with the camera copy.

Work Marks

From the approved rough layout of a page or copy unit the artist prepares the mechanical on smooth-surfaced illustrator's board or, for booklet pages, frequently on bristol board. Corner marks are drawn to indicate the work area and page size; for multicolor work center marks are added as in Fig. 6-5. These work marks guide the platemaker and the binder.

Outside the work area of the paste-up the artist indicates in light blue or in pencil the margins, column width, and height for positioning type repros and other elements, squaring them with a T square and triangle. All trim margins should be ⅛ inch (3.175 millimeters). Work marks for bleed trim and folds are shown in Fig. 6-6.

PHYSICAL MAKEUP OF A MECHANICAL

The form of a mechanical varies with its size and the expense incurred in its preparation. Usually a mechanical must withstand considerable handling in the printer's shop as it is sent from one department to another with other copy. Ordinarily it is prepared on an illustrator's board, with a tissue overlay for instructions and a kraft paper protective cover, which is fastened to the back of the mechanical so that it can be folded back and under when the mechanical is placed on the camera copyboard.

Illustrator's Board with Tissue Overlay and Protective Cover

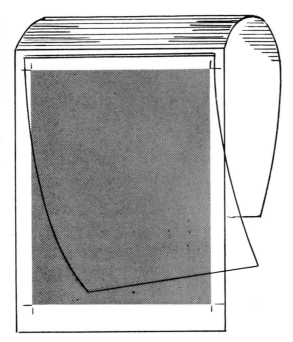

Fig. 6-4 A mechanical that entails much work is prepared on board with a tissue overlay for instructions and a kraft cover.

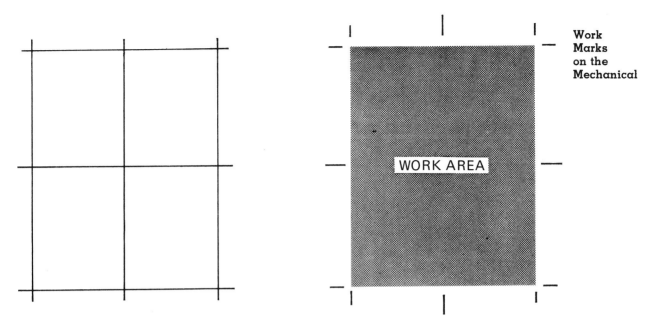

Work
Marks
on the
Mechanical

WORK AREA

Fig. 6-5 The work, or design, area of a copy unit, such as a page, is shown at left with center lines added for possible later use. In practice, only the ends of the lines are drawn, as shown at right. Center lines are used on multicolor copy and booklet pages or for jobs on which the vertical position is not evident. Work marks are removed when the paper is trimmed or are opaqued on the negative.

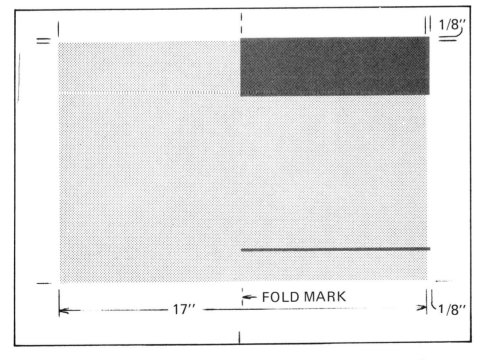

Trim and
Fold Marks
for a
Bleed Design

1/8"

← FOLD MARK

17"

1/8"

Fig. 6-6 The front and back of a four-page folder with a bleed design are shown. The shaded area is the work area of the paste-up, as indicated by corner marks. The bleed copy is extended ⅛ inch (3.175 millimeters) for trim with an extra work mark added. The bindery needs the fold marks (lines of short dashes) outside the work area, and after folding it will trim the page to the corner marks.

There are a wide variety of illustrator's boards, surfaces, and thicknesses; the larger the mechanical, the thicker the board. Separate artwork is apt to be submitted on a rag-content surface of the cold-press type, which is not too rough for pen and ink. Plate-finished bristol board, which is available in 1- to 4-ply thickness, takes fine line detail and is frequently used in 2-ply for copy supplied as a separate element. Other types of paper and board may be used for artwork and positioned on the mechanical: kid-finish bristols, watercolor papers, Ross or coquille boards, and scratchboards.

A single copy overlay on film or parchment is apt to be fastened with tape to the top of the mechanical in such a way that the camera operator can slip paper under it to photograph it and then fold it back to show the mechanical of the key copy. If there are two or more overlays, the pin register system described in Chapter 9 is generally used so that the camera operator can take them apart and photograph all copy as a group.

For ordinary copy without pen or wash drawings, a heavy offset stock or bristol index stock is often used for the paste-up. Photos supplied as separate elements should be mounted to avoid damage and fingerprints. The job and position in which they are to be used should be identified.

Hand opaquing is being replaced by the use of red masking film, which is cut and positioned on the copy. Art supply stores sell such materials as well as colored art papers, tone sheets, and the like.

A smooth illustrator's board is used to take ink and any hand opaquing. For paired booklet pages consisting mostly of text, 2-ply bristol board with modest margins is apt to be used so that many pages will fit on the copyboard of the camera.

The cover should bear the customer's name (the department and the individual if the company is large), the job identification, a list of separate elements, and the delivery date of any copy that is to come.

TWO BASIC FORMS OF MECHANICALS

The type of organization and the quality of a job have a bearing on the details of copy preparation for the camera. The method of estimating plate costs should also be considered.

As we have explained, the purpose of the mechanical is to transfer to the copy preparation stage some of the work that otherwise would be handled by the engraver or the printer.

There are two basic forms of mechanicals for a single color. These are shown in Figs. 6-7 and 6-8; Fig. 6-9 is a variation of Fig. 6-8.

We have always considered that opaquing of halftone areas on the mechanical for offset should be limited to ordinary-grade printing. The resulting "window" in the line negative makes it simple to strip a halftone negative on top, but this does not permit emulsion-to-emulsion contact printing for the offset press plate. There is some loss of tonal quality from light undercutting the dots.

If an offset printer requests the opaquing of tone areas for a long-run printing job, it will be for deep-etch press plates, which require the image reversal (mirror image) of halftones. On special thin film the printer will strip the halftone negatives under the windows of the unit negative; this gives a left-reading image as for photoengravings. If by chance a mechanical has halftone positions opaqued instead of outlined, it makes no difference to the offset printer.

USE OF MASKING FILM BY THE ARTIST

Masking film was originally developed to avoid much brush opaquing on photographic negatives by the offset platemaker. Its use prevented light from passing through clear portions of film in contact printing—negative to positive or positive to negative. It wasn't long before the user's mechanical artist started employing this film on mechanicals instead of brush-opaquing when a solid area, either black or a flat color, was desired. This camera copy gave a clear area in the platemaker's negative needed for a solid printed area, or the user could mask a photo image for a silhouette halftone, permitting the printer to brush out the background.

Masking film is a thin, translucent red or amber film with a temporary adhesive backing on a heavier clear film carrier sheet. When it is placed on top of any form of artwork, the image beneath is visible. The masking film can be cut with a sharp knife or razor blade along a line or the edge of a design, care being taken not to cut the carrier film.

HANDLING TONE ELEMENTS ON THE MECHANICAL

TROUBLE SHOOTING AT 611

Any customer with a problem telephone can call 611 for repair service any time, night or day. And they'll get help fast. Our cover and inside photos show how. How long does a repair take? Usually less than four hours. But this depends on the type of problem. And on how busy our 26 local repair bureaus get.

For example, the big ice storm last December knocked out nearly 41,000 phones, necessitating longer waiting periods for some people.

Keeping SNET's 2¼ million telephones working is a big job. In 1973 there were 1,041,464 calls to 611—about 3,000 a day. This is the second lowest rate of repair calls in the Bell System.

It averages out to about one call every two years for each phone.

Of these calls, one quarter were because of no dial tone. In 22 per cent of the cases the customer couldn't receive outside calls.

Transmission noise and not being able to call out each bothered 15 per cent of 611 callers. About 10 per cent of the troubles stemmed from a physical condition—like a frayed cord a dog chewed on, coin phone vandalism, etc. The remaining 13 per cent were for miscellaneous reasons and conditions.

It all added up to a repair bill of $48 million for 1973. Repair service at no additional charge is, of course, included in the monthly rate for basic phone service.

Cover: At a repair bureau, a repair service clerk (top) takes the particulars of a 611 call and picks out the customer's card from the files. Both go to a special test position (below). There a testman electrically pinpoints the problem and dispatches a repairman to correct the trouble wherever it lies.

Inside: Repairs are made either at the customer's home (top), in the switching system itself (above left) or outdoors. The testman runs a final check to make sure the phone is working properly again before calling the customer with the news.

Fig. 6-7 Tone elements scaled and positioned with line copy for a combination line-and-tone copy unit. This form is widely used by advertising departments and agencies when the mechanical must be sent out for approval. If the tone elements are to be supplied separately for reduction or are proportioned for various pages of a booklet, Photostat copies are positioned on the mechanical, but before it is sent to the printer, X's, meaning "Not for camera copy," are marked on them. It would be hazardous to use the form in Fig. 6-8 accompanied by the art, for some pieces might be damaged or lost.

Fig. 6-8 Tone elements indicated for size and position by a red outline and keyed for identification to tone elements supplied separately. This method is often used within an organization or in cases when only departmental approval is required. For some ordinary-quality work, small halftones may cost no more than Photostat positives.

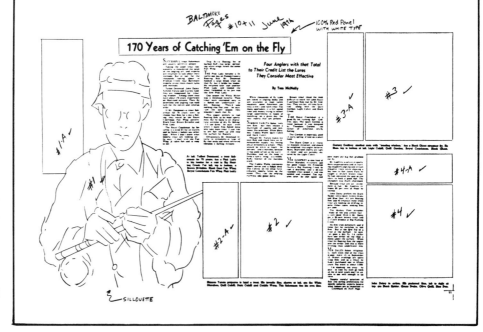

Plant's Exhaust System

The original ductwork has been retained and is used as a vent relief system discharging to the roof top penthouse and thus outdoors. The lavatories are served by this exhaust system and volume dampers and back pressure dampers in the penthouse control it. The cooling tower by which 95% to 98% of the water used for refrigeration condensing is saved is located out of sight from the street over a central stairway. This makes it possible to exhaust the building by using the cooling tower fan and closing the ouside air intake damper. Any one area can be handled in this manner by leaving its door to the stairway open and closing those for all other departments.
A view of the composing room makeup department is seen in Fig. 2, which shows the same Weathermaker unit as in Fig. 1 in the far right background plus an exhaust hood, also at the right, connected to the existing ventilating system. This view clearly shows the discharge. plenum of the self-contained Weathermaker extending above the fluorescent lighting. Linotype machines are located in the left background. ·
ployees throughout the plant and has increased cleanliness and production.

Fig. 6-9 The opaquing of halftone areas on the mechanical is a photoengraver's technique (the photoengraver flops the negative to get emulsion-to-emulsion contact printing). This method is not recommended for offset for any but ordinary-quality work because it does not permit emulsion-to-emulsion contact printing in the platemaking. There is some loss of tonal quality.

Transparent Overlay

Fig. 6-10 The artist often uses a transparent film or a parchment overlay on the mechanical or on an element to separate line and tone copy that are to be combined or to carry the color copy. Masking film on a clear overlay is widely used to silhouette halftone elements.

The mask can be left over the design or an area and the rest of the masking film peeled off the carrier sheet. Used this way with a photograph, the mask would produce a silhouette halftone. The carrier film with the mask still on it could be cut to a practical size for an overlay positioned with register marks on the photo. The printer's camera operator would burn out the background (show black on the negative). Later, working with groups of such copy, the operator would fold back the mask overlay and make a halftone exposure to get the halftone image; the rest of the negative would be black just as if it had been brush-opaqued to get rid of the background.

HANDLING PASTE-UP COPY

As an adhesive for paste-ups, a special melted wax has replaced rubber cement for volume work. A hand applicator with an electric heating unit is sold at art supply stores, and sheet-waxing machines are available for volume use with repro proofs or galleys of metal or phototype. The advantage is that copy can be waxed in batches and positioned later; removal or repositioning is easy. Since 5 or 10 minutes are required to melt the wax, a machine is not practical unless the heat is left on, as is customary in an art department. Wax stick applicators are available for corrections. Galleys should be trimmed after waxing. Always burnish down both wax and rubber adhesive.

Elements positioned on a paste-up mechanical should not be trimmed closer than 1/8 inch (3.175 millimeters). Hairline rules should always be drawn on camera copy with a pen. A hairline printed from a metal rule is apt to be gray in spots, and the line will drop out in the photographic negative.

The trim size of a printed job should be able to be cut efficiently from a standard size of the paper selected (Chapter 3 lists the standard sizes for different kinds of paper). Book paper sizes are now the same for offset as for letterpress.

PRINT PROOFS

Since the paste-up artist should see proofs of his or her paste-up copy before press plates are made, the subject of offset proofs is timely. With offset printing, various types of photoprints are made from the negatives and positives of copy as supplied for the camera so that work may be checked before plates are made.

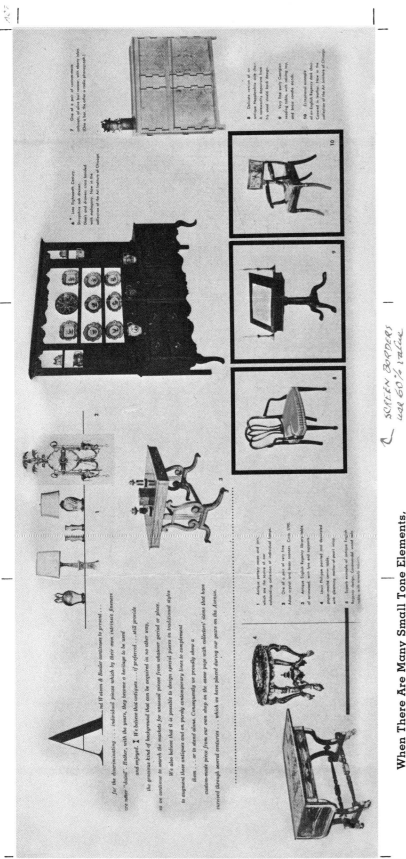

When There Are Many Small Tone Elements, Prepare a Line-and-Tone Mechanical.

Fig. 6-11 Camera copy prepared as a complete unit with all copy elements scaled and positioned avoids much stripping (positioning of negatives) and the chance of error. Such a mechanical is termed "copy in one piece." The three box borders were done in black with a note requesting 60 percent tint. The copy is marked for two folds to get a six-page folder.

For a budget job, the use of screened Velox photoprints of the halftone elements would make this an all-line mechanical and thus save plate costs.

When a panel or heavy border is wanted in a tint instead of a solid, copy is prepared the same, but for the tint a notation on a tissue overlay or in the margin tells the printer the strength of tint wanted.

TO AVOID STRIPPING MANY REDUCED SEPARATE TONE ELEMENTS, UNIT TONE MECHANICALS ARE USED TO PROVIDE FOR REDUCTION

Tone Mechanical

Size-and-One-Half Camera Copy

Fig. 6-12A When there are many small halftones on a page and details are important, planning may provide size-and-one-half projection prints from the original negatives of the photographer. These prints are positioned on proportioned paste-ups, and the copy units are handled in groups by the platemaker to keep stripping costs to a minimum.

Type proofs in reproduction size are pasted up for each page: the tone negative and the line negative for each page are combined for stripping the flat, or a tone flat and a line flat are made and printed down separately on the press plate.

With the above catalog each tone illustration was placed against a black background. In making the projection prints from the original 8- by 10-inch (203- by 254-millimeter) negatives, the photographer put in the background.

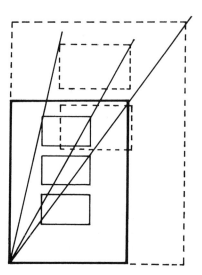

Fig. 6-12B How to get the element position on enlargement for size-and-one-half separate elements as a tone mechanical for reduction. For an irregular layout, use a ghosted Photostat as a guide to position.

Catalog Page

Fig. 6-12C

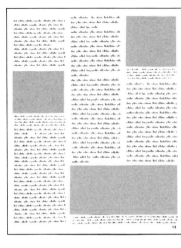

Fig. 6-13 Publications often use pieces of masking film with pressure-sensitive adhesive on its back to mark the position, size, and shape of halftone elements on page mechanicals. This procedure produces windows on the page negatives on which the halftone negatives can be stripped. Time is saved, but as mentioned earlier, there is some loss of tonal quality because the method does not permit emulsion-to-emulsion printing of the press plate.

from this art...

Use of a Mask Overlay Gives a Silhouette Halftone

...you get this effect

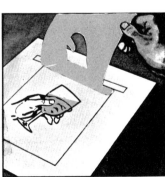

Fig. 6-14A Masking film being removed from a clear carrier base film after the mask has been cut along the outline, leaving just the mask on the subject. The mask on a suitably sized piece of carrier film is placed as an overlay on the photo with register marks for positioning.

Fig. 6-14 To make a silhouette halftone the offset printer usually uses masking film on a clear overlay to mask the wanted image and burn out the background by overexposure in the camera, making the unwanted area black on the negative. The printer can then fold back the masking overlay and make a halftone exposure to get the silhouette halftone.

Or with the use of a sheet of halftone-tint film the printer can produce a uniform gray background. If the subject is to be inserted into a color background, the printer will use masking film to trap the color to the subject.

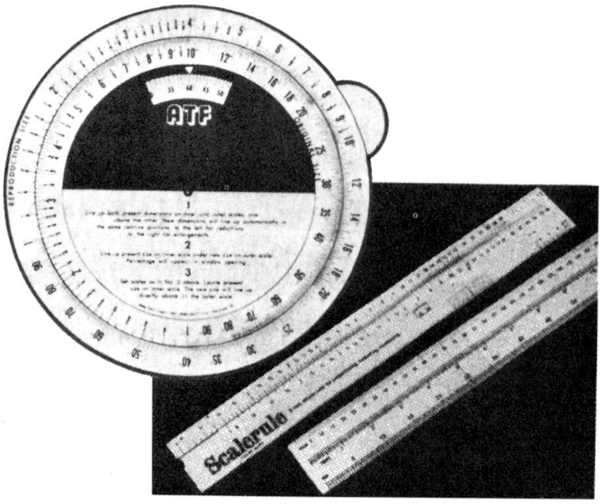

Fig. 6-15 Scaling instruments are used to determine the percentage of reduction or enlargement and to proportion multiple copy elements for same-focus economies.

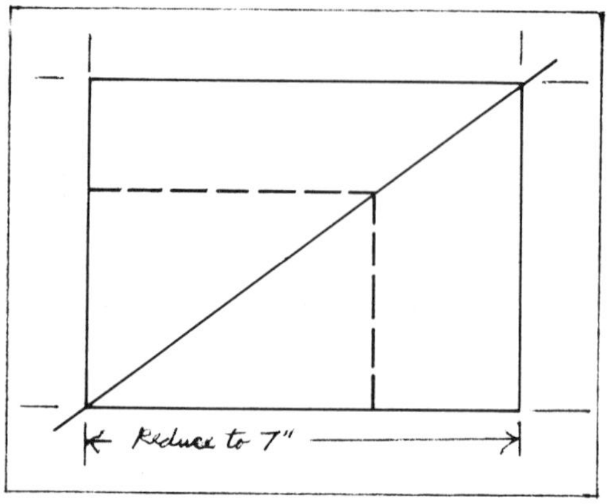

Fig. 6-16 The diagonal-line method of proportioning is not used with offset.

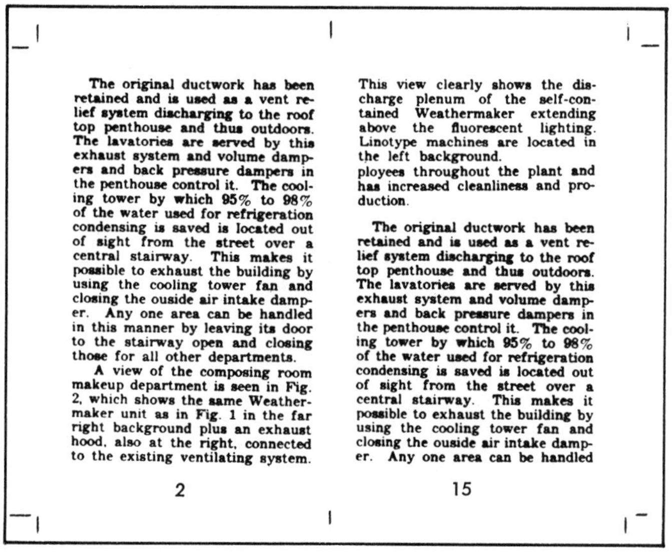

The original ductwork has been retained and is used as a vent relief system discharging to the roof top penthouse and thus outdoors. The lavatories are served by this exhaust system and volume dampers and back pressure dampers in the penthouse control it. The cooling tower by which 95% to 98% of the water used for refrigeration condensing is saved is located out of sight from the street over a central stairway. This makes it possible to exhaust the building by using the cooling tower fan and closing the ouside air intake damper. Any one area can be handled in this manner by leaving its door to the stairway open and closing those for all other departments.

A view of the composing room makeup department is seen in Fig. 2, which shows the same Weathermaker unit as in Fig. 1 in the far right background plus an exhaust hood, also at the right, connected to the existing ventilating system.

2

This view clearly shows the discharge plenum of the self-contained Weathermaker extending above the fluorescent lighting. Linotype machines are located in the left background.

ployees throughout the plant and has increased cleanliness and production.

The original ductwork has been retained and is used as a vent relief system discharging to the roof top penthouse and thus outdoors. The lavatories are served by this exhaust system and volume dampers and back pressure dampers in the penthouse control it. The cooling tower by which 95% to 98% of the water used for refrigeration condensing is saved is located out of sight from the street over a central stairway. This makes it possible to exhaust the building by using the cooling tower fan and closing the ouside air intake damper. Any one area can be handled

15

Fig. 6-17 Paste-up of pages to be bound. Pages of printed jobs to be bound are pasted up in pairs, either as facing pages with even page numbers on the left or in binder's imposition form according to the imposition obtained from the printer or bindery. If binding is in facing pages, the printer strips the page negatives in imposition form when stripping the flat used for the press plate. Except for simple jobs, the printer's advice should be obtained.

For all but the simplest work, blueprints should be ordered and checked by the paste-up artist to see that no copy has become detached from the paste-up, that separate elements are positioned correctly, and that reverses and other work by the platemaker have been done. After the proof is approved, plates can be made.

For booklets, catalogs, and the like, blueprints of the flat are made and folded into a dummy to check imposition, margins, and simple color breakup, particularly subheads in color. Two different colors on the same blueprint are handled by separate exposures of each flat—for the black, a longer exposure for a dark print; for the colors, a shorter exposure for a lighter print.

To check exact measurement or fit, such as that of a book jacket or catalog cover, undeveloped blueprints are supplied, for if they are developed in water and then dried, the paper shrinks.

Prints of separate copy elements are termed "loose" blueprints. These are sometimes used by the layout artist in determining just where a title or headline should go when positioned on a design, or the pages of Christmas and fashion catalogs may be laid out with the loose prints of illustrations and type blocks, and the flats stripped to the paste-up of prints as the layout.

To check the quality of a halftone negative made from doubtful copy, a silver print (black on white) is used. A Velox print also is suitable but is more expensive.

Much process color work is checked with prepress color proofs consisting of a lamination of four thin sheets of clear plastic in each color. The cost is 10 cents on the dollar, as compared with ink proofs from proof plates. The latter are used in critical color matching.

Today various new forms of prints such as Xerox are used to scale and position elements for layout approval, even for some color work, but not for camera copy.

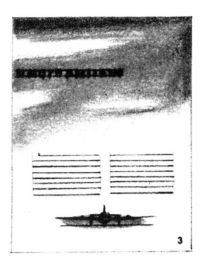

Fig. 6-18 Pages of a spread are usually separated in the imposition layout. Single-color or simple color spreads should be prepared with at least a 1-inch (25.4-millimeter) center spread for the stripper's tape; otherwise two negatives must be made. The figure shows how pages 2 and 3 would be handled; it also provides for color areas and for type that crosses the fold. Even pages are always on the left.

Fig. 6-19 A copy unit such as this for covering one side of the press sheet is equivalent to a flat. In such a case the stripper's work or control marks are frequently used; a ¼-inch (6.35-millimeter) line is a fold mark, and an ⅛-inch (3.175-millimeter) mark is a cut mark. Thus the fold trim is a combination of the two marks, as shown; the spine fold is indicated by ¼-inch marks, and the corner marks are ⅛-inch cut marks.

DIAGRAMS OF BINDER'S IMPOSITIONS EXPLAINING PASTE-UPS IN IMPOSITION PAIRS

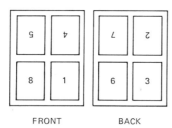

SHEETWISE IMPOSITION

FRONT   BACK

Fig. 6-20 Run sheetwise, the front of the sheet is printed. The plate is then changed for the backup, and the reverse side is printed.

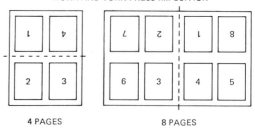

WORK-AND-TURN PRESS IMPOSITION

4 PAGES   8 PAGES

Fig. 6-21 Run work-and-turn on a larger press, both front and back are printed on one side of the paper; the pile of printed sheets is then turned over and run through the press again. The sheet is cut in the middle as indicated, producing two complete eight-page booklets ready for folding. This procedure saves a plate and a makeready by offset.

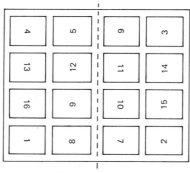

16-PAGE BOOKLET
WORK-AND-TURN IMPOSITION

Fig. 6-22 For short and medium runs, work-and-turn imposition is apt to be used, with the cut sheet folded as shown. This job could also be planned for binding two deep.

Folded Signature Impositions

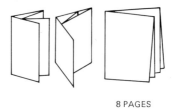

8 PAGES

Fig. 6-23 Three impositions for an eight-page signature.

How to Determine a Simple Binder's Imposition

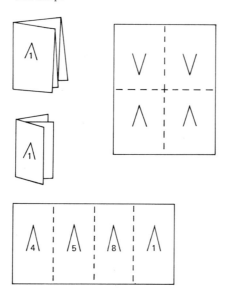

Fig. 6-24 Make a tissue dummy. With a razor blade cut a V, point up, all the way through the folded paper. Number the front and back of the V's as 1, 2, 3, and so on. Open the dummy, and you have the imposition.

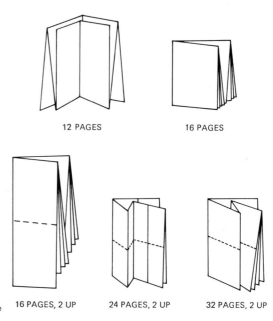

12 PAGES   16 PAGES

16 PAGES, 2 UP   24 PAGES, 2 UP   32 PAGES, 2 UP

Fig. 6-25 The larger the press sheet and the longer the folded section, the greater the bindery economy. Small booklets may be folded six deep.

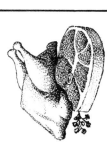
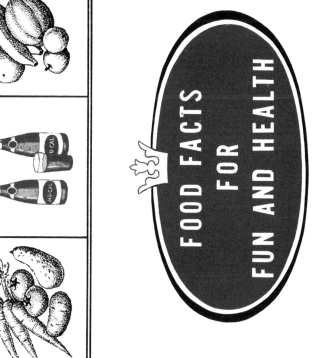

Fig. 6-26   Print proof of booklet cover in two colors. This was a blueprint made from two separate negatives, one for black and one for the color. Full exposure for black gave dark color; less exposure of the color negative gave a lighter tone so that color could be identified.

LISTING OF ALL SEPARATE ELEMENTS

The cover of a mechanical should list any separate elements and the name and telephone number of user's contact person. In process color work, artwork should not be held for submission with the mechanical. Send artwork to the printer as early as possible to avoid the possible need for overtime.

New Technology and the Absence of Economic and Technical Restrictions

Before we continue with the preparation of copy components and the paste-up mechanical to obtain camera-ready copy and the many how-to instructions entailed, let's stand back and see things in perspective. Let's consider why the character of commercial art and its procedures have changed, the importance of time and cost factors, the need to specify type and calculate the space it will occupy, and why all restrictions on the choice of art media for uncoated paper have been removed. In Chapter 10 we shall explain a new procedure, now used by all printing processes, for preparing process copy for reproduction.

There is a general impression that the form of camera copy is determined by the printing process used. Actually, it is determined by the resulting plate costs. If these costs are disregarded, copy prepared for one process can be used for either of the other major printing processes. For example, a combination line-and-tone copy unit with offset involves only the cost of the halftones in addition to the basic plate charge; and the same is essentially true of gravure because both processes use the time plate estimating method. Under the Photoengravers' Standard Scale (Item 2) the cost of both line and tone areas was double the halftone scale cost.

The reason that we discussed the proportioning of multiple tone elements was that same-focus economies are allowed under the time method. These economies also apply to the process color art. For letterpress process color photoengravings, Item 2 of the former scale method is absent, and camera copy is frequently submitted in the form of a mechanical to take advantage of economies available. The alternative is a proof of the made-up type page because photoengravers now use photocomposing methods and no longer accept type metal for combination with process engravings for electros.

Because of new capabilities and procedures in the area between the original artwork and that prepared for the camera, a category called "art production" has developed, transferring some of the steps formerly handled by the engraver or offset platemaker to the art department in order to save time and costs. This form of production starts in the creative planning stage, which now has a wide choice of methods, particularly for process color copy. The proportioning of tone elements and composition methods are a part of art production.

Last and most distinctive are recent and continuing developments in phototypography and photocomposition with its speed and economies through electronics and the computer. Typography has moved into the editorial office and the art department.

Comparable to the draftsman in engineering and architecture is the "production artist," for both prepare working drawings from designer's sketches. With aptitude and work all can advance in their chosen fields.

TOOLS OF THE TRADE ARE HANDLED BY THE LARGER ART SUPPLY STORES

Technical Drawing Pens

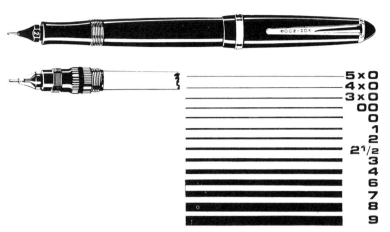

These pens have long, hollow drawing points for use with rulers, templates, and mechanical drawing aids. The nibs are interchangeable for width of line (as shown) and are coded by color to indicate size.

Fig. 6-27   The Koh-I-Noor Rapidograph individually interchangeable drawing-point tips are designed to meet the special needs of the professional, who requires frequent changes in line widths, as shown. No. 2 is widely used for commercial lap register.

Image projector for studios and publications, used in tracing artwork for enlargement or reduction.

Hand waxer, used to coat proofs and other material with adhesive wax for paste-ups.

Sheet waxer, used to coat entire sheets of proof and other art for paste-ups.

Desk-top light table, used for tracing, for checking the fit of film overlays, and for alignment over a grid.

Swivel-tipped knife, designed for cutting masking film.

A twin-line cutter is helpful in correcting type composition.

This drawing pen repeats the same line width after refilling.

Lucidas Save Artists' Time for Sketching

Fig. 6-28   Art departments usually have some type of lucida, an instrument which projects an image of an illustration, photo, or object onto the drawing board in enlarged or reduced size. This one, by Art-O-Graph, Inc., can be clamped to any drawing board and has a normal projection range of 3 times up or down, with a possible extended range to 6 times. Art supply stores usually have several models for sale.

7

PREPARATION OF SINGLE-COLOR ELEMENTS

SINCE WE ARE DEALING WITH copy in paste-up form, we are now concerned with the preparation and assembly of elements suitable for camera-ready copy, positioned on the mechanical according to the rough layout supplied. The accompanying instructions should include the kind of paper to be employed, for the contrast of the printer's negatives differs slightly according to whether coated or uncoated paper is to be used. The mechanical artist should also get any original contact photos and artwork.

If composition has not already been specified, the mechanical artist may have to handle this problem. In any case, the production artist should check the layout for copy fitting. Some adjustments may be necessary. The "rough" in a large art department usually contains a rubber-stamped imprint giving the delivery dates for art, composition, proofs, and delivery of the job.

Most illustrations will be photographs and various forms of line copy; the latter must be scaled for positioning on the mechanical. Contact photoprints are scaled or proportioned with projection prints made by the photographer from original negatives, as described below. Line elements are usually scaled or reversed by Photostats or comparable types of prints. If a mechanical involves only a single halftone, the size and position of the original photo or art is merely indicated on the mechanical by a red outline, and the photo itself marked for cropping and size. The photo goes as a separate element with the mechanical to the offset printer. Multiple tone elements are usually scaled and positioned on the mechanical; line elements are always scaled and positioned. If any multiple tone elements are to be reduced in size by the camera to hold better detail, they should be proportioned for about size and one-half of the reproduction size and supplied as separate elements in one or more groups for same-focus camera economies. The user can get a better price if the same-focus reduction is for 60, 70, or 80 percent of the original size rather than an uneven figure such as 63 or 78 percent. How to proportion a group for same-focus economies with a scaling instrument is described below in Fig. 7-2.

CROPPING AND SCALING PHOTOGRAPHS

The cropping and scaling of photographs are the same for all printing processes: the area to be reproduced is indicated by crop marks in soft pencil on the white edge of the photo for both width and height. With offset the width wanted is shown by marking the percentage of the original size, sometimes by inches.

The diagonal-line method of determining proportioned height when area width is reduced or enlarged for reproduction size is used chiefly for letterpress (Fig 6-16). The reason is that each subject is priced separately by

CROPPING PHOTOS

8- by 10-Inch
(203- by 254-Millimeter)
Photoprint

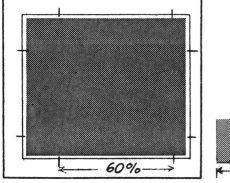

60%

Scaled Print

3"

Fig. 7-1   Crop marks indicate the wanted area; 60 percent means that percentage of the original size.

size in engraving and there usually are no same-focus discounts.

Offset frequently proportions multiple tone elements for the unit or job because same-focus economies are allowed. The cost of a camera focus can thus be divided among the group. The method of proportioning such tone elements is shown in Fig. 7-2.

The most common error with camera copy for the photomechanical processes is that the photo and specified reduction do not fit the space provided on the mechanical, usually for height. It occurs because both scaled sizes have not been checked.

WORKING WITH THE PHOTOGRAPHER

For persons without a background in a commercial art department, the following will be helpful. In advertising, most photographic illustration is handled by professionals, much of it on location rather than in the studio, and a lot of it is produced with small hand cameras such as the 35-millimeter and 2¼- by 2¼-inch (57.15- by 57.15-millimeter) sizes for convenience. The greater part, however, will be in the form of 5- by 7-inch (127- by 178-millimeter) and 8- by 10-inch (203- by 254-millimeter) contact prints—the prints from the camera negatives. The photographer usually knows nothing about the reproduction size to be used. These contact prints (sometimes already crop-marked by the rough layout artist) go to the mechanical or production artist making the mechanical, who has the rough layout of the copy unit or dummy.

If the photos are to be scaled and positioned, as is usual with most commercial printing by offset, the contact prints are marked for cropping and size wanted and returned to the photographer, who positions the original negatives in a vertical projector, makes the projection prints in wanted sizes, and delivers them to the customer. The cost for a projection print is about $1.50 to $2.

When there are two or more tone elements on a copy unit, an art department usually positions them on the mechanical for a combination line-and-tone copy unit. Subjects in different sizes are thus reduced to one camera focus, and the printer need not strip them to position. This procedure is usual for the photomechanical processes, and agencies like to use it for letterpress in magazine ad schedules because copy in one piece reduces errors and the number of approvals by clients.

Some small offset printers and shops use a price list based on the size of negatives. Here nothing is gained by scaling and positioning; the cropped contact prints are supplied separately for camera copy.

COLOR TO BLACK AND WHITE

Frequently a color subject is to be reproduced in black and white. For the mechanical it should first be photographed on panchromatic film, like that used for snapshots, to reduce the colors of the print to gray tones. If time is short, the printer can readily handle this job.

If you want a black-and-white illustration

SCALING INSTRUMENT USED TO PROPORTION COPY ELEMENTS FOR SAME-FOCUS CAMERA GROUPS

The inner (original-size) scale rotates.

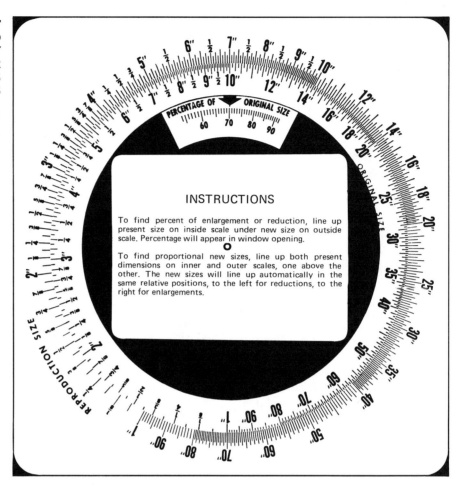

Fig. 7-2 Proportioning a same-focus group of tone elements for 70 percent of the original size for group reduction by camera. The rough layout shows the reproduction sizes; the proportioned sizes for cropping for the group are directly opposite on the inner scale.

If, for example, a photo is to be reduced to a 4-inch (101.6-millimeter) reproduction width, it should be cropped for a 5¹¹/₁₆-inch (144.5-millimeter) width. Height cropping is determined in the same way. Keep the instrument at 70 percent to figure the sizes of the other subjects for the group. To handle many subjects, two or three groups may be necessary: 60 percent, 80 percent, and so on.

Proportioned tone elements can be intended for a copy unit, for various pages of a booklet, for related jobs on one order, and for process color copy.

A single tone element on a mechanical that is not part of a large job is merely marked for cropping and reproduction percentage and sent to the printer as for letterpress.

of a large color subject such as a window display, a matte-finish Photostat will show all colors except red in gray tones. Red photographs as black; the solution is to outline red with white to show the boundary and on the negative (white area) to paint in a light gray. The positive print will show a darker gray for the red.

When copy is sent out for Photostats, prints, or composition, be sure that it is identified by the customer's name. If the customer is a large organization, add the department and the individual's name. Use a rubber stamp or a sticker label, for often work lies around for days because the studio does not know to whom it belongs.

DON'T MIX RETOUCHING GRAYS

The whites and grays used in retouching may contain pigments that absorb different amounts of ultraviolet light. When the retouched photoprint is illuminated on a process camera copyboard with ultraviolet-rich light, the retouched areas may photograph darker than the visually equivalent silver-density areas. Retouching artists should know how their whites and grays photograph on different types of photographic paper. To determine how paints will photograph, the retoucher should put samples on fixed-out photographic papers and have them exposed in a process camera. The exposures will show which brand of paint is suitable for a particular paper. Or a Velox print of the halftone negative will show the result when the retouched photograph is printed.

In retouching photos it is very important not to use grays of a different cast on the same job; for example, a blue gray in some spots and a brownish gray in others. The retouched photo may look fine, but the camera operator must resort to different emulsions and a filter to get a good negative. This is a long and costly procedure. The same brand and cast of grays should be used on the same subject or on a group of photos for same-focus work.

CHINESE WHITE NO LONGER USED FOR SILHOUETTE HALFTONES

A photoprint which is to be reproduced as a silhouette halftone is no longer outlined in white for the wanted area. A piece of amber masking film on its carrier sheet is positioned on the print and carefully cut for the silhouette, and the unwanted masking film (over background) is then peeled off. The mask (over subject) on its carrier sheet is positioned as an overlay on the photo to produce camera-ready copy and marked "Silhouette." The background is thus burned off.

COMBINING LINE AND TONE FOR A COPY ELEMENT

Quite frequently an illustration is a combination of line-and-tone copy, either a design or type matter such as a headline running across a photograph. One kind of copy, usu-

Handling Type Proof or Lettering to Go on Halftones

Fig. 7-3 The problem is illustrated with the artist's camera copy (left). The type proof can be attached as an overlay in position on the photograph with tissue instructions for the effect wanted. The clear overlay shown here helps present the procedure plainly.

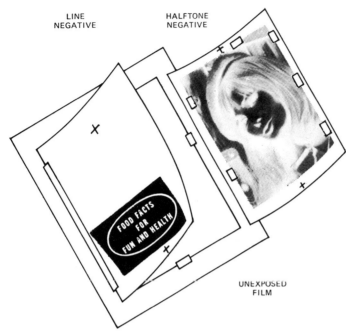

LINE NEGATIVE

HALFTONE NEGATIVE

X

FOOD FACTS FOR FUN AND HEALTH

UNEXPOSED FILM

Fig. 7-4 The printing user's camera copy is the photo or art in scale with the line copy (often a headline to be reversed or printed) on an overlay. The platemaker has a film carrier to position line and tone negatives. Each is exposed separately in the dark on unexposed film, which remains light-sensitive under the black of the negatives.

Reversed Type into Tone

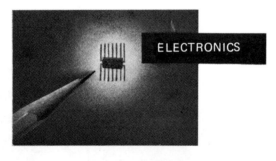

ELECTRONICS

ELECTRONICS

How Copy is Prepared
Tone element outlined in red on copy and supplied as a separate element.

Fig. 7-5 Reversed-type panel inserted into a same-color halftone. An exception to the use of a film carrier for combining line and tone copy occurs when a reversed element goes on tone of the same color. If any tone would show in the white type of the reverse, the platemaker removes the tone underneath.

ally the line element, must go on an overlay in position to keep it separate from the other. The platemaker combines the two negatives to obtain the desired result.

In Fig. 7-4 the oval with type matter within it would print as black on the halftone. If the type or design appeared as white on the halftone, this method would not be necessary—a positive film of the type would be positioned on the tone negative for a contact print, thus providing a mask to make the type show in white on the halftone. The printer, of course, handles this work.

HALFTONE TINTS BY THE PRINTER

If a halftone tint is wanted on an area such as a border, it can be indicated by an outline on the camera copy with a notation on the strength of tone wanted—30 percent, etc. If the edge outline is in black, it will be held; if the outline is in red, it will be dropped. For a border to be tinted, as in Fig. 6-11 (about 6 points), all that is needed is a note that it is to be screened. See Fig. 7-6.

For newspapers and inexpensive utility printing the artist can use tone sheets purchased from an art supply store. Pieces of the sheets are positioned on the desired areas of copy for the camera. See Figs. 7-29 to 7-32.

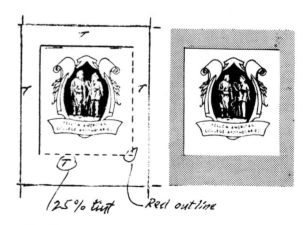

25% tint   Red outline

Fig. 7-6 Any instructions in the work area of the copy are made in light blue; on a black reverse, in yellow. The holding line of the tint area is in red if it is to be dropped and in black if it is to be held.

**When Tint
Covers Line Copy,
Put a
Red Outline
on the Overlay**

Fig. 7-7 When a tint area is to be combined with line copy, as in this example, or is to be surprinted with a different color, the holding line should go on the overlay. This procedure makes it simple for the printer to combine line and tone.

If a halftone tint covers part of a line image, the holding line should be prepared on a clear overlay, for a halftone tint is in a 133- or 150-line screen and is treated as a halftone which is combined with the line copy, as shown in Fig. 7-7.

PHOTOSTATS

In the larger cities Photostats are available in two types: glossy Photostats which reproduce dark tones as black (not grays), generally used for type reverses, and matte-finish Photostats. The latter will show tones and colors (except red, which photographs as black) in gray tones. The blacks are not quite as sharp as in the glossy Photostats, but the matte-finish Photostats can be used for reverses. Photostats of reproduction quality cost about twice as much as ordinary Photostats of readable quality.

Photostats come in standard paper sizes such as 8½ by 11 inches (216 by 279 millimeters) or 11 by 14 inches (356 millimeters) and are priced accordingly. The standard maximum reduction is 50 percent, but a smaller size can be obtained by reducing the half-size negative. Frequently the mechanical artist can do some work on the negative before sending it back for the positive copy.

Photostats can be used in many ways to save time. Users should obtain informative material published by a large reproduction Photostat service.

NEWER FORMS OF PRINTS

The newer forms of prints, such as Xerox, have largely replaced ordinary Photostats in two standard sizes, 8½ by 11 inches (216 by 279 millimeters) and 8½ by 14 inches (356 millimeters), but without change in image

**Proper
Contrast
Important for
Type Printed
or Reversed
on a Tint
or a Tone**

Type on White Background
Type on White Background
Type on White Background
Type on White Background

NO SCREEN

Type on Tint Backgrounds
Type on Tint Backgrounds
Type on Tint Backgrounds
Type on Tint Backgrounds

25% SCREEN

Type on Tint Backgrounds
Type on Tint Backgrounds
Type on Tint Backgrounds
Type on Tint Backgrounds

50% SCREEN

Type on Tint Backgrounds
Type on Tint Backgrounds
Type on Tint Backgrounds
Type on Tint Backgrounds

75% SCREEN

Type on Black Background
Type on Black Background
Type on Black Background
Type on Black Background

SOLID REVERSE

Fig. 7-8 Legibility is reduced when type is used in reverse or is combined with halftone tints. These examples show the importance of selecting the proper size and style of typeface to ensure easy reading.

size except with more sophisticated copiers. The cost is about 10 cents per single copy (one to nine copies) with a reduction for quantity.

The makers of the newer prints generally also produce reproduction-quality Photostats and Velox prints in a glossy or a matte finish, in the same size, larger, or smaller. There is a small charge for focus change and an extra $1 for screens or Veloxes. Sizes generally range from 8 by 10 inches (203 by 254 millimeters) to 20 by 24 inches (508 by 610 millimeters), with costs ranging from $1.75 to $10 for positive-to-positive prints.

TECHNIQUES

Fig. 7-9 Pen-line drawing used for shading and values.

Fig. 7-10 Pen-line drawing excessively reduced.

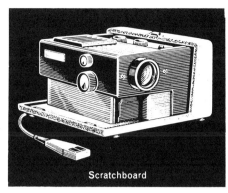

Fig.7-11

Fig. 7-12 Pen-line drawing with solid blacks.

Fig. 7-13 Carbon pencil drawing on textured paper.

Fig. 7-14 Line-tone by pencil on frosted acetate, a book illustration technique obtained by a dark pencil, such as Ebony 6325. Texture and pressure provide the desired tones; a contact negative gives the right-reading image. This technique has been used for simple color work.

WORKING WITH PHOTOSTATS

Fig. 7-15 By use of a prism on the camera lens, a lateral reversal to face left instead of right is obtained even with a Photostat.

Perspective

Fig. 7-16 A sketch or an object can be angled in a Photostat to assist the artist in gaining perspective. A photolettering service is used for type camera copy.

Fig. 7-17 A line vignette created by a Photostat from a tone vignette with the help of an artist's stipple in black and in white. There is a substantial plate cost economy.

NEW FAST COLOR COPIES

Helpful for many uses, including rough layouts, manuscript illustrations, and any nonreproduction purposes, are full-color, two-color, or one-color paper copies measuring 8½ by 11 inches (216 by 279 millimeters) or 8½ by 14 inches (356 millimeters). Prices range from $1.75 to $1.25 per copy, with quantity discounts reducing the cost to as low as $1 each for eleven or more copies. If a change in size is needed for scaling, the copy must go on acetate, which costs about $2 more per copy.

SCALING LINE ELEMENTS

Most original line artwork is done 2 to 5 times the reproduction size. It is scaled to the size indicated by the rough layout by means of Photostats or equivalent inexpensive photoprints. Art studios are now installing a special type of daylight camera, such as the POS ONE shown in Fig. 7-23, which can make any form of print from a Photostat to a halftone negative on film in one step, either enlarging or reducing. The Polaroid industrial camera is also widely used for reducing line copy.

PREPARING COPY FOR TYPE REVERSES

A widely used method of preparing copy is to cut the Photostat negative to the wanted size and blacken the white cut edge, but it is risky because of the danger of dog-eared corners, for mechanicals get a lot of handling at the printer's shop. The safest way is shown in Fig. 7-18. If the copy to be reversed includes fine serifs or lines, it is best to rule in the boundaries of the reverse and let the platemaker handle with film without the Photostat reverse. The tissue overlay should carry the instruction "Reverse this element." Film can hold a fine line.

NEWER FORMS OF COPY PRINTS

In discussing the reduction of line art to scale size for a paste-up, we have referred to Photostat prints, first the negatives and then the positive copies from them. These are rapidly being replaced by special photographic papers which produce positives in one step. Art studios are installing special daylight cameras which will make any form of print from a Photostat to a halftone negative on film by selecting the type of photographic material needed. The speed and economy of this development are replacing outside services.

The Right Way to Prepare
a Type Proof for a Reverse

Fig. 7-18 Opaquing a border around cut proof avoids dog-eared corners and shadow lines. An irregular border to a reversed element requires this method.

Fig. 7-19 If a Photostat negative is trimmed for a type reverse, blacken the paper edges. There is a risk of dog-eared corners.

Fig. 7-20 This clipping from a weekly newspaper reminds us that typefaces with fine serifs and hairlines should not be used. Square-serif or sans-serif faces, not smaller than 8 points, are best for reversing.

Fig. 7-21 Plan for making Photostats in groups when there is room to do so.

Newspapers Have Their Own Forms of Line and Tone Prints

Offset newspapers usually prepare page mechanicals and use a special form of photographic paper to get either line or 100-screen halftone positives in one step. With their cameras, subjects can be enlarged or reduced in size and positioned.

CONVERTING TONE COPY TO LINE
Screened Photoprints

For budget jobs requiring many small halftones, the use of screened Velox prints of original photos or art is one solution. These are line copy and are scaled and positioned on the paste-up. They can be outlined with Chinese white, or the artist can add line art for a combination line-and-tone effect.

Such prints are now made by Velox specialists using the proper density for offset. Originals should be cropped and supplied in proportioned groups so that an 8- by 10-inch (203- by 254-millimeter) Velox can be cut apart for the individual subjects; the cost is about 8 to 10 cents a square inch. Prints from two-color work are also supplied by Velox specialists, with the screen angled for color.

Making Your Own Screened Prints

If you have continuous-tone negatives, contact prints on Kodak Autoscreen Ortho Film will have the halftone dots in them. Union shop regulations usually require prints of these on the paste-up. This film gives excellent definition and sharp detail. The use of a projector will permit a change in size.

**CONVERTING AN
OBJECT OR A
PHOTOGRAPH TO
LINE COPY**

Perspective Photostat   Bleached Photostat

Fig. 7-22 The object positioned on a bracket for angle and perspective is sent to the Photostat service for a "ghosted" matte Photostat. The artist works on this in india ink to produce the effect wanted in line. The Photostat is then bleached, leaving only the india ink image. Areas can be left unbleached. To mask an area, dissolve a small quantity of paraffin in carbon tetrachloride. The resulting solution will repel bleaching solutions or watercolor on the Photostat. When the Photostat is dry, a cotton swab soaked in plain carbon tetrachloride will remove the masking solution.

The POS ONE Daylight Camera with Special Paper Produces Any Form of Print in the Art Department

Fig. 7-23 Visual Graphic's POS ONE desk-size, automatic-focus camera and processing system is used for a broad range of copy preparation services. Its positive-to-positive single-step process requires no negative, darkroom, or plumbing. A mobile unit, it has a self-contained camera, lights, and processor. The copyboard measures 16 by 20 inches (406 by 508 millimeters) and accommodates film or paper in sizes up to 11 by 17 inches (279 by 432 millimeters). Enlargements can be made to 200 percent and reductions to 50 percent. The paper exits dry. The POS ONE 720 model does full color on paper or film.

The CPS 516 model offers many creative options—photoprints, Veloxes, and Photostats in the same size, enlarged, or reduced—thus dispensing with outside services. Photos, wash drawings, and color transparencies are reproduced as black-and-white position Photostats in sizes up to 11 by 14 inches (279 by 356 millimeters). The machine produces 100-line–screen prints, and special-effect screens are available to convert photos or tone art to line. Desired color overlay copy of type or art can be created.

By twisting a lever this POS ONE model can be converted to a processor for the RC paper used by phototypesetting machines.

Fig. 7-24 This Kodak PMT material produces a positive photograph in one shot of the camera. Selected material produces either a line or a halftone print in scaled size. The photo is developed for newspapers in a 100-line screen.

The availability of a photographic department also permits use of another method.[1] Your negative is positioned in a projector, and a piece of magenta contact halftone screen is placed on top of the photo paper. The resulting print, in the size wanted, will be in halftone screen ready for the paste-up. With offset, the usual 110-line screen limitation does not apply.

Screened Prints from Polaroid Cameras

Fast prints for news bulletins and catalogs can be made with the use of a photoscreen adapter attachment for the Polaroid or any 4- by 5-inch (101.6- by 127-millimeter) camera that will accommodate the No. 500 Polaroid sheet film holder. High-contrast film, now available for Polaroid cameras, should be used.

Photostats Save the Artist's Time

Photostats can be made of tone art or of the actual object to serve as a base on which the artist works in black for a line drawing, later bleaching out the unwanted tones of the Photostat. This can also be done with photoprints, using a potassium oxalate bleach (Fig. 7-22).

The use of Photostats as an aid in preparing illustrations is so widespread that obtaining informative literature from at least one large Photostat studio is recommended. Since Photostats are also made on acetate, they may be used as overlays for loose register.

---

[1] *Halftones and Combinations with Positive Screen Prints,* Bulletin 12, Eastman Kodak Company, 343 State Street, Rochester, N.Y. 14608.

Halftone reproduction from continuous-tone originals.

Tone-line reproduction made with an 80 to 90 percent mask on the negative.

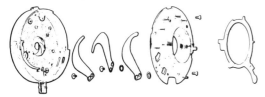

Tone-line reproduction made with a 100 percent mask on the negative.

Tone-line reproduction with added artwork. Production time is one-third to one-half of the time necessary for complete hand drawing or tracing.   **Fig. 7-25**

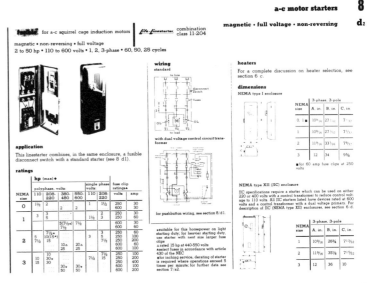

Fig. 7-26 This prizewinning Westinghouse catalog containing many small halftones and line illustrations was produced as line copy. Screened Velox prints of photos were positioned on the page paste-ups to get all-line copy.

Kodak Tone-Line Process Saves Time

Fig. 7-27 From a photograph to a line illustration by a photomechanical process.

A Clear Acetate Overlay with Self-Adhesive Transparent Proofs

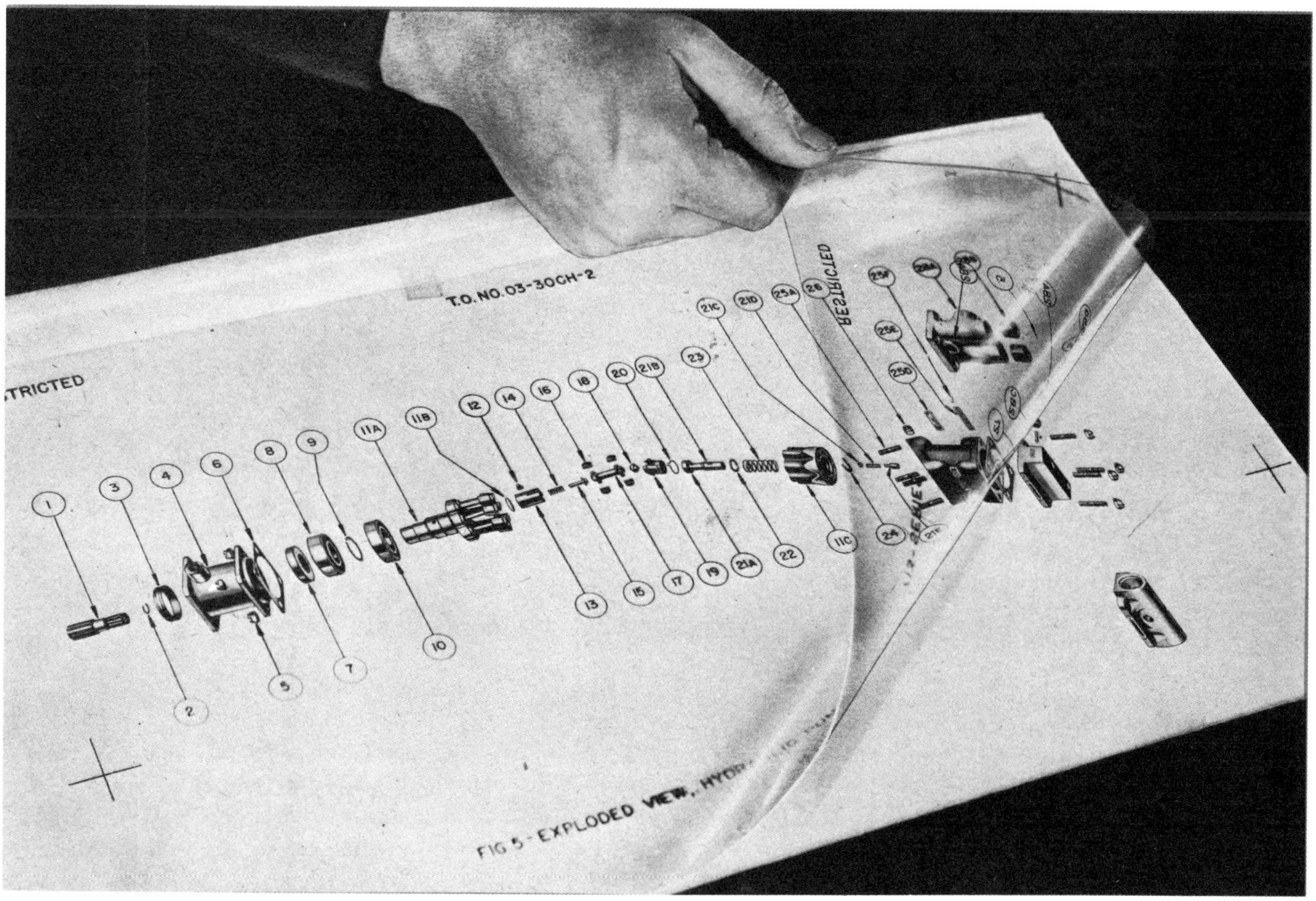

Fig. 7-28 Technical illustration frequently requires combined line-and-tone illustrations using symbols, arrows, codes, and so on, which must be positioned accurately. This job is handled with a clear (not frosted) overlay and a special kind of transparent proofs of line work with pressure-sensitive adhesive on the back.[2] Accurate positioning of the small proofs from the typographer's sheet of line proofs is very simple. Copy for map work is also handled in this way on transparent material; a name in type does not mask any lines or copy beneath on the key copy.

In some commercial printing a transparent proof (black or white ink) is positioned on the tone copy for a surprint or type reverse. The typographer should get a layout for position, for the proof material must extend beyond the edges of the tone copy; otherwise a faint line will show in the halftone. Because of the halftone screen, type edges are not sharp. This, of course, is an economy method.

Kodak Tone-Line Process

In preparing technical illustrations, a time-saving method is to convert photos of equipment of exploded views of parts to preliminary line copy to be touched up and completed by the illustrator. Photo studios and some photocompositors perform this service, as illustrated in Fig. 7-25. An unsharp positive mask is made and superimposed on the negative to get the line print.

[2]Composition, symbols, and so on may be ordered in black or white ink on clear adhesive-backed acetate from Monsen Typographers, 22 East Illinois Street, Chicago, Ill. 60611, and 928 South Figueroa Street, Los Angeles, Calif. 90015; and from Service Composition, 3928 Marlton Pike, Camden, N.J. 08109.

Peel away protective backing sheet and place Craf-Tone pattern over parts of the drawing to be shaded.

Rub down with a cloth, starting from the bottom and rubbing from left to right, moving upward as the pattern sheet adheres to the drawing.

Fig. 7-29

With a Craftint cutting needle, cut and strip away parts not desired. Rub the surface with added pressure to make secure. Now the art is ready for the engraver.

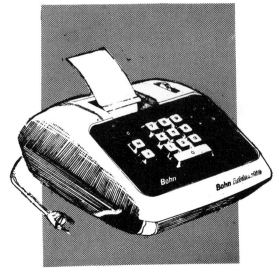

Fig. 7-30 Background tint makes an illustration stand out, projecting it from the background.

A Few of Hundreds of Tints and Patterns Available to the Artist

Fig. 7-31 Art supply stores carry these shading sheets on clear self-adhesive plastic ready to be added to line art for tones and backgrounds.

Velox Halftone Prints and Printed Halftones Are Line Copy

For a budget job (Fig. 7-26), screened Velox prints were scaled and positioned to avoid halftone costs.

Used only with offset, printed halftones can be reproduced with very little loss of tone and reduced or enlarged by a line camera exposure.

TONES AND PATTERNS ADDED TO COPY BY THE ARTIST

For newspaper illustrations and routine printing quality, rough tone can be added to line copy by portions of stock tone and pattern sheets obtained from an art supply store. This line copy involves no extra cost.

The printed tone sheets on transparent paper are usually in 65-line screen, in strengths from 20 to 80 percent tone. When pasting the material down on line copy, take care that there are no paper edges under the tone sheet area because these would produce a shadow line when printed. You may have to use a Photostat positive copy to avoid this problem. When pasting elements on newspaper stock, be sure that the rubber cement or melted wax is not too thin, for it tends to soak through the newsprint and make a brown spot which will be reproduced.

Fig. 7-32   With patterns and tones printed on special paper with invisible inks, the artist adds several tones to pen-and-ink drawings with brush developers. [*Courtesy Craftint Manufacturing Company*]

Fig. 7-33   This example shows the use of two tints between black and white. For technical illustration both transparent tone and pattern sheets and Craftint invisible-pattern papers afford as many as two different tones with brush developers. The artist can thus increase the contrast between different parts. The work is frequently done twice size and reduced for printing.

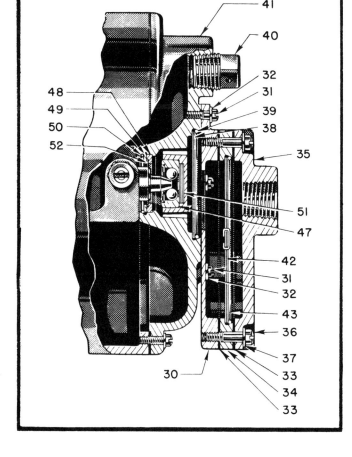

Line drawing using transparent pattern sheets.

Fig. 7-34   The artist's use of tone or pattern sheets for advertising is generally limited to conventional newspaper production. In commercial printing halftone tints made by the printer are used. Such areas are outlined in red, and the tint strength is noted.

Pen-line drawing without shading.

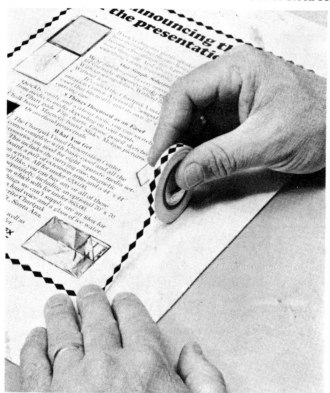

Fig. 7-35   Illustration from the Chart-Pak catalog.

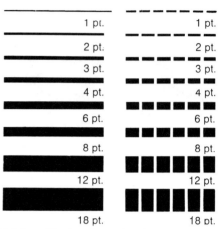

Solid- and broken-line point-size tapes.

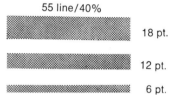

Benday pattern tapes printed in black on transparent or opaque material.

Tint areas in most advertising material and publications are handled on the mechanical with a red outline for boundary and a note for tint strength: less than 50 percent if the tone is to be surprinted and over 50 percent if there are to be type reverses. The printer uses halftone tint film in 150-line halftone.

Art supply stores sell a wide variety of tone and pattern sheets as well as the Craftint materials. See Figs. 7-29 to 7-32.

There are many forms of rules, borders, symbols, register marks, and numerical characters in constant use. Time is saved by the use of these stock items, which are available from art supply stores.

Technical fountain pens have largely replaced ruling pens, particularly in working with French curves and templates. Koh-I-Noor's Rapidograph with interchangeable nibs for different line widths is popular. The No. 2 line is often used for holding line (color lap) when two colors touch.

8

MECHANICALS FOR SIMPLE COLOR PRINTING

THERE ARE TWO KINDS OF color printing: *simple* color, for which opaque inks are generally used; and *process* color, for which transparent inks are used. For the first, the ink selected is to give the color wanted. Most simple color work is in black and one color, but it can be in more than one color. Where two colors touch, the camera copy should provide for a "color lap" because moisture causes the paper to expand. This is termed "color register." Without the lap of inks, there are apt to be "leaks," white lines between the two colors because the paper expands between printings.

THREE TYPES OF COLOR REGISTER

For simple color printing there are three types of color register: (1) *loose register,* in which colors do not touch or are surprinted; (2) *lap register,* in which colors touch; (3) *hairline register,* a method of providing a very fine ink lap of transparent inks to avoid a noticeable secondary color at the ink lap. This last type is used for incidental backgrounds or color spots when the main illustration is in process color. Process printing requires the use of transparent inks to get the secondary colors of the four-color process.

Loose color register does not require color register; lap register does. Hairline register is used only with the transparent inks employed for process color printing. The lap must be very fine because with transparent inks lapping produces a secondary color, such as green, formed by yellow and blue.

The general principle with offset and the other time-estimated processes is to provide copy for the camera in such a form that platemaking operations—the number of camera focuses, the amount of stripping, and, to a limited extent, the amount of work indicated for the platemaker to finish—will be kept to a minimum.

For simple multicolor work, copy can usually be prepared in *one piece,* much as single-color copy is, with the platemaker making a (duplicate) negative for each color and completing the work indicated by the tissue overlay for each color. Special copy techniques (keylining or outlining in red) are frequently used. The advantage is accuracy of color register.

LOOSE REGISTER: COLORS NOT TOUCHING OR SURPRINTING

Some two-color copy is so simple (Fig. 8-1) that camera copy is all in black with the tissue overlay indicating work to be in color. The platemaker can handle this with two negatives, opaquing unwanted work on each. The Railroad YMCA billboard poster camera copy

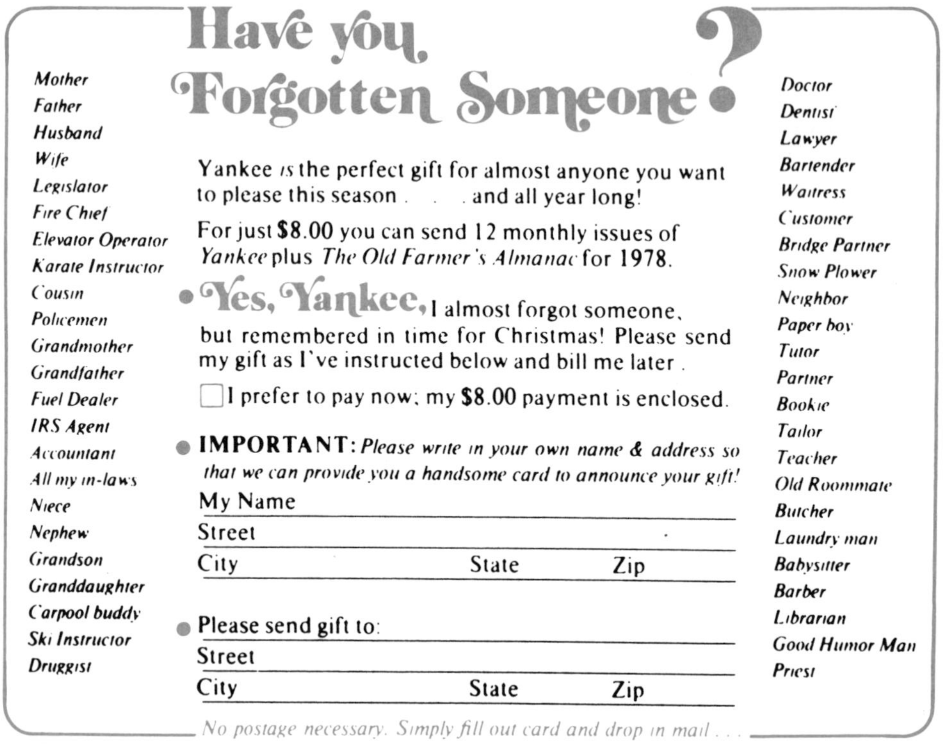

Have you Forgotten Someone?

Mother
Father
Husband
Wife
Legislator
Fire Chief
Elevator Operator
Karate Instructor
Cousin
Policemen
Grandmother
Grandfather
Fuel Dealer
IRS Agent
Accountant
All my in-laws
Niece
Nephew
Grandson
Granddaughter
Carpool buddy
Ski Instructor
Druggist

Yankee *is* the perfect gift for almost anyone you want to please this season . . . and all year long!

For just **$8.00** you can send 12 monthly issues of *Yankee* plus *The Old Farmer's Almanac* for 1978.

• **Yes, Yankee,** I almost forgot someone, but remembered in time for Christmas! Please send my gift as I've instructed below and bill me later.

☐ I prefer to pay now; my **$8.00** payment is enclosed.

• **IMPORTANT:** *Please write in your own name & address so that we can provide you a handsome card to announce your gift!*

My Name
Street
City State Zip

• Please send gift to:
Street
City State Zip

No postage necessary. Simply fill out card and drop in mail . . .

Doctor
Dentist
Lawyer
Bartender
Waitress
Customer
Bridge Partner
Snow Plower
Neighbor
Paper boy
Tutor
Partner
Bookie
Tailor
Teacher
Old Roommate
Butcher
Laundry man
Babysitter
Barber
Librarian
Good Humor Man
Priest

7BYY7–

Fig. 8-1 Copy in one piece for loose color register. The tissue overlay indicates elements in color; black and color are handled with two negatives.

(Fig. 8-2) was just a type proof with instructions on the tissue overlay.

Quite frequently surprinting (usually in black or a dark color) runs across the edge of a regular-shaped color area. In such a case, you should leave a gap in the color boundary line, which the platemaker can close on the color negative (Figs. 8-3 and 8-4). If, however, irregular color is to be surprinted, as in Fig. 8-7, color copy should go on an overlay with the art in black.

In the retail direct-mail field there is some two-color printing that is rather rough, flat color being kept within an outline of the subject or background, as in Fig. 8-8. In this case the artist could use red masking film as an overlay. Since the film is translucent, the artist can see the holding lines and cut and remove the red film on the carrier sheet within the indicated areas. The resulting overlay is equivalent to a printer's negative; color areas are clear film. Alternatively, color areas could be indicated on the camera copy in light blue, or instructions put on the tissue overlay.

A printer would probably make a contact positive from the line negative. Using an overlay on the positive, the printer would strip in pieces of halftone tint film for the color. If the illustration in Fig. 8-8 were for an offset newspaper, the mechanical artist would use an overlay and position pieces of tone sheet for the color. On the mechanical

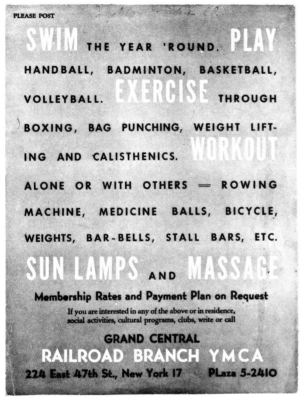

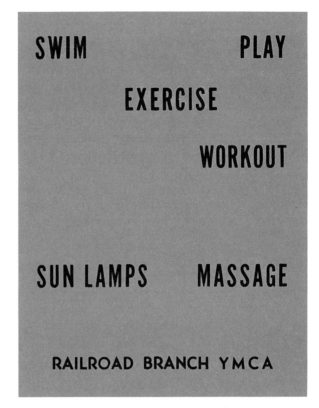

Type Proof Provides Two-Color Copy; Tissue Overlay Indicates Red Background with Words in Reverse, Surprinted in Black

Fig. 8-2 A repro proof of type matter with a tissue overlay, indicating the color background and which type is to be reversed and which is to be in black, serves as the copy for the camera for this two-color piece. The platemaker makes a contact positive for the color and reversed type, removing the image for the type in black. The camera negative is opaqued to eliminate the reversed type and is used for the black plate. Black overprints on the red.

The red plate is made from a contact positive of the original negative of type proof after all type matter in black has been opaqued on the negative. For the black plate the large reversed words are opaqued on the negative.

Surprinting across Color Boundary

TYPOGRAPHY IS ARCHITECTURE, AND THE TYPOGRAPHER IS THE ARCHITECT. THE BUILD-ING BRICKS HE USES ARE THE TYPEFACES, AND THE MORTAR IS THE SPACING HE SELECTS FOR HIS COMPOSITION.

TYPOGRAPHY IS ARCHITECTURE, AND THE TYPOGRAPHER IS THE ARCHITECT. THE BUILD-ING BRICKS HE USES ARE THE TYPEFACES, AND THE MORTAR IS THE SPACING HE SELECTS FOR HIS COMPOSITION.

Fig. 8-3 With regular-shaped color designs formed by using a straightedge or a compass, copy can be prepared in one piece with a gap. The platemaker makes two negatives or positives, one for each color. Guided by a tissue overlay or dummy, the platemaker completes each of them, masking unwanted images or type.

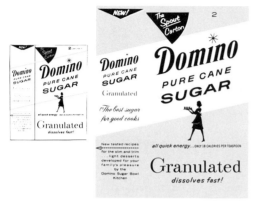

Fig. 8-4   Copy for this Domino sugar carton, in loose register, was probably prepared in this form. The background is in yellow, the reverses in red, and the type and the woman in dark blue. Gaps in the red holding lines (figure and reverse above) would be completed by the platemaker.

One-Piece Copy and Keylining Handle Reversed Element and Type Surprinting

Fig. 8-5   Copy in this form serves for both colors and saves camera work by the platemaker. Duplicate negatives are made. One is prepared for color in loose register, and the other has all work removed except for the bug and type matter to surprint in black. Black is always printed last.

The reversed headline was handled with a Photostat negative; the wavy edges signal "Work to be completed." The printer's negative produces the positive to go on the color negative, resulting in the reversed headline. This procedure is equivalent to an overlay knockout.

Surprinting or Reversing Type or Design on a Color Panel

> ### ORDER YOUR COPY NOW!
>
> *These actual pages serve as your introduction to the new, 1971 Ayer Directory — bigger, more complete than ever before!*
>
> ● If you have never used the Ayer Directory you owe it to yourself, and to your organization, to buy one now.
>
> ● If you have an old copy of the Directory, update your Information Center now with the new, 1971 Ayer Directory.
>
> **$42 plus 63c postage and handling, within the U.S.**

Fig. 8-6   Color or tint panels can merely be drawn with red boundary lines, but sometimes they are keylined inside lines as shown here. The tissue overlay gives the instructions. A Photostat negative can handle a reverse.

A Word on Offset Platemaking

The great majority of press plates are "surface" plates made from a flat of page negatives. This flat is contact-printed on a large sheet of aluminum, as shown in Chapter 1. The light passing through the clear parts of the negatives develops the printing image (type, lines, halftones, and backgrounds) on the press plate by hardening the light-sensitive plate coating.

Using a Photostat negative on the mechanical or masking or opaquing an area gives the clear areas on the platemaker's negative. The platemaker may mask your camera copy if you have not done so or may go back and forth from negative to contact positive, mask the desired area, and then return to the negative form to get the clear area on the negative for platemaking.

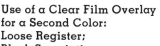

Use of a Clear Film Overlay
for a Second Color:
Loose Register;
Black Surprinting

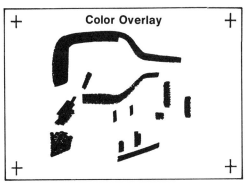

Fig. 8-7 With an irregular design and black surprinting color, an overlay is used for the color copy. For loose color register (not touching or surprinting) there is no provision for ink lap. [*Lawrence, Inc., Chicago*]

the artist would use a tone sheet for the 30 percent tint in black for the handkerchief background.

Fig. 8-9 shows the handling of all elements as a unit for both black and a second color, a light brownish tan which was overprinted by black. The second color was virtually a tint block of pages and of regular shape, with colored areas indicated by a tissue overlay. The platemaker handled the negatives for the second color from the copy supplied.

A parchment overlay with a line ruled on it was sufficient for the diagonal white line. This copy provided the line knockout to be handled by the platemaker. The parchment overlay was cut to show the corner marks and fold for the page on the key copy. These served as register marks, which were sufficient here but are not recommended for exact register because of the danger of the overlay's shifting slightly.

LAP REGISTER: WHERE COLORS TOUCH

Lap is the most widely used type of color register with simple color printing. Unfortunately, there is a widespread belief that color copy (in black or gray tones) goes on an overlay registered to the mechanical for black and that the artist makes his or her color copy slightly wider to go under the touching darker color or black reverse. A producer will advise against this procedure for most advertising printing because it often is not done accurately and "leaks" occur if moisture causes the paper to spread between printings. Correction requires extra expense.

Nevertheless, the overlay method is used for plate economy when a series of mailing pieces is prepared as a copy unit. All go on the same paper with the same inks (Fig. 8-15), generally with just one color touching black because the lap can be wider to go under the black. The producer just places a sheet of white paper under the overlay for the color negative, then folds back the overlay, and photographs the mechanical for the black.

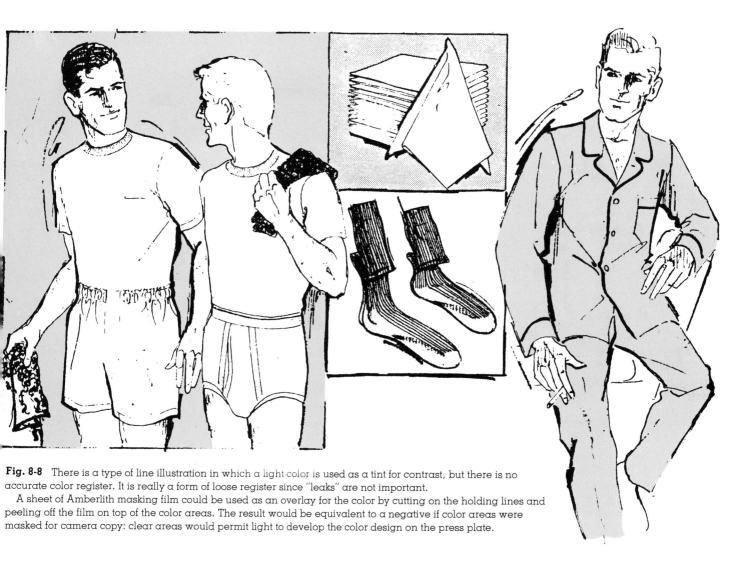

Fig. 8-8 There is a type of line illustration in which a light color is used as a tint for contrast, but there is no accurate color register. It is really a form of loose register since "leaks" are not important.

A sheet of Amberlith masking film could be used as an overlay for the color by cutting on the holding lines and peeling off the film on top of the color areas. The result would be equivalent to a negative if color areas were masked for camera copy: clear areas would permit light to develop the color design on the press plate.

Commercial lap register is generally ¹⁄₃₂ inch (0.8 millimeter).

Copy in One Piece Preferred

For lap register offset producers have always preferred handling copy in one piece. This method goes back to the days of stone lithography, when a *key-line* litho transfer sheet was traced where colors touched on the original artwork, then flopped for left reading, and transferred to each color stone for a key-line color boundary. For solid color, the proper area on each stone was painted in with tusche right up to the line. Since the key line was litho ink, it reproduced, and since it was common to both colors, its width gave the lap of the touching colors. Figure 8-11 may clarify this old technique.

With photography replacing the stone procedures and the mechanical providing camera copy in place of work done on litho stones, the mechanical artist now draws the key lines of simple color boundaries. The old lithographer brush-opaqued to ⅛ (3.175 millimeters) of the key line, with a wavy edge to the opaquing. This device served as a signal to the platemaker: "Provide for color register."

In recent years adhesive-backed masking film has replaced brush opaquing. Since the film is translucent, the mechanical artist can cut it halfway into the line, the line width providing the lap width. When color touches a black or dark-color reversed area, the platemaker adds the lap on the negative for the touching color.

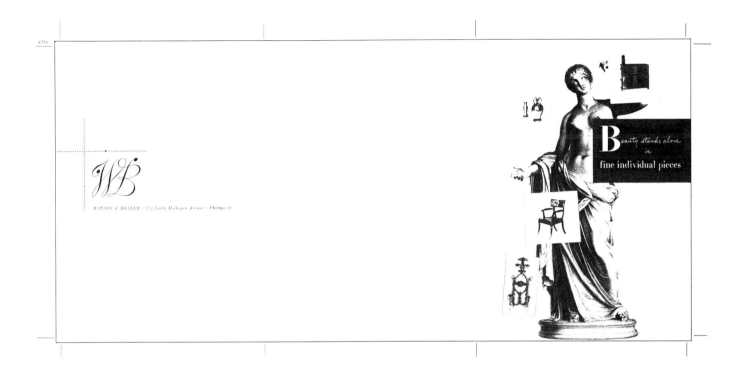

Fig. 8-9   The paste-up was not the same size but permitted a reduction in width from 8⅞₁₆ to 6¾ inches (from 214.3 to 171.5 millimeters) folded so as to hold details better in the small halftones. The dummy indicated not only color pages but the reversed initials *WB* with the horizontal dotted line in white. Since the squares for merchandising boxes on copy were color boundaries without an edge in black, this was loose register. The platemaker completed the work required.

Black Surprinting Color: One-Piece Copy

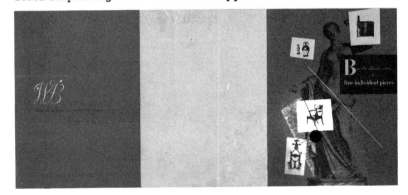

Precautions

With lap register, the quality of the printing and light colors have a bearing on ink lap, which for commercial grade is ½₃₂ inch (0.8 millimeter) and for top quality is ½₆₄ inch (0.4 millimeter). For light colors that have so little pigment that they are almost transparent inks, the lap should be finer. When the overlay method is used for small subjects, as it fre-

Key-Line Width for Lap Register

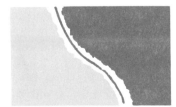

Fig. 8-10   One-piece copy for commercial-quality lap register uses a key line of about ½₃₂ inch (0.8 millimeter). The No. 2 nib of a technical fountain pen is widely used.

As mentioned in the text, simple color areas are no longer opaqued. The holding lines of the color areas, with a tissue overlay indicating colors, are enough (see Fig. 8-15).

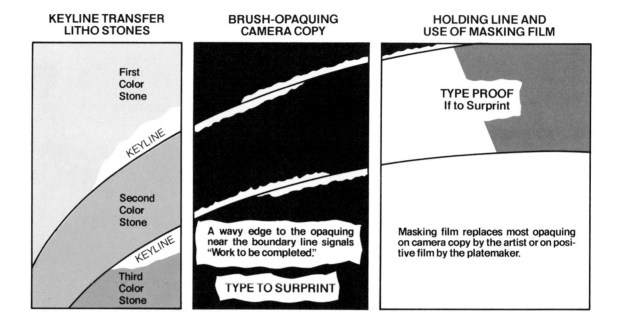

| KEYLINE TRANSFER LITHO STONES | BRUSH-OPAQUING CAMERA COPY | HOLDING LINE AND USE OF MASKING FILM |

**The Development of Keylining
as a Camera Copy Technique**

Fig. 8-11   Stone lithography was the original color-printing method. To provide for the color lap (register) of touching colors, the litho artist made a key stone by drawing lines in litho ink or crayon. By using transfer paper, the artist could transfer this key drawing to other stones, one for each color. Since the key lines were common to each color, the width of a line determined the ink lap of touching colors.

quently is in preseparated color illustrations by the artist, the size should be at least size and one-half. Sometimes small subjects are done 4 times the reproduction size to get a wider holding line. (See also Fig. 9-15.)

The purpose of Fig. 8-11 is to show the development of keylining techniques for lap color register, from the transfer of the litho artist's key-line drawing to each color stone to the touching (painting in) of the color area on each stone. With the introduction of photographic methods of platemaking, the mechanical artist in the user's art department was taught to brush-opaque up to ⅛ inch (3.175 millimeters) of the key lines; the technique signaled the platemaker to provide for color register. The white area around the type to surprint was opaqued out on the color negative.

The use of masking film replaced brush opaquing. Since the film was translucent, the mechanical artist or the platemaker could cut the film into the key line. Its width determined the ink lap of the color register.

KEYLINING COPY TECHNIQUES

"Keylining" is a rather ambiguous term that refers to methods of preparing copy for the camera in one piece—techniques that not only provide the camera copy but avoid complicated copy preparation by indicating and facilitating operations to be completed by the platemaker, usually for simple color work. Keylining is used by all the printing processes for copy in paste-up form. We shall see how these copy methods signal the platemaker: "Colors touch; provide for register," "This element surprints," or "Reverse this element."

Keylining is actually an old trick of the trade. The techniques go back to early stone color lithography in which outlines of the art to be reproduced were traced and then transferred to the various litho stones to key the design for each color. A black crayon transfer key reproduced; the width of the line was common to both touching colors and provided the amount of color lap desirable for register. A red key outline, made with

Overlay Method

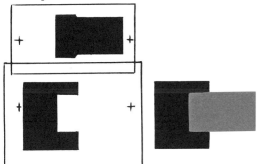

Fig. 8-12 Lap register by the overlay method is used mostly to save money on plate costs, since register of touching colors is provided for in the camera copy. For copy involving more than black and one color, this method requires accuracy to avoid leaks where colors do not lap because of the shrinkage of paper or overlay material. Its use is generally confined to small-size jobs printed in groups, as in Figs. 8-16 and 8-17.

The artist handling preseparated colors for illustrations uses the overlay method but generally works in 2 to 4 times size. This procedure gives a holding line of at least 1/16 inch (1.6 millimeters), making it easy to bring color images into the line for irregular register.

LAP REGISTER

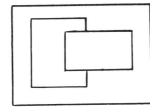 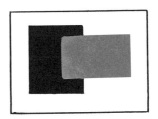

Copy in One Piece

Fig. 8-13 The copy above in regular-shaped register of touching colors just gives the boundary, or holding, lines of two touching color areas; composition and Photostat reverses can be positioned within them for any surprinting or reversed elements. On the photographic positive film, the platemaker strips in the red masking film for the flat color areas for each color press plate. The holding lines where the two colors touch are common to both colors and determine the width of the ink lap. The register is very accurate.

Fig. 8-14 The example with a woman introduces a keylining technique used for colors registering in an irregular shape or for a reversed black into color. The background color is opaqued (or masking-filmed) to 1/8 inch (3.175 millimeters) of the inserted image; this signals the platemaker: "Colors touch; provide for register." See applications of the technique in Figs. 8-21, 8-26, 8-27, and 8-28.

Opaquing of Color Areas Close to Key Line Is Now Usually Omitted

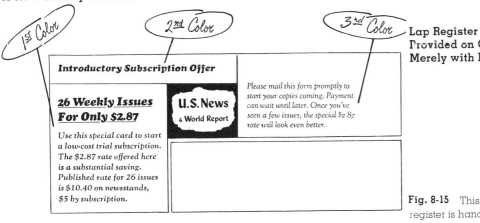

Lap Register Provided on Copy Merely with Lines

Fig. 8-15 This very simple example shows how lap register is handled merely with holding lines: the artist cuts the masking film halfway into the line for both touching colors. The width of the line determines the width of the ink lap. To lap the color under the reverse, the artist cuts the masking film for a 1/32-inch (0.8-millimeter) lap. If the mechanical artist does not use masking film, a tissue overlay shows what is wanted, and the printer's stripper will use the mask on the color positive.

Type to surprint is trimmed with a wavy edge and pasted in position on the mask or area. For a reverse a Photostat negative is trimmed with a wavy edge and positioned by the artist.

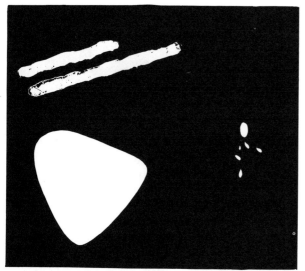

Overlay Copy for Color

**Four Folders Prepared as a Copy Unit;
Overlay for the Color**

Fig. 8-16 This very simple illustration in line with a background in light green was handled with an overlay for the green. It could have been done with copy in one piece and a tissue overlay to show the color area and handling of reversed type panels, but the overlay for the color avoided handwork in the platemaking. Since there were four folders, each with the same layout and color and only the front illustration different, the four subjects were handled as a group and the saving was multiplied more than 4 times. If the color had been in tone, the use of the overlay would have been the only method of handling the job.

Key Copy for Black

Front Page of Folder

dragon's blood powder, would not reproduce and so served only as a temporary guideline for the litho artist, a copyist. Today, therefore, in copy preparation a line in black is held, while the platemaker understands that a line in red is a temporary guideline. Although the red line is picked up by the camera and shows on the negative, it is not held after work has been completed.

The litho artists and transfer men completed the work indicated for each color stone; they reversed elements, touched in backgrounds, completed work for the key lines, provided for type and designs to surprint, and so on, using their craft skills in the various steps that came between the designer's stones and transfer proofs and the large press stones.

COPY FOR FIVE SMALL FOLDERS PREPARED AS A UNIT

Second imposition of this half of the press sheet.

The five folders, measuring 5½ by 3⅜ inches (139.7 by 85.7 millimeters) with one fold, were printed in black and yellow on one side and in black and red on the reverse side of the sheet.

Half of 17- by 22-inch (432- by 559-millimeter) press sheet, two on; flat made from copy unit of multiples.

Copy: paste-up with overlays, one for the color and one for halftone tints.

Fig. 8-17   An example of copy preparation that handled five small folders. It provided the flats for black and color, run two on the press plate without stripping.

The job run was black and red on one side and black and yellow on the reverse side of the sheet. Overlays were used for colors and halftone tints; lap register was provided in copy for touching colors, and black was surprinted on color.

When there are a series of printed pieces, they usually are planned for a combination run using the same stock and colors. Note that by planning the single fold on the side of the piece instead of on top, ten pieces were cut from the sheet instead of eight. This is an example of good planning for ordinary quality at a minimum cost.

One-Piece Mechanical for Two Colors, with Tissue Overlay Indicating Color and Surprinting

Fig. 8-18   Here is another example of camera copy for black and one color prepared without the use of an overlay for color copy, as is typical of contemporary procedures adopted to avoid bad register and hand opaquing. The boundaries of color areas and tint panels were drawn in red, indicating "Drop line." Lines to be held, such as the box under the blue "ticket" panel, were drawn in black. The circle around the offset symbol was marked "Drop line" on the tissue overlay. *X*'s on the tone elements (Photostats) mean "For position and subject only." Photos were supplied as separate elements for reduction.

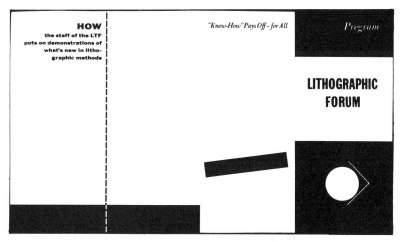

Two Positives
Made by the
Printer from a
Mechanical

Fig. 8-19 Positive prepared for blue.

Fig. 8-20 Positive prepared for black.

Inserting Irregular Line Element into Color Area

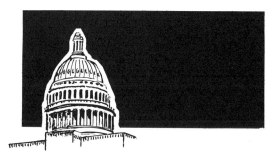

Fig. 8-21 The line element is positioned, and the background is opaqued to ⅛ inch (3.175 millimeters) of the element with a wavy edge to the opaquing. This provides camera copy for the element and signals the platemaker "Colors touch; provide for register."

Inserting a Regular-Shaped Flat Color into a Halftone; Copy in One Piece

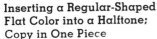

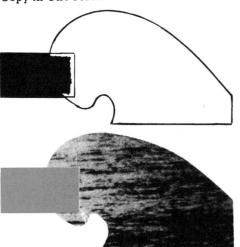

Fig. 8-22 Where color touches a halftone, draw a fine line on tone copy; insert color element, keylined on the color side of the line copy.

What Is a Knockout?

The Overlay   **The Knockout**

Fig. 8-23 The above illustrates one form of what a platemaker terms a "knockout." A knockout may be just a line, as in Fig. 8-9, or a reversed type of lettering, but usually it is an irregular-shaped copy element to be inserted into a background—flat color or halftone. A scaled positive of the element contact-printed with a negative of the background gives the platemaker an exact outline for color register when a copy element is to register into the background.

An Irregular Tone Element Inserted in a Color Background; No Provision for Register Required

Fig. 8-24 Scaled tone element positioned on an overlay. Usually the tone element is not in scale; so a pencil sketch is used for size and position.

When process photoengraving first came into commercial use, lithographic craftsmen were hired by the engravers because they were the only printers experienced with color. These men naturally applied many of their litho techniques to the new photographic methods, working on negatives or positives instead of on stones. Work was added or removed to complete the images for each color.

The preparation of copy in paste-up form for the camera gradually moved from the art department of the litho producer to the user's art, advertising, or editorial departments, and the keylining copy techniques accompanied the transfer of this work to the user. In some areas the producer still does the copy preparation for many customers or for specialized forms of production.

The techniques described here demonstrate the usual keylining applications, with examples in which these techniques have been used. As we have mentioned, the kind of ink and its color have much to do with the provision for color lap and have a bearing on the preparation of keylined copy.

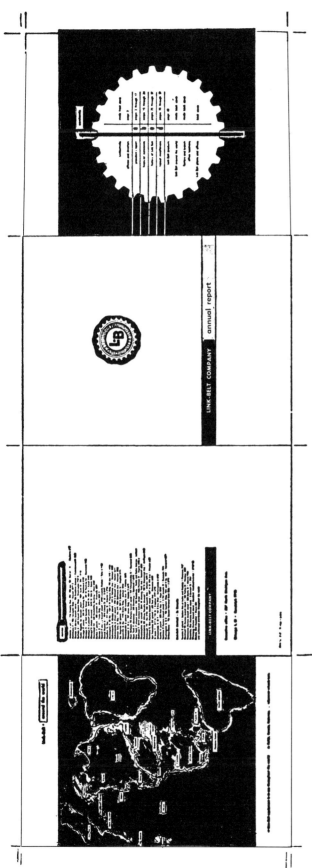

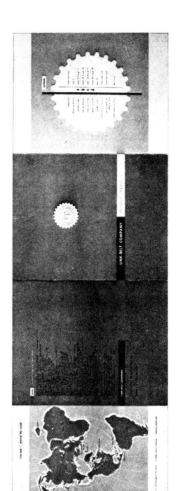

**Gatefold Cover in Two Colors and Black:
Copy in One Piece, Using Keylining and Overlay**

Fig. 8-25 Copy was prepared in one piece, with a tissue overlay to indicate colors; an acetate overlay was used for positioning small type proofs of names surprinted on the map in two colors. A knockout overlay handled the radial design on the blue of the oceans.

Since colors were separated by white, the map was handled as one-piece copy. A brown-red background was used on the front and back covers, the left gatefold was brown-red and blue, and the right gatefold was light blue overprinted with a black bar.

Note the keylining for both front and back covers for the platemaker to handle the reverse background with "service" line reversed and an emblem in blue inside the white gear wheel.

Copy for the gatefold on the right was handled by a negative Photostat because horizontal rules in white ran to the left edge of the background and were blue in the white center area. The heavy vertical bar in black was keylined at the ends for copy for camera and lap register, but the job was done in loose register at these two spots because black could overprint light blue.

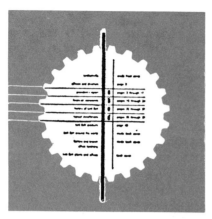

Fig. 8-26 This keylining technique was used in Fig. 8-25 to handle the vertical black bar extending into the light blue background. Actually, the platemaker used a loose register and merely surprinted the black on the blue. If the choice of inks had made it necessary, copy provided for lap register.

Fig. 8-27 Keylining handles an irregular outline against a flat color. Note also how the irregular design in white in Fig. 8-25 was handled to go into the background color.

Four-Color Copy for Camera Prepared in One Piece with a Tissue Overlay Indicating Color Areas and Surprinting of Type

Fig. 8-28 [*Courtesy Stecher-Traung Litho. Corp.*]
This example shows how copy can be prepared in one piece, using the red outline for color boundaries and keylining techniques for lap register and surprinting type on background in place of color overlays. Copy in this form is usually preferred by the producer because it fits more accurately than overlays. Since the platemaker completes the work indicated, the plate cost is slightly higher than that of accurate overlays.

With this form of copy, the platemaker usually makes a positive for each color. In this example, the yellow background and panel outlined in red on copy and the type in the right bottom (blue) panel, "12 Beautiful Models for the Modern Kitchen," were printed in yellow; the platemaker filled in the red outline areas and provided for the type matter on the yellow positive. The work indicated in blue was handled on that positive, all else being blanked out. On the red and black positives everything was blanked out except what was to appear in those colors. For the "Save" panel in red, the keylined type "With a brand new" was filled in solid and provision made for lap register of red to the woman's head and shoulders.

Most simple color work is prepared by this method or the overlay method to avoid the cost of finished art and color separation by the camera.

Keylining around Type Matter on an Opaqued Area
Means "Surprint on the Color"

Fig. 8-29 Copy in Fig. 8-28 contains the line "With a brand new" in black on a red background, with the copy handled as shown here. This provided camera copy for the type in black, and the platemaker merely filled in the white area when completing the negative for the red plate.

Fig. 8-30 Keylining around type matter on an opaqued area means "Surprint on the color." When masking film is used instead of brush opaquing, the type to surprint is merely pasted on the film.

 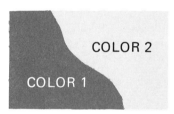

Hairline Register Is Required with Transparent
Inks Used for Process Color Printing

Fig. 8-31 Since the lap of these inks results in a secondary color, incidental illustrative treatment in simple color requires a fine holding line when two colors touch. Much collateral printing requires hairline register because of process color illustrations.

Copy Prepared
for the
Use of Photographic Spread
or Masking Film

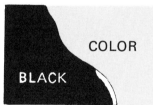 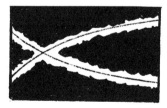

HAIRLINE REGISTER

This type of register, which is required with transparent inks, uses only the one-piece copy method. When simple color printing is handled with transparent inks, often because the main artwork of a campaign is in process color, the lap of registered colors must be very fine to avoid a noticeable secondary color from the lap. To get such a fine lap of touching colors, particularly for an irregular shape, a keylining copy technique is used, as illustrated in Fig. 8-31. The fine holding line is common to both colors in this example, and its width therefore determines the amount of ink lap.

Fig. 8-32 Camera copy is prepared here in a variation of hairline register. For black or a dark color, paint or mask up to the line, and merely outline the boundary of the color area if there are only two colors. If more than two colors are to register, mask or opaque each up to 1/8 inch (3.175 millimeters) of the line, as shown.

This form of copy is suitable for the platemaker's use of either "photographic spread" or masking film. The platemaker will paint up to the line of selected color areas, depending on which color is to lap under, according to the sequence of printing the colors.

With more than two colors the technique is the same as the old brush opaquing close to the key line.

Fig. 8-33   Box wrap: hairline color register by keylining.

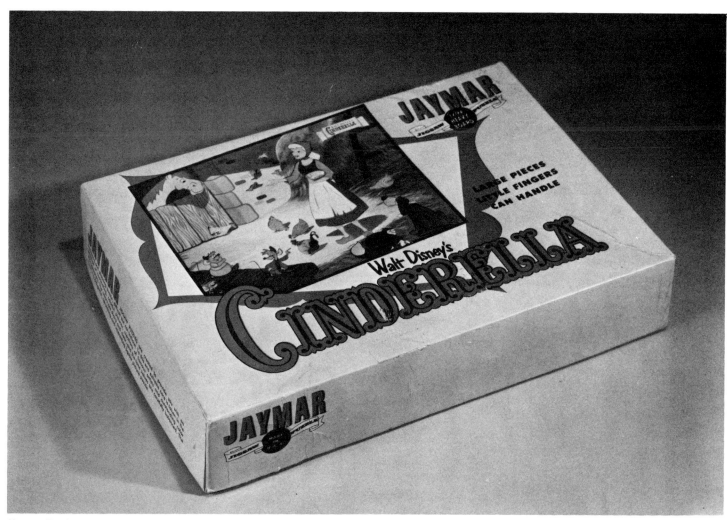

Use of Keylining for Hairline Register
Copy Prepared in One Piece for Four Transparent Colors

Fig. 8-34 This example illustrates a common problem: the principal illustration is process color (in this case the separations were picked up from a previous job), which required transparent process color inks. Because of the transparent inks, the supplementary art had to be prepared for hairline color register. A tissue overlay in color indicated the color breakup for the platemaker. The overlay method is not accurate enough for hairline color register. Incidental color treatment of supplementary art and headlines is usually handled in flat color by the artist to avoid the cost of larger process plates, as in this example.

Provision for Color Lap
Unnecessary for Type Matter

GRAPHIC

ARTS

MONTHLY

Fig. 8-35 This example illustrates how type can be "spread" by the camera to give a lap for color register. Other methods are used by the printer for some types of production.

**How to Handle Copy
for Shadow Lettering**

RIGHT   WRONG

Fig. 8-36 A common error in handling headlines in color, whether type or lettering, is to outline the black shadow area. Just the opposite should be done. If the shadow is also a color, keyline where the colors touch.

DESIGNING FOR
SPLIT-FOUNTAIN WORK

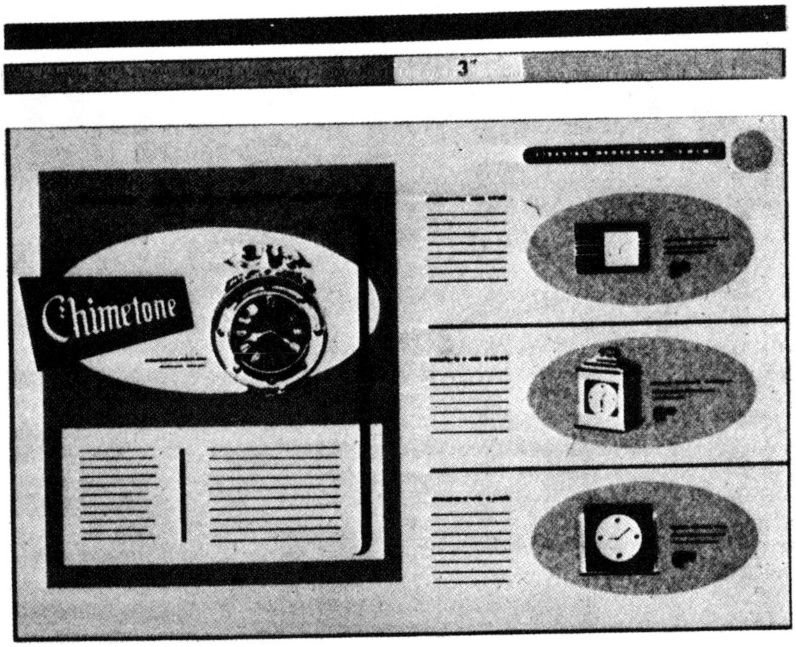

3"

Fig. 8-37 In this illustration the bars at the top represent the ink rollers of the press. The separation between colors never need be more than 3 inches (76 millimeters); for color tints, the separation can be as narrow as 1¼ inches (31.75 millimeters).

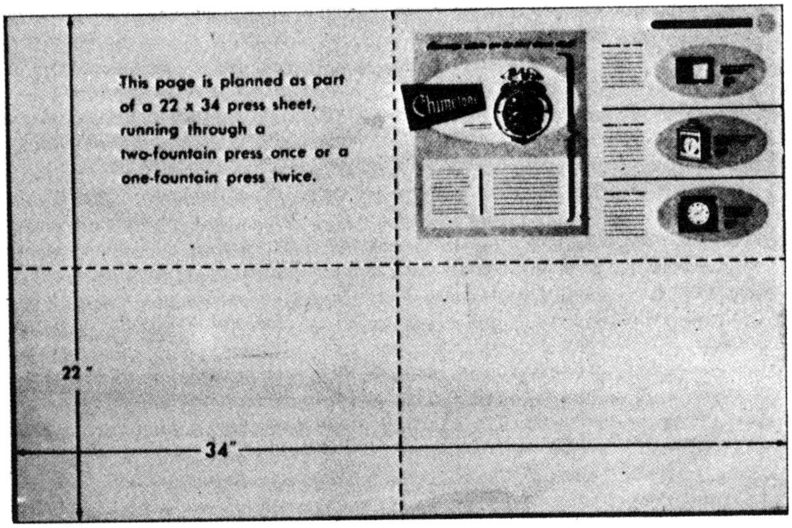

This page is planned as part of a 22 x 34 press sheet, running through a two-fountain press once or a one-fountain press twice.

22"

34"

HEADLINES IN COLOR ON A
DARK BACKGROUND

Frequently display type or lettering in color is placed on a dark background color. To get contrast for visibility and to avoid a possible secondary color by surprinting, a silhouette of the type or lettering is removed from the background by the printer so that the type color will go on white paper to get the reflection for contrast. Any necessary lap of inks is handled by the platemaker, who takes care of this problem in the camera operation or in exposing the flats for the press plate. The type matter is handled on an overlay for position.

9

USE OF THE COPY OVERLAY

We Have Touched on the use of the overlay: for combining line and tone copy in a single-color printing; for providing camera copy for a knockout, with the film positive serving as a mask when positioned on a negative for contact printing; and for handling an irregular design in color that is to be surprinted with black type or design. Figure 7-7 is an example of the last of these uses. Because the black surprints or does not touch the color, color register is not a problem.

The major use of overlays is to provide separate camera copy for color, usually for the copy unit when opaque inks are employed. However, we have seen that some mechanicals can be prepared either by the overlay method or by the one-piece–copy method. The overlay method is chosen if plate economies are important, particularly if several small printed pieces are to be prepared as a copy unit, as in Figs. 8-16 and 8-17, but the artist's work must be accurate; otherwise, charges for corrections will cancel much of the economy.

COLOR REGISTER AND INK LAP

You may recall from Chapter 8 that the overlay method is used for loose register (color surprinted). With lap register there must be some ink lap because the paper may expand or shrink in printing between pressruns. Copy in one piece with keylining is best for accuracy of lap.

Later in this chapter, in the section "Preseparated Color by the Artist," the use of the overlay for book illustration is discussed (Figs. 9-14, 9-15, 9-16, and 9-17). Usually there is just a holding line, and the lap is halfway into the line. The mechanicals are prepared 1½ to 4 times size in order to facilitate provision for the lap.

USES OF OVERLAYS WITH COLOR

Generally, overlays are employed for color for the following purposes:

- Irregular color design to be surprinted by black or dark color (Fig. 7-7). Overlays are not used with transparent inks unless special watercolors keyed to process ink colors are worked on thin film overlays to obtain secondary colors in design, as for greeting cards.
- Handling color in tone to be surprinted with black or another color (Figs. 9-4, 9-5, and 9-12).
- Handling a reverse design or type running across touching colors (Fig. 9-6). The overlay provides copy for a knockout of design for a reverse image.
- Reversed type on a very dark airbrush background should be handled with the Photostat negative on an overlay but not on the airbrushing. Dark tones are apt to be only 80 or 90 percent, and the difference in tones of the two ele-

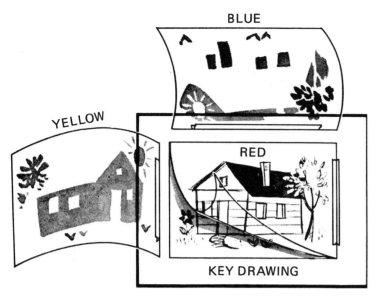

Fig. 9-1 The old flap method of handling overlays shows how copy for each color is prepared on a separate overlay by the artist, who works in black or in grays for tones.

ments is likely to be noticeable in the printing, particularly on coated paper.

- Individual overlays on elements widely scattered on a large copy unit are generally used instead of a unit overlay (Fig. 9-13). The size and position of any elements to be reduced are outlined in red, and such elements supplied separately with an overlay.
- Camera copy for multiple halftone tints should have different overlays for each tint strength unless there is at least 1 inch (25.4 millimeters) for stripper's tape between the tint areas. A single tint strength can go on the mechanical; it is just opaqued or indicated.
- Preseparated colors by the artist for illustrations. A blueprint of key copy on the film overlay helps to get good lap register (Fig. 9-15).
- If separate small printed pieces are to be handled on same paper and inks and loose or lap register is to be used, they can be prepared as a copy unit (Figs. 8-16 and 8-17).

Color Areas on One-Piece Copy

When an artist opaques color areas with copy in one piece, he or she frequently works in red. Red, which photographs as black, indicates a color area.

Figure 9-5 includes type overlays for surprinting and reversing type on tone, as handled for gravure. This could be used for offset, but usually one positioned type proof would be supplied with the reversed type circled. The producer would make two negatives, opaquing one to leave only type to surprint. On the other negative the producer would opaque all but the type to be reversed and from this make a knockout positive by contact. The rough tissue overlay indicates the final result wanted. Or the producer may just circle the reversed type.

PRESEPARATED COLOR BY THE ARTIST

The principle of mechanical color separation by placing the design for each color on a separate overlay (black or gray tones) is also used by the creative artist for simple forms of color illustrations. The major purpose, particularly for book illustrations, is to avoid the cost of process color plates. Since only a rough color sketch is required for approval, the artist's expense may also be smaller. The procedure goes back to the days of stone lithography, when all paintings were reproduced by litho artists (copyists) who made a key outline of the design, which was transferred to many litho stones, one being required for each ink color in the painting. Guided by the original artwork, the litho artist worked on each stone with litho crayon, tusche, and ink to get the tones and details in black. Many ink colors were necessary because all the pigments were opaque. The Metropolitan Museum of Art in New York has a lithographed reproduction of a watercolor with a proof book showing the nineteen different inks used in its preparation.

The modern procedure, of course, uses separate overlays instead of separate litho stones. Alternatively, an artist using the original stone techniques makes a keylined mechanical signaling the platemaker to complete indicated work and to provide a negative for each color, as shown on the tissue overlay or the dummy.

Fig. 9-2 Top half of a two-page spread, 10 by 7½ inches (254 by 190.5 millimeters), in two colors.

Line Mechanical

Fig. 9-3

**The Overlay
for Color**

Fig. 9-4 A Magic
Marker in red on a clear
film overlay supplied
camera copy for tones
(both color and black)
shown by a tissue
overlay.

HOW COLOR ART WAS PREPARED

The planning for several million booklets in color called for minimum cost. With offset, an inexpensive uncoated stock permitted fine halftone work. The thirty-three illustrations in two, three, and four colors required the use of an inexpensive art medium and freedom from process color costs.

The job was planned for key-line drawings in black with a tone overlay for each color. Working on clear Vinylite material with felt-tip applicators (red, yellow, and blue), the artist got both the primary and the secondary colors. For example, viewing the blue and yellow overlays in contact, the artist saw the green which would be obtained. (These colors are transparent and produce the tonal qualities of watercolors, avoiding any "mechanical" tonal qualities.) Handling the color copy in groups of the same focus reduced plate costs. Tone in black was obtained from overlay duplicate halftone negatives by opaquing unwanted color design.

Eleven illustrations were in four colors, five in three, and twenty-two in two. Planning saved both time and money. [*Client: Aluminum Limited Sales, Inc.; agency: J. Walter Thompson Company; art: Alfred Avison Studio, New York*]

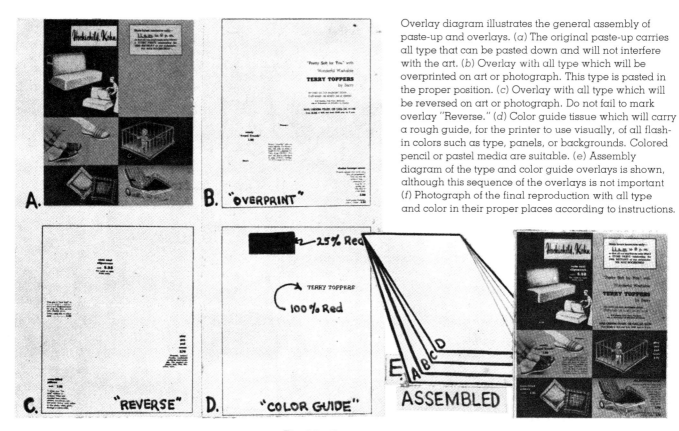

Overlay diagram illustrates the general assembly of paste-up and overlays. (*a*) The original paste-up carries all type that can be pasted down and will not interfere with the art. (*b*) Overlay with all type which will be overprinted on art or photograph. This type is pasted in the proper position. (*c*) Overlay with all type which will be reversed on art or photograph. Do not fail to mark overlay "Reverse." (*d*) Color guide tissue which will carry a rough guide, for the printer to use visually, of all flash-in colors such as type, panels, or backgrounds. Colored pencil or pastel media are suitable. (*e*) Assembly diagram of the type and color guide overlays is shown, although this sequence of the overlays is not important (*f*) Photograph of the final reproduction with all type and color in their proper places according to instructions.

Fig. 9-5 Copy overlays save platemaking time. This copy with overlays prepared for gravure simplifies the operations of the platemaker and thus saves time. In gravure plate costs are estimated by time. [*Courtesy Gravure magazine*]

When an Element Runs across Two or More Colors, It Is Handled on an Overlay

Fig. 9-6 In this illustration the "Swift's Premium" cartouche oval reverse running across two touching colors would be handled on an overlay. The stripper would position the two negatives (colors) and then with a positive of the overrunning design knock out the reverse image to get proper fit on the two colors.

**AIRBRUSH ART FOR COLOR REQUIRES
BLACK SURPRINTING FOR SHADOW DETAIL**

Black Key Copy

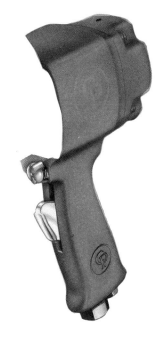

Fig. 9-7 Two original photoprints of this tool, one in normal tone and one in high key to surprint color, were cut and combined. The normal print was greatly retouched for black with highlights, and the light half was retouched for shadow detail to surprint color.

Fig. 9-8 Overlay color copy prepared by masking to produce an airbrush silhouette of color to be surprinted by high-key black for shadow detail.

Procedures in Use

Most colors preseparated by the artist are prepared on film overlays for opaque ink by line copy, including tints and patterns applied by the artist. Any tone copy is put on the mechanical or on a separate overlay. For the illustration in Fig. 9-17, there were a mechanical for the brown tone and an overlay for the green.

Guided by the approved rough color sketch, the artist prepares the key copy for the black on illustrator's board, usually proportioning it for size and one-half, a practical work size that facilitates the provision of any needed color lap. If the illustrations are to be small, as in Fig. 9-15, the work is frequently done 4 times the reproduction size. All camera copy is executed in black or gray tones. When the copy is in line with only a few tone elements, these are scaled and positioned as

Velox screened prints, which are classed as line copy. Such prints are also available for two-color work, screen-angled and registered.

The use of preseparated color with opaque inks can be almost an art technique in itself because of the extra color strength as compared with process inks for simple color printing.

Preseparated Color for Transparent Inks

To handle a volume of artwork requiring the usual secondary colors with process inks, such as art for greeting cards, special art techniques are available. With special watercolors keyed to standard process inks the artist, guided by a rough color sketch, works each primary color on a separate thin film overlay. Positioned in register sandwich-style, the secondary colors thus formed can be seen. The printer photographs batches of same-

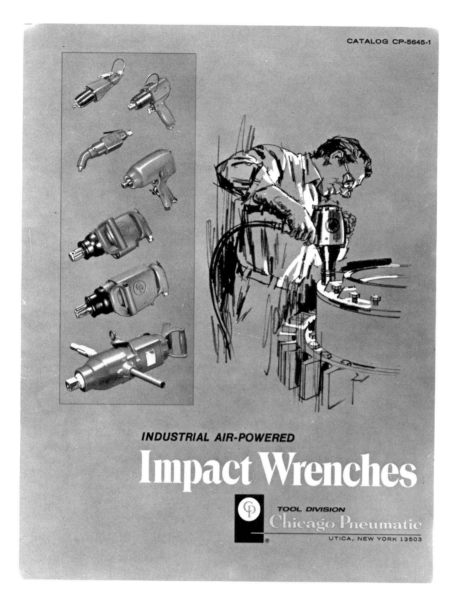

Fig. 9-10   Key copy: black.

Fig. 9-11   Red plate.

**Highlight Dropout Overlay
Prepared by Artist with Illustration**

Fig. 9-9   The illustration of the tool operator in scale on the key copy was prepared separately in 120 percent of scale size with a dropout mask overlay on clear film, in register, to be contact-printed on the red negative for the result shown in the cover reproduction. The panel background with pictures of tools and the company name were printed in a light olive green (not shown).

Fig. 9-12   Highlight dropout mask overlay for white areas of the red plate, prepared on key copy for black.

color overlays in groups. All the colors have been separated, and no color correction is required.

Bourges Color Corporation's Colotone sheets perform the same function except that unwanted color areas are removed by brushed solvent or a scraper. Tone art can be added with special colors. Each colored sheet comes in five different tone values: 10, 30, 50, 70, and 100 percent. Besides the standard process colors, the standard (opaque) poster red, yellow, orange, and green ink colors of the business paper associations are available.

Supplementing Process Subjects with Preseparated Color Design

Frequently with collateral printed material and sometimes with publication ads, the key illustration is in full color and so must be printed with regular transparent process inks. Often the key illustration is picked up from another job, and the separations are available, or conversions of color photoengravings may be used for offset production.

Incidental illustrative color treatment such as color spots, backgrounds, and tints is often added. To avoid additional process color expense, preseparated color camera copy is prepared. Remember that hairline register must be employed because of the transparent inks being used.

LOW-BUDGET COLOR COPY

Every artist runs into situations in which little money is available for artwork or in which much is expected for the money allotted, particularly in book design. These needs created the "contact autopositive technique," of which an example in single color is shown in Fig. 7-14. The artist works with a dark pencil on the rough side of frosted film overlay material and by the pressure of the pencil stroke on the abrasive texture obtains the desired tones. The pencil should be hard enough not to smear: the jet-black extra-smooth Ebony pencil 6325 is recommended and was used for this illustration. This technique has been used for book illustrations in several colors.

Note that there is no halftone screen and that the result approaches the texture of stone lithography. The artist works in the same size in the usual right-reading manner, and from the artwork a contact negative is made and

positioned as a halftone negative would be. The reproduction will also be right-reading. Since camera expense is avoided, you can't get much lower plate costs.

Tissue Overlays in Pencil

It is quite simple to take a black-and-white photo and add one or two colors for a Multilith job. The artist merely uses the broad strokes of a graphite pencil or crayon on tissue overlays to add tone color where it is wanted.

For commercial work you can add color to a black-and-white photo by sending the photo to an offset producer with instructions to make a halftone negative and blueprints on overlay material that you supply. Each blueprint supplies the holding lines for a color as you work in black or wash for the color.

At this time we should mention that new developments in process color—photographic masking for color correction and automated procedures developed for short-run process color—have superseded some of the low-cost, manual, preseparated, simple color methods. This subject is covered in Chapter 10. Fig. 10-2 shows such a process illustration for which color separations cost about $75.

PIN REGISTER SYSTEMS

When the camera operator photographs key copy and overlays, the usual practice is to handle all copy as a group. This requires flap overlays to be torn apart.

Various makes of pin register systems are coming into use. Snug-fitting holes in the overlays fit over pins or dowels fastened to the key copy on illustrator's board.

Rapidly superseding the old flap acetate overlays and the more recent pin register and punched-hole method is the use of round "button" dowels on the black key copy and fitters on the overlays, as shown in Fig. 9-18. This patented method avoids the awkward flaps (which in any case the producer frequently removes for photographing all copy as a group) and the punching of illustrator's board and the acetate.

Register marks are placed on the key copy. The overlay is frequently notched as shown or cut to give clearance for the dowel button. With the overlay in place, the notched fitters are positioned to register lines and taped to the overlay. An adhesive-backed dowel is

USE OF INDIVIDUAL ELEMENT OVERLAYS

Overlay

Fig. 9-13   When a color mechanical is large, as for a 25- by 38-inch (635- by 965-millimeter) broadside, separate overlays are usually made for each element carrying a second color. This procedure avoids the danger of the film overlay's shrinking. The platemaker detaches the overlays to photograph them as a group, and the stripper positions them by register marks.

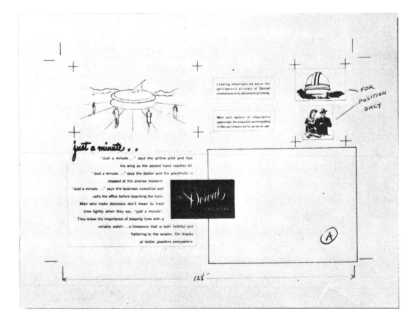

Overlay

Note that register marks are kept close to the copy to save film in group camera work. Two register marks are sufficient with small elements.

A PICTURE IN FOUR COLORS IN "THE FOUR CORNERS OF THE WORLD" (Knopf)
Written and illustrated by Roger Duvoisin

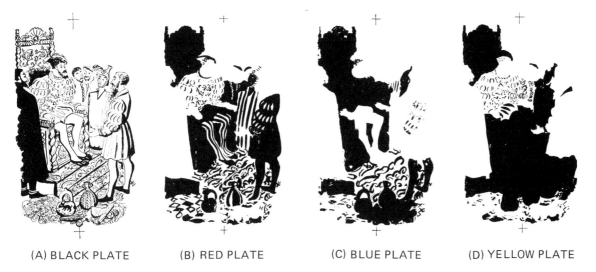

(A) BLACK PLATE   (B) RED PLATE   (C) BLUE PLATE   (D) YELLOW PLATE

Preseparated Colors by the Artist Widely Used for Book Illustrations

Fig. 9-14   These illustrations demonstrate the usual procedure of a book illustrator when he or she is required to preseparate four flat colors in order to avoid the cost of finished art and process color engravings. Working from an approved rough color sketch (above left), the artist first has a line print made of the rough sketch to serve as the key black plate (A). Then with three separate overlays in line copy, one for each of the three colors, the artist executes the artwork in black for B, C, and D. This procedure avoids the need for color filters by the printer's camera operator. This subject required considerable surprinting of colors: the chair received three colors to get a reddish brown light enough to take the black design of A.

then placed through each fitter to stick to the key copy sketch; the oblong fitter should point toward the round dowel to allow for expansion or contraction. Additional overlays have fitters positioned on the dowels of the key copy before they are taped in place.

The fact that illustrator's board expands and shrinks $\frac{1}{16}$ inch (1.6 millimeters) or more in large sizes is the reason for the use of oblong fitters. It takes time to get overlays and key copy back into register. It is suggested that old aluminum press plates be obtained from a regular producer. These can be cut to the desired size with scissors and laminated to drawing paper with shellac to get a dimensionally stable illustrator's board, or Precision Art Board can be purchased. It is important that the overlay material used be dimensionally stable; ordinary acetate dries and shrinks.

Caution: For Acetate Overlays Use a Dimensionally Stable Material

There are many types of acetate material, both matte- and clear-finish. The type used for copy overlays should be of a quality that will not shrink from drying out or expand from moisture. Work is held up when the platemaker finds that the overlay copy has shrunk $\frac{1}{16}$ inch (1.6 millimeters) and does not fit the key copy. Dimensionally stable brands include Vinyline and Cronar; art supply stores usually also offer other brands. A thickness of 0.005 inch (0.127 millimeter) is generally used. Acetate inks, opaque thinner, and opaque removable solution are available.

MATERIALS THAT FACILITATE PREPARATION OF OVERLAYS AND MECHANICALS

The volume of artwork on overlays, as well as the use of coated sheets of acetate in colors, has resulted in the development of dimensionally stable materials and a variety of surfaces and coatings, ranging from clear, transparent sheets that take ink or wash to removable opaque coatings and colors.

Some of these materials avoid brush-opaquing by the artist, and others permit the artist to see the black key underneath as he or she works the color area on the overlays. Standard color sheets that permit seeing the results of combining colors are available, and yet the artist can remove unwanted areas and even add tone with color and brush.

Continuous-tone illustration is obtained by contact negatives from pencil on grained acetate. The result resembles stone lithography.

The larger art supply stores sell many of the materials listed below. The number at the end of each paragraph is the key to the name and address of the manufacturer offering informative literature.

Clear Acetate Sheets

These take all types of inks and colors and pen, brush, or airbrush. They will not chip or crawl. (1), (2)

Matte-Surface Acetates

There are many types and degrees of roughness; the acetates take pencil, pen, brush, and blueprint coating. They are used for scribing. The underside is opaque, and the top is white. (3)

Masking Film

This film is translucent but photographs as black. Mounted on a base, it can be hand-cut for a clean line and removed if desired. It is used for opaque areas and adheres to illustration board with rubber cement. (4), (5), (6), (10)

Transopaque Overlay Sheets

They have a red coating that photographs as black; it is removed by scraping small areas and by dissolving large areas. The sheets are widely used for design in black and white on a colored background; also with adhesive tape for cutting and positioning. There is a liquid coating for corrections and added pen or brush detail. (2)

Bourges Colotype Overlay Sheets

These are transparent plastic sheets that match twelve basic standard transparent inks

PRESEPARATED COLOR TECHNIQUES
AS USED BY THE READER'S DIGEST

Fig. 9-15   A large portion of the editorial content is offset on uncoated paper. Until the present use of process color most of the color illustrations were prepared by artists as shown here.

A comprehensive sketch is planned on the basis of a key plate (usually black) and three or four *Digest* colors selected from twenty-eight special hues and supplied to the selected artist with instructions to render an overlay for each color on textured Vinylite or on matte-finish acetate in register on the key drawing.

(A)

(B)

(C)

(D)

(E)

(F)

A. Jordan plate is bluish green.
B. Mountain plate is purple blue.
C. Key plate is black.
D. Cameo plate is a dark flesh tone.
E. Pink plate is a light coral red.
F. Finished proof with all colors in register.

PRESEPARATED LINE AND TONE COLORS

Brown (Tone)   Green (Line)

Fig. 9-16   A two-color illustration by Roger Duvoisin for *Bhimsa*, by Christine Weston (Charles Scribner's Sons, New York, 1945), was done in watercolor for the brown and with an overlay in flat color for the green, thus avoiding the cost of separating colors photographically. The resulting illustration is shown below in a black-and-white halftone.

Fig. 9-17

REMOVABLE COPY OVERLAYS ARE NOW USED

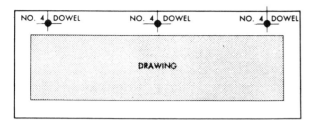

Drawing Board for Oblong Work; Dowels
Positioned with Ruled-Line Fitters

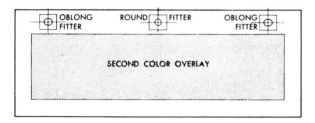

Overlay Film with Fitters Attached, on
Clear or Matte; Second-Color Overlay
Worked on While Held in Register with
the Dowels on the Artwork

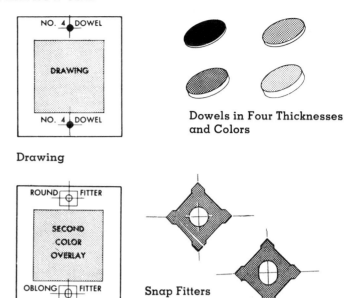

Drawing

Dowels in Four Thicknesses
and Colors

Overlay Film

Snap Fitters

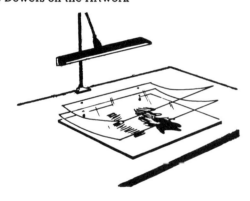

Fig. 9 18 [*Accurate Step & Repeat System, Inc., 858
Sussex Boulevard, Broomall, Pa. 19143*]

in five different values. By working each color as an overlay, the artist can visualize the result of combining these colors for secondary colors. The artist then removes any unwanted color and adds with pencil, pen, or brush. (2)

Colored Acetate Sheets

These come in transparent colors, grays, and black to match standard inks and are used to visualize results in flat colors with secondary colors. The sheets have an adhesive backing.

Reds are used for overlay sheets; there are also pattern sheets in color applied by the artist. (2), (7), (9)

Blueline Emulsion Film

Dino blueline prints of the black key provide an overlay on which detail for color can be turned to black in selected areas by applying a chemical with a brush; the rest of the design in blue will not photograph. After a print has been made, hydrogen peroxide applied to black lines turns them back to blue for reuse for a second color. Brush-opaque areas for solids; the film is accurate for color lap. (8)

Tints and Patterns

These provide invisible tones on either film or drawing paper that are developed chemically where wanted by brush application. Multicolor types are also available. (9)

Sources of Materials If Art Supply Stores
Are Not Available

(1) Abraham Seltzer & Co., Inc.
     231 West 54th Street
     New York, N.Y. 10019

(2) Bourges Color Corporation
     20 Waterside Plaza
     New York, N.Y. 10010

(3) Henry P. Korn Associates, Inc.
     300 Park Avenue South
     New York, N.Y. 10010

(4) Ulano Products Company, Inc.
     210 East 86th Street
     New York, N.Y. 10028

(5) Morley Associates
     273 Columbus Avenue
     Tuckahoe, N.Y. 10707

(6) Separon Co.
     56 West 22d Street
     New York, N.Y. 10010

(7) Cello-Tak Manufacturing, Inc.
     35 Alabama Avenue
     Island Park, N.Y. 11558

(8) Di-Noc Division, 3M Company
     1700 London Road
     Cleveland, Ohio 44112

(9) Craftint Manufacturing Co.
     18501 Euclid Avenue
     Cleveland, Ohio 44112

(10) Serascreen Corp.
     5-25 47th Road
     Long Island City, N.Y. 11101

10

PREPARATION OF PROCESS COLOR ART

To Reproduce Full-Color Artwork such as paintings and transparencies, the colors are separated photographically by the use of color filters in front of the camera lens to get color separation negatives of the three primary colors and black. Process artwork is not positioned on the mechanical along with text and headlines; its size and position are merely indicated by Photostats or inexpensive color prints.

The original artwork, whether a transparency or a watercolor, now is rarely used for camera copy in commercial printing but instead passes through intermediate photo steps to produce "prepared" copy for the camera. Thus mixed art media are reduced to one of two forms; either they are proportioned for same-focus economies with offset, or the process elements are scaled for positioning. All groups of process elements are, of course, put in tonal balance. The intermediate photo steps are undertaken with reproduction-quality color photoprints or with duplicate transparencies produced by photo color laboratories.

The purpose of these operations is to transfer to the copy preparation stage by the user work which formerly was done by the offset platemaker at a much higher cost; time also is saved. Since with offset the process plate size is not limited, process mechanicals are frequently used to avoid the individual stripping of each subject on all four press plates. Color camera sizes range to a 60-inch (1524-millimeter) circular halftone screen.

Most full-color printing is done by the four-color process. The artist should understand that the process has limitations—some colors can only be approximated, particularly in publication advertisements because of the use of standardized inks.

LIMITATIONS OF THE FOUR-COLOR PROCESS

When working with colors, the artist should be aware that there are limitations to the colors that can be reproduced, imposed mainly by the process red and blue. For example, you cannot get a good Persian blue or emerald green. Since both the process red and the process blue are cold in hue, you cannot get a warm Christmas red or a royal blue; the red and blue can only be darkened with a black tint.

These limitations are particularly stringent in publication printing, for which standardized process inks are used. Various publication associations publish color charts showing the results of combining tones of color on both coated and uncoated papers. Most of the larger consumer magazines also publish their own color charts on the paper they use.

In commercial printing process inks can be changed to suit job needs, or a fifth or a sixth color can be used to meet exacting requirements. In the cosmetic industry as many as eight colors are used to match hair tints and the colors of lipsticks and nail polish. Some fine arts reproductions are printed in ten colors.

A commercial artist working in color should understand that his or her artwork must be suitable for reproduction by the four-color process. If the work requires six colors,

Process Mechanical and the Reproduction

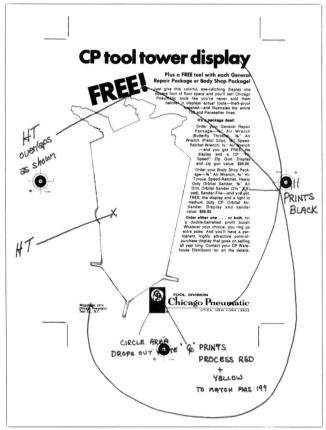

Fig. 10-1A Mechanical with a single process color element. This Chicago Pneumatic mechanical gives a good idea of how instructions are handled on a tissue overlay. The single process color subject was merely outlined in red for size and position: the artwork was a 3¾- by 4¾-inch (95.25- by 120.65-millimeter) transparency supplied as a separate element.

Fig. 10-1B   The completed advertisement.

it may be rejected. Here are some tips for the artist:

Process Red

To reproduce purples, dark blues, cold browns, and cold pink tones the ink must be close to the magenta or cold red, whereas to get clean oranges, warm Christmas red solids, and extremely clean flesh tones the ink should be cleaner or toward the warm red. The artist should avoid mixing any of the two groups of colors in the same painting. For example, if there are clean oranges, avoid purples, dark blues, and so on.

Process Blue

To get the dark blues, purples, and royal blue tones of a painting, the printer's ink should

be of a reddish cast, but if the subject has much clean green, the blue ink used should be closer to peacock or greenish blue. If the artwork contains both clean greens and cold purples, one of the two colors must be sacrificed if only one blue is to be used in the printing. Otherwise, either the greens would be too olive, or the purples would be too dirty.

Other Problems

The few limitations of process red and blue inks mentioned here do not cover all the problems of four-color reproduction, but they do point the way to closer cooperation between the creative artist and the reproduction technician. When on unfamiliar ground, consult one of your producers for guidance and procedure before artwork is prepared. This is standard procedure in the book-publishing field, in which time and budgets are always tight. Get the producer's recommendations on problems: there are art techniques and color processes that save time and money and may be suitable for the desired quality. In advertising, production time and cost usually have priority over quality.

ADVICE ON PAINTING AND PIGMENTS

Avoidance of Overpainting

To make a correction or a change in an oil or opaque watercolor painting the artist should remove the old work first. Otherwise some of the rays of the copyboard arc lamps will penetrate the paint and bounce back from the canvas to register on the color separation negatives. This produces a muddy spot on each of the four color separations that must be corrected by hand, resulting in extra charges.

Do not letter on top of artwork. Position lettering or type proof on an overlay; it will be handled by the platemaker.

Choice of Pigments

Almost any form of art can be color-separated photographically, but the platemaker's charges may vary greatly with the pigments used and the secondary colors required. In artwork transparent pigments are the simplest to color-separate. There are watercolors keyed to standard process colors, and if these particular colors are suitable, no color correction will be required.

Color reproduction is frequently unsatisfactory when an artist varies the type of paint. The change may not be apparent to the eye, but when the colors are separated photographically, each type of paint—acrylic, tempera, casein, and so on—may require special handling with filters and different developers. The same type of paint should be used throughout the subject or group to be color-separated.

Both type matter and lines reproduced in process colors should be limited to one or two colors. The use of all four colors causes unnecessary register problems with a large press sheet.

White pigment should be used sparingly to lighten colors, and the same brand should be used throughout a painting or group. Different brands may reflect different light rays from the arc lights and add to the correction time because different filters and developers are needed to get good separations. You will find that the work of the best artists saves several hundred dollars in plate costs because they know the requirements for four-color reproduction and the methods to be used for different grades of quality.

NEW PROCEDURE WITH PROCESS COPY

Prior to World War II reproduction color photography was generally limited to 35-millimeter Kodachromes or their equivalents, which were too small for color correction, and for all printing processes the color camera operators had to follow an involved procedure to obtain scaled color-corrected separations. The results were not seen until color proofs of the plates were made.

Carbro prints, the only form of reproduction-quality prints available, were made by layers of primary colors on separate tissues; all had to be originals. Duplicates could not be made. The available photo color prints were not of reproduction quality.

In Chapter 1 we explained how offset plate costs were estimated on the basis of time— the amount of time required to make the press plates by the form of camera copy prepared by the printing user and supplied to the printer. In Chapter 2 we discussed the extra capabilities of the offset process, due largely to the absence of economic and technical restrictions.

To understand the new procedures with process color copy and their advantages to the user it is well to know something of former methods. With four-color process copy, the camera operator separated the colors photographically with the aid of color filters and the subtractive color process. For the yellow, the filter used in front of the camera lens held back the other two primary colors; the procedure was then repeated for the blue and the red separations. A plate for the black was made with a special filter to accentuate details and secure a better black for type and other line copy.

For various reasons the color separation negatives usually required tonal adjustment by changing their opacity in some areas. In order to get more color a litho artist dissolved a little of the black emulsion on the film to let more light through when the negative was contact-exposed on the light-sensitive plate coating. To get less color the artist added to the opacity of an area with a stain. His or her skill was to judge color by tones of gray.

In advertising, many illustrations were, and still are, made up of components requiring inserts, changes, combinations, and so on. Under the old methods much featheredging of the cut lines of the films was required so that the lines would not show in the reproduction. This featheredging was a time-consuming and costly operation by engravers or strippers when printing plates were made.

Then, too, practically all process elements had to be scaled and positioned to the layout supplied. With process color printing this had to be done in register on separate plates for each of the four color elements.

BEGINNING OF THE NEW TECHNOLOGY

An early development was the densitometer, an instrument for measuring the tonal qualities of artwork and halftones (both reflection and transmission types) which was much more accurate than the human eye. The result was less manual time spent in color correction. This advance was soon followed by "photographic masking," a technical procedure for determining and supplying the needed tonal correction of color separation negatives, a more accurate procedure than the manual methods of the litho artist. The result was pleasing-picture–quality color separations at a cost of less than $100 a set. Top-quality color producers generally do not use this procedure because it does not meet their standards, but it is a real economy in publication printing (see Fig. 10-2).

PHOTOGRAPHIC MASKING FOR COLOR CORRECTION

Formerly the engraver or platemaker handled most color correction on the color separation negatives; this was a hand operation. With offset, at least 60 percent of the work was done on the continuous-tone negative separations, and the rest by dot-etching the screened positives. New technology substituted photographic masking for hand tonal changes on the negatives and made possible a greater degree of correction. Such masking is now widely used by all three major printing processes. A rush photoengraving set of color engravings can thus be made in 2 days instead of the usual 10 days.

With offset, masking not only has reduced the number of hours required for color correction but has opened the door for short-run process color (1000 sales portfolio sheets in full color for $200) and permits pleasing-picture–quality separations (limited color correction) for less than $100. An example is the *Electrical World* ad promoting the magazine's offset section (see Fig. 10-2).

Five different masking techniques are used in offset; some require reflection, or opaque, camera copy, and others need transparencies. Art production therefore ascertains from the producer which form of copy is desired.

RANGE IN PROCESS QUALITY AND COST

Thus we see that with offset printing there is a range in quality and cost of process color work, running from less than $75 to more than $1000. This range extends from the use of masking alone for color correction to the conversion of color separations by other printing processes, the use of multiple plate sizes from a single set of color separations, and either unscreened or screened color separation negatives produced by the new electronic scanning machines. Planning of collateral printed material makes full use of offset's capabilities.

FLEXIBILITY OF PROCESS BROADENS CONTROL

If we review Chapter 2, "Offset Production Planning," and consider copy preparation in the light of the form in which the copy may be prepared, we shall realize that the flexibility of the process (due to the estimating method and capabilities) adds to cost control the advantages of time and quality control in planning. Moreover, the form in which copy is prepared for the camera takes into consideration its use for related pieces of an advertising campaign in addition to the initial printing job.

For composition, there are not only additional cost controls but additional forms—

phototype, different faces, styles, tricks, spacing, and measures—not practical with metal type.

OFFSET'S EXTRA CAPABILITIES WITH PROCESS COLOR

In the following pages we shall illustrate many of offset's extra capabilities:

- The enlargement or reduction of size from same process halftone negatives (Figs. 10-12 and 10-13).
- Multiple plate sizes from one set of color separations (Fig. 10-14).
- Large process color plates (Figs. 10-14 and 11-1).
- Conversion of process photoengravings and gravure plates (Figs. 10-15, 10-16, and 10-17).
- Process color proofs before plates are made (Fig. 10-20).
- Fine halftone screens on uncoated and rough-textured papers (Fig. 10-19).
- No restrictions on the use of modern typefaces on uncoated paper.
- Low-cost process color plates (Fig. 10-2).

BREAKTHROUGH IN PROCESS COLOR PLATE COSTS

Formerly all procedures involved in process color copy—scaling and positioning color elements, as well as keeping the color elements of an assembly in tonal balance plus any requirements for photocomposing—had to be handled by the printer. A change came in the late 1940s with the development of reproduction-quality color photoprints, first dye-transfer imbibition prints and later the Type C color print. Eventually, with the availability of color film in larger sizes, reproduction-quality transparency duplicates were developed at a usable cost. Color photo laboratories or studios took the original artwork with a layout and instructions and produced prepared camera copy, complete with any color adjustments needed to suit the art director. Today such work is often done overnight. Very important, duplicate print copies can be made for a fraction of the initial print cost.

Thus the user's art director can see the result of creative planning before plates are made. All preliminary work has been done; the camera copy supplied the printer is the

Fig. 10-2 Low production cost for a full-color page. To promote the economy of full-color production costs for advertising in the offset section of *Electrical World*, a promotion to agencies showed that costs for this house ad were less than $275. The costs included separations and Color Key print proofs as well as photography and composition.

final version, with no further changes. Obviously, both time and money are saved by offset's time plate estimating method because so much of the preparatory work has been done.

As you may recall from the list of extra capabilities of offset in Chapter 2, with process color assemblies (units of two or more elements) there are no size restrictions on process plates. This means that a large printed piece, such as a 25- by 38-inch (635- by 965-millimeter) broadside, containing process elements can be handled as a process mechanical. The individual stripping of each process element separation negative on the four press plates is thus avoided, and many hours are saved (see Fig. 10-3).

BEGINNING OF PREPARED CAMERA COPY

In the early 1940s the use of color photography for advertising was just beginning. Most national advertisers employed from six to ten printers for the various types of production; not only did the 35-millimeter Kodachromes then in use have to be enlarged for color correction, but multiple copies were needed for the various printers. Carbro prints were the only form of reproduction-quality photoprints suitable for scaled size, but inexpensive duplicates were not possible.

This problem was solved with the development of dye-transfer color photoprints; duplicates could be supplied for about 10 cents on the dollar. One international advertiser required thirty-two copies of all artwork. Equally important was the fact that the imbibition prints made from three-color separation positives permitted rapid color adjustment to suit the art director; colors could be changed to show the colors available in a line of merchandise, and inserts and combinations of separate elements could be photocomposed. This was the beginning of prepared camera copy, which was much faster and less costly than the previous method of having the platemaker handle the equivalent operations.

A few years later Type C color photoprints were developed by Kodak. These prints are made from copy in negative form such as Ektachrome color film; otherwise there is the cost of converting copy in positive form to negative to make the prints. This form of color photoprint has endured because it can be made overnight in several grades of quality. The standard sizes are 8 by 10 inches (203 by 254 millimeters), 11 by 14 inches (279 by 356 millimeters), 14 by 17 inches (356 by 432 millimeters), 16 by 20 inches (406 by 508 millimeters), and 20 by 24 inches (508 by 610 millimeters).

Early users of reproduction color prints preferred the dye-transfer type when there were changes in color or when work involved inserts or combinations by photocomposition. Such work was more difficult with Type C prints, but if camera copy in negative form was available, the cost was about one-third less.

COST OF REPRODUCTION COLOR PRINTS

Since dye-transfer prints require manual operations by technicians for changes, the cost now is about $250 for 8- by 10-inch (203- by 254-millimeter) and 16- by 20-inch (406- by 508-millimeter) sizes, and their use is limited to critical color matching. In recent years the LaserColor Print was developed, making fine-quality prints available for about $25. They are widely used because they can be made overnight.

TYPE C AND OTHER REPRODUCTION PRINTS

Widely used for reproduction and other purposes, such as presentation prints, are various quality grades of Type C and newer forms of color prints. The time required may range from "in by 4 P.M., ready 9 A.M." to 2 or 3 days. Prices for 24-hour prints range from about $20 for 8 by 10 inches (203 by 254 millimeters) to $55 for 20 by 24 inches (508 by 610 millimeters), with an extra $5 for overnight delivery. Reproduction-quality C prints range from about $40 for 8 by 10 inches to $95 for 20 by 24 inches, with delivery in 2 or 3 days. Some color studios offer additional larger sizes: 24 by 30 inches (610 by 762 millimeters) and 30 by 40 inches (762 by 1016 millimeters). A few duplicate copies of reproduction quality cost about half the price of the original print; in quantity each may cost as little as $5.

COLOR TRANSPARENCIES

Small photographic color transparencies were used for printing before color prints were developed. Such transparencies went directly to the platemaker to be scaled, color-corrected, and positioned on the layout. The procedure was so complicated that high extra costs resulted. If copy components were to be inserted or combined for an illustration, expensive featheredging was required at the joining line of the negatives.

With the postwar development in color photography came color film in sizes up to 14 by 17 inches (356 by 432 millimeters) for transparencies, used mostly by a new type of photographic service, the photo color laboratories. The laboratories converted the 35-millimeter transparencies, any other form of artwork, or original transparencies of another size to scale size, color-adjusted as desired for the art director.

Transparencies frequently require color adjustment, and retouching is in order. If the retouching is poorly done, a transparency can be ruined. With a costly transparency, printers advocate using a duplicate for retouching. They use the original to make the color separations and the duplicate as a guide for any necessary color correction.

If the transparency on hand is too strong or too weak in a color, it can be color-adjusted by using Bourges color masking filter overlays, even for spot areas such as a fashion model's dress against a background. The filter overlay that makes the desired adjustment is fastened to the transparency.

Use of a Viewing Light

The color values seen in a transparency depend on lighting conditions. These conditions must be the same when user and producer judge the color values; the same type of viewing light should be used by both. At least one brand of light has a dial control; when the user obtains the desired result, the dial setting is noted on the edge of the transparency so that the engraver can duplicate the lighting. Official standards have been established.[1]

Cost of Duplicate Transparencies

Duplicate transparencies of reproduction quality made from any size of original transparency or artwork are usually based on two sizes for cost: any size up to 8 by 10 inches (203 by 254 millimeters), $50; any size up to 11 by 14 inches (279 by 356 millimeters), $75 to $100. Some color studios offer transparencies in sizes smaller than 8 by 10 inches at $10 and up.

[1]These are contained in a folder obtainable from the American Association of Advertising Agencies, 200 Park Avenue, New York, N.Y. 10017.

CHOICE OF COLOR TRANSPARENCIES OR PRINTS

Advertising photographers work closely with art directors in the creative stage either in the studio or on location. In the field 35-millimeter and 2¼- by 2¼-inch (57.15- by 57.15-millimeter) hand cameras are widely used for convenience; some have motor-drive attachments for eight frames per second. To get the expression or element of believability wanted by the client, 100 or more pictures may be taken.

The brilliance and purity of colors of a transparency cannot be reproduced with four-color printing by any process, for the color quality of three pigments on paper cannot match the qualities of dyes on transparent film with transmission lighting. For this reason some printing users prefer color prints, the qualities of which are closer to the reproduction on paper.

Printing technicians seem to agree that a good color transparency in proper register for sharpness and with proper focal depth will give the best reproduction, particularly in the highlights. However, many camera operators will tell you that a print is preferable in order to hold important details in the shadow areas.

The degree of color fidelity required also has a bearing on the form of camera copy. For example, medical literature directed to doctors that shows the color of diseased tissue must be exact. A microphoto in color would be converted to a large dye-transfer print, the visual quality of which would be closer to the printed reproduction than a transparency. Moreover, the print could be color-adjusted to suit the requirements of all concerned and would provide for reduction. The reproduction of accurate color is the objective in this field.

With the use of such forms of camera copy, particularly transparencies, electronic scanning machines (described below) were subsequently developed to obtain color separations in hours rather than days for any of the printing processes. The machines can take even a 35-millimeter transparency and enlarge and color-separate it. This procedure for the production of prepared camera copy is now the standard for use with all printing processes.

MEASUREMENT OF TONAL QUALITIES BY INSTRUMENT

A major reason for the improvement of process color reproduction is the use of the densitometer to measure the density, or tonal qualities, of selected areas at both ends of the gray scale on reflection or transmission copy. A reflective type of densitometer is used to measure art and prints and the reproduction. A transmission type measures transparencies and photographic negatives and positives. With a viewing eye on the end of a cord, tones on the ground glass of a process camera can also be measured. Science has replaced the human eye in judging tones because visual perception varies widely from person to person.

DISPATCH OF ARTWORK

Color separations take time. To avoid the extra cost of overtime to meet a specified delivery date, send artwork to the platemaker before the mechanicals are finished. This is also the case with a color photo laboratory preparing camera-ready copy.

WORKING WITH THE PRINTER

Don't forget that an offset printer should always be told the *kind* of paper to be used for tone printing. The printer adjusts the halftone dot size for the difference in light reflection from smooth-surfaced and from rough-surfaced paper. It is best to attach a swatch of the paper to the mechanical. The printer orders

Ordering Photo Color Transparencies and Prints

If you want	And you have	Order
A color print or color transparency for reproduction (one or several)	Color transparencies	Repro dye-transfer prints Repro duplicate transparencies
	Color negatives	Repro Type C prints or duplicate transparencies
To make a selection from a number of color originals to preview an ad	Color transparencies	Internegatives and Type C prints
	Color negatives	Type C prints
To produce a color assembly ready for reproduction	Color transparencies and color artwork	Color-corrected duplicate transparencies of all, scaled and positioned on film
A color layout for presentation	Color transparencies and color artwork	Presentation dye transfers plus Type C prints or Ektachrome paper prints
	Color negatives	Type C prints
Finished artwork for reproduction, needing retouching and correction	Color transparencies Color artwork Ektacolor negatives	Retouched repro duplicate transparencies; in extreme cases, repro dye-transfer prints plus retouching
To produce color plates for an ad in several places simultaneously or by more than one process	Color transparencies Color artwork	Repro duplicate transparencies or repro dye-transfer prints
	Ektacolor negatives	Repro duplicate transparencies or Type C prints
To present a new advertising program or idea to a client or to reproduce an ad or ad campaign in jumbo size for sales presentation	Color transparencies, finished art, tear sheets, or proofs	Comprehensive dye-transfer prints; Ektachrome paper prints
	Ektacolor negatives	Type C prints
Display pieces for point-of-purchase or exhibit	Color transparencies Color artwork Ektacolor negatives	Color "printparencies" Color display duplicates (print on translucent base)

Courtesy Robert Crandall Associates, New York.

the mill brand and the paper size, for different mill brands have different color casts, frequently bluish or pinkish; this is particularly important with process color copy.

Color samples of nonprocess printing should appear on the kind of paper to be used. Don't send a color sample on coated paper if an uncoated paper is to be used: the same ink will look different.

Matching ink colors is expensive and time-consuming; the Pantone® ink-matching system, which is covered in Chapter 12, is widely used today. Ink color is specified by number.

For process color printing, the printer orders the inks specified for the mill brand except for publication advertisements. The artist should be guided by the chart of the standard inks used by all publications.

The size of a printed piece should be determined by standard paper sizes and by the efficient press size for the quantity ordered. Most large multicolor jobs are now printed on offset web (roll) presses. Since these presses are custom-made, unit sizes vary (mainly according to standard publication sizes), as do folding and binding capabilities, which offer important economies.

When large jobs are to be printed, they are usually designed for the press to be used. Chart I (Fig. 12-4) in Chapter 12 shows comparative press times for a single-color, 17- by 22-inch (432- by 559-millimeter) unit run on different press sizes to produce 100,000 sheets for 11- by 17-inch (279- by 432-millimeter) folders. If the unit size was changed to 11 by 16 inches (279 by 406 millimeters), a different press would save $200.

Services of Color Photo Studios

By means of photo color prints or transparencies:

- Original process copy can be scaled or proportioned.
- Mixed art media can be reduced to a single medium for group color separation, with all elements put in tonal balance.
- Color can be removed or added, strengthened or adjusted, and contrast added.
- Any colors can be added to black-and-white photos. This is a form of the Flexichrome method.
- Assemblies of process elements can be scaled and transparencies "floated" to their position on film for color separation by electronic scanners or contact separation.
- Opaque copy can be converted to transparencies, or vice versa.

- Material can be composed creatively to make an illustration of separate units by combining, inserting, or surprinting them.
- Duplicates of the prepared copy can be made available.
- The 35-millimeter and 2¼- by 2¼-inch (57.15- by 57.15-millimeter) color transparencies are too small for color correction. These are enlarged or scaled as transparencies or color prints to make correction possible. Small hand cameras are widely used in advertising photography.

Thus the use of intermediate photo steps between the original art and that supplied for the camera saves much time and cost. All changes and adjustments can be made before copy goes to the printer, in one piece exactly as it is wanted.

PROCESS ELEMENTS SCALED AND POSITIONED FOR CAMERA COPY
BY THE USE OF REPRODUCTION-QUALITY COLOR PHOTOPRINTS

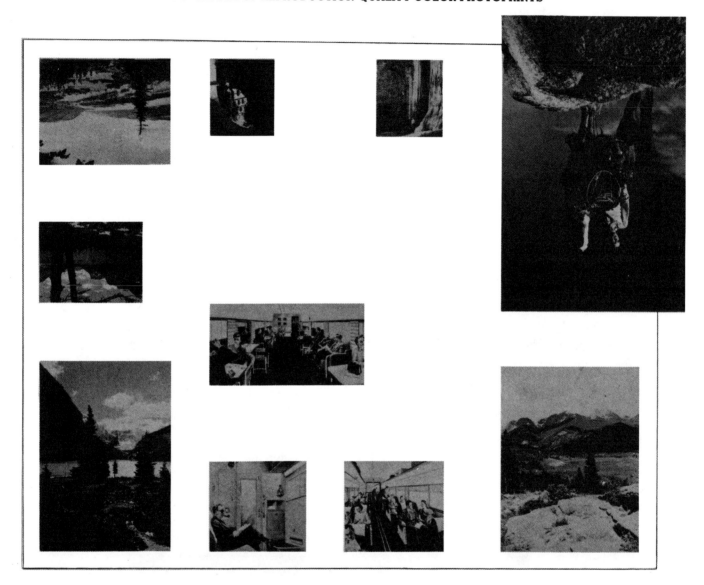

**Mixed Art Media Reduced to a Single Medium,
with Elements in Tonal Balance and Color-Adjusted**

Fig. 10-3 For process color, the expense of only one set of color separations is necessary when art elements are assembled on the mechanical by means of professional color prints, scaled and positioned. Artwork for the above included three 35-millimeter Kodachromes, one 8- by 10-inch (203- by 254-millimeter) and three 4- by 5-inch (102- by 127-millimeter) transparencies, and three 16- by 20-inch (406- by 508-millimeter) paintings. This mechanical provides color copy for client approval with an opportunity for color correction.

Fig. 10-4 The subject with its lilliputian scale obviously involved scaling and combining several color elements. Such preparatory work to get copy in one piece for the camera is usually handled by a photo color laboratory.

Fig. 10-5 The problem in handling the Betty Crocker spread was to get favorable perspective for each element and avoid shadows of one element falling on another. Separate color separations were made of most of the elements, and eight prints then were made and stripped in the form of a one-piece montage copy for the platemaker. [*Courtesy* Art Direction]

How Elements Are Assembled for Camera Copy in One Piece

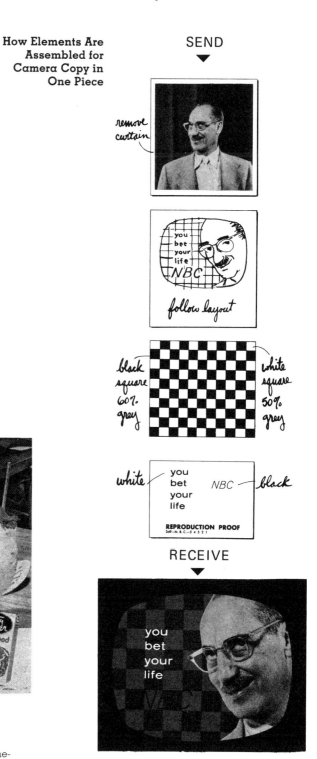

Fig. 10-6   [*Courtesy Edstan Studio, New York*]

Fig. 10-7 The twelve transparencies above were made for use with the two advertisements at the right. The ad at the upper right was made from the figures of the five women in bathing suits and the beach background. Each figure was duplicated in the exact size, color-corrected and density-balanced, and then stripped into the beach background to produce the complete page. The ad at the lower right was made from the figures of the six women in dresses and duplicated to the exact size. The figures were then color- and density-corrected, retouched and silhouetted, and stripped into the exact position. [*Courtesy Robert Crandall Associates, Inc., New York*]

WORKING WITH COLOR PHOTO STUDIOS

Informative literature obtainable from the larger color photo studios is recommended. A list of such studios follows.

Authenticolor
227 East 45th Street
New York, N.Y. 10017

Berkey K & L Custom Services, Inc.
222 East 44th Street
New York, N.Y. 10017

Color Central, Inc.
612 North Michigan Avenue
Chicago, Ill. 60611

The Color Wheel, Inc.
227 East 45th Street
New York, N.Y. 10017

Robert Crandall Associates, Inc.
(Sales representative of
Color Corp. of America)
306 East 45th Street
New York, N.Y. 10017

Diversified Photo Services
30 Werman Court
Plainview, N.Y. 11803

Evans-Avedisian Color Lab, Inc.
342 Madison Avenue
New York, N.Y. 10017

Kurshan An'Lang Color Service, Inc.
222 East 44th Street
New York, N.Y. 10017

Newell Color Laboratory, Inc.
816 Seward Street
Hollywood, Calif. 90038

Pic Color Corp.
25 West 45th Street
New York, N.Y. 10036

Rapid Color, Inc.
1236 South Central Avenue
Glendale, Calif. 91204

Stewart Color Labs, Inc.
563 Eleventh Avenue
New York, N.Y. 10036

Stowell Studios, Inc.
11 West Illinois Street
Chicago, Ill. 60610

Streisand, Zuch & Freedman, Inc.
40 East 49th Street
New York, N.Y. 10017

REFLECTION AND TRANSMISSION COPY NOT GROUPED TOGETHER FOR THE CAMERA

In art production you must not overlook the fact that reflection (opaque) camera copy goes on the camera copyboard and transparent copy goes into a transparency holder in the copyboard for backlighting. For offset and rotogravure, to which same-focus economies apply, do not supply a transparency and a watercolor for group separation, for they must be photographed separately. A color photo laboratory can convert the watercolor to a transparency, or both can be converted to color prints, scaled and positioned or proportioned for reduction. If there are a number of process subjects, you can plan for two groups, one of transparencies and the other of reflection copy, to obtain same-focus economies. See Figs. 10-8 and 10-9.

ELECTRONIC SCANNING MACHINES FOR PROCESS COLOR SEPARATIONS

The invention of electronic scanning machines, or scanners, to make process color separations for any of the printing processes is an example of new technology in the development of reproduction-quality color transparencies and photo color prints. The purpose of these machines is to automate the manual methods of photoengravers and other platemakers, particularly the scaling and positioning of process elements in an assembly for a copy unit as well as necessary color adjustments for the art director. Their use with transparencies avoids most of the extra cost of mixed-art media.

The mechanical principle of a scanner is similar to that of a machinist's lathe. The transparency is wrapped around a glass cylinder that revolves, but instead of a cutting tool a light beam inside the cylinder passes through the transparency, and the colors are separated for each of the four separations as the revolving transparency moves laterally, several hundred lines per inch. Pushing buttons determines the suitability of the continuous-tone separation negatives for the different processes.

The platemaker formerly made the final screened halftone negatives, but now a laser scanner is widely used for process color separations. Some scanners use the contact half-

**Color Transparencies
and Reflective
Artwork
Cannot Be
Color-Separated
Together**

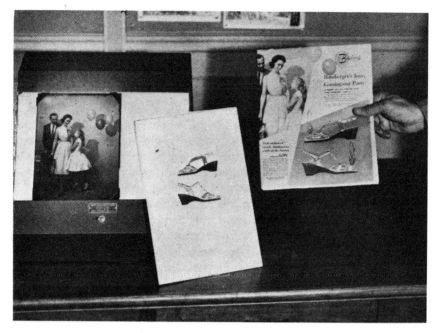

Fig. 10-8   A combination of opaque art (direct lighting of the copyboard) and a transparency (backlighting) requires two sets of color separations and extra color stripping to obtain the ad shown above. A proportioned transparency of the shoe artwork positioned with the transparency of the people would permit both elements to be handled by one set of color separations.

**Process Color
Elements Proportioned
for the Copy Unit
or Job**

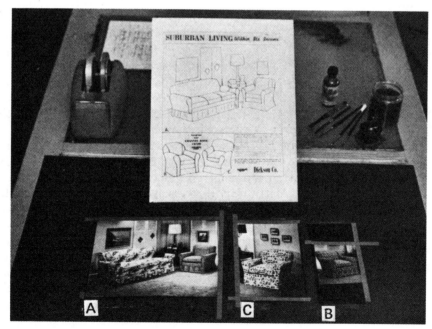

Fig. 10-9   If process color elements are not scaled or proportioned for gravure or offset (time method), extra color separations will be required. For this layout only the *A* and *B* elements were scaled; the *C* element had to be color-separated separately.

tone screen; others do not. The maximum size of screened laser separations is about 24 by 24 inches (610 by 610 millimeters). For larger-size work, large process color cameras are still used if blowups are not suitable. The screened image is projected for large poster plates.

Special Transparencies for Assemblies for Use by Scanning Machines

Many full-color advertisements contain several process color illustrations. Under standard production procedures the engraver would scale and position these elements on all four process engravings. At $20 an hour the job would be quite expensive. Today special camera copy is prepared for the use of scanners, which are almost standard for full-color magazine advertisements. The original artwork goes with the layout to a color photo studio, which reduces all elements to scaled transparencies. The result is good copy for scanning machines under any printing process. The platemakers handle all the color elements (an assembly) as one transparency, avoiding time-consuming scaling and positioning.

For electronic scanning machines color transparencies are usually required so that they can be wrapped around a glass cylinder. A copy unit which contains several process elements (an assembly) is prepared by a color laboratory: the emulsion of each subject transparency is floated to position on a piece of film. This copy is suitable for scanning, for contact separations, or for the color camera. Color transparencies are the best form of copy for good color reproduction in highlights.

Reproduction-quality color prints are widely used by advertising agencies for much of the collateral material of their clients. A color mechanical made with these prints permits a single set of color separations to handle all process elements without the usual stripping of each element to the four flats. Duplicate prints are available for other producers and processes for simultaneous production.

RANGE OF SIZES BY ENLARGEMENT OR REDUCTION

Figures 10-12 and 10-13 exhibit one of the extra capabilities of the offset process, resulting from the fact that the offset halftone,

whether process color or not, has the final tones in the screened negative. Therefore, enlargement or reduction is practical within reasonable limitations.

When color separations are made for a full-color magazine advertisement, the other sizes needed for related collateral material are also made. For such pieces as window displays and window strips, which are viewed at a distance, blowups are frequently made.

CONVERSION OF PROCESS PLATES OR SEPARATIONS FOR PRODUCTION BY ANOTHER PROCESS

Both the time and the cost factors of process work require avoiding the duplication of plate costs when more than one printing process is required. Magazine color plates have always been converted for the production of collateral printing by offset since both processes use the halftone method. The simplest form of conversion consists of clean black proofs of the color plates for camera copy. The resulting negatives can be enlarged or reduced for a change in size. Usually just the artwork is wanted for the different layouts. Special transparent proofs made on a Vandercook offset press give the equivalent of same-size screened positives. Now there are also specially developed conversion methods, such as Ludlow's Brightype and the Minnesota Mining and Manufacturing Company's Scotchprint and DuPont's Cronapress, both for same-size prints. The latter two methods are also used to get duplicate "original" process plates required by some magazines for further etching to suit their paper and inks.

It is not unusual for a full-color advertisement in a national advertising campaign to be reproduced by all three of the major printing processes in various publications and editions. Conversion methods have been developed for all processes to avoid duplicating process plate costs. For gravure halftones are converted by a "split-dot" method and a fine grid screen. Offset material is converted to photoengraving by a slight enlargement of the dot structure. See Figs. 10-15, 10-16, and 10-17.

Applications

Process separations by conversion cost about 25 cents on the dollar. Since commercial art is

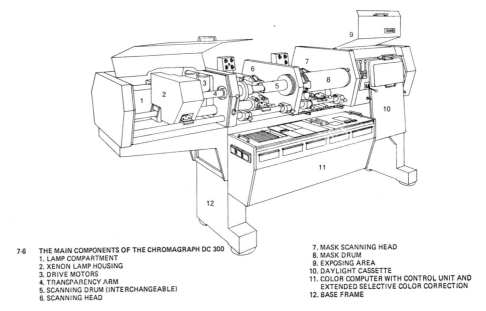

7-6   THE MAIN COMPONENTS OF THE CHROMAGRAPH DC 300
1. LAMP COMPARTMENT
2. XENON LAMP HOUSING
3. DRIVE MOTORS
4. TRANSPARENCY ARM
5. SCANNING DRUM (INTERCHANGEABLE)
6. SCANNING HEAD

7. MASK SCANNING HEAD
8. MASK DRUM
9. EXPOSING AREA
10. DAYLIGHT CASSETTE
11. COLOR COMPUTER WITH CONTROL UNIT AND
    EXTENDED SELECTIVE COLOR CORRECTION
12. BASE FRAME

Fig. 10-10   Schematic drawing of the Chromagraph DC 300 laser scanning system.

Fig. 10-11   The Chromagraph DC 300, a daylight-operated electronic scanner to produce color-corrected continuous-tone or direct screened separations from various color originals. The scale of reproduction in relation to the original is continuously adjustable between 33.33 and 1600 percent. Any portion of the original can be selectively enlarged. The scanner has a separate programming mask cylinder to combine pictures, lettering, backgrounds, and so on. The maximum original and recording size is 16 by 20 inches (406 by 508 millimeters).

MULTIPLE PLATE SIZES FROM ONE SET OF COLOR SEPARATIONS

Fig. 10-12 A calendar in several sizes, such as this one with twelve pages of color, is a standard item with many companies. Offset handles all sizes from the original color separations; the jumbo wall calendars are usually blowups. TWA specified that all process color was to be in a 150-line screen or finer.

Fig. 10-13 The General Electric pages are center spreads of a sixteen-page full-color magazine insert. The problem was plate costs for the two sizes needed: *Business Week* had a smaller page size than *Fortune*. Offset handled both sizes from the original separations.

OBTAINING MULTIPLE PROCESS PLATE SIZES
FROM ONE SET OF COLOR SEPARATIONS IS A MAJOR PLATE ECONOMY

Color separations, 12 by 16 inches (305 by 406 millimeters)

Yellow  Red  Blue  Black

Half-page
magazine ad

Dealer folder

Annual report, 8½
by 11 inches (216
by 279 millimeters)

Postcard

Fig. 10-14 This magazine ad shows how publication advertising is integrated with collateral printed material through the use of key artwork in all parts. In an advertising campaign, the same artwork in many different sizes is required for both the dealer and the prospective customer. With offset, one set of color-corrected separations (usually continuous-tone positives) permits the camera operator to make all plate sizes in the same halftone screen. All pieces shown and the four separations are in proportion. The large window strip is a blowup of the small one. [*Lamport, Fox, Prell & Dolk Inc.; Western Printing & Lithographing Co.*]

Window display, 21 by 31 inches (533 by 787 millimeters)

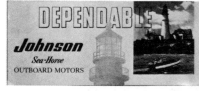

Small window strip

Large window strip, 41 by 17 inches (1041 by 432 millimeters)

Fig. 10-15 Conversion process: (1) original four-color process advertisement that appeared in magazines; (2) blowup of the ad to be used as a mailing piece, window display, or poster; (3) featured subject lifted from the original background and inserted in another for the front of a catalog and price list; (4) another use of this feature, as an envelope stuffer.

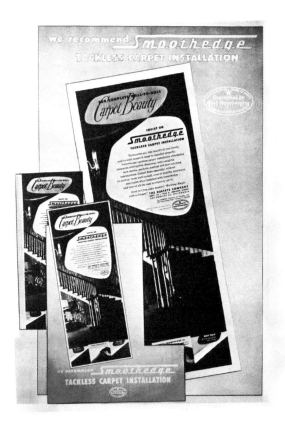

Figure 10-16 A magazine's editorial promotion booklet printed by offset in color from gravure color separations.

Conversions Cut Plate Costs to 25 Cents on the Dollar

Conversion of Gravure to Offset

Fig. 10-17 Window poster produced with conversions of process art from color plates and enlarged.

Fig. 10-18 Half-page color ad and two of several dealer displays. Consumer publications cooperate with advertisers on such merchandising aids.

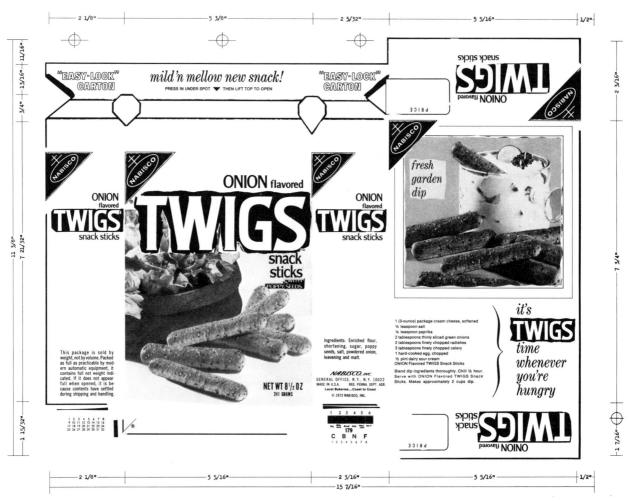

Fig. 10-19A   A repro mechanical for a folding carton. [*Courtesy Metro Litho Inc.*]

**Folding-Carton
Mechanicals
Require
Extreme Accuracy**

Fig. 10-19*B*

a practical business, with the limitations of budget and delivery dates, much collateral material is produced by conversion not only because it saves money but because it integrates all parts of an advertising campaign by repeating key illustrations in each of the various parts.

Thus the layout of a magazine page may be influenced by the use of the artwork for dealer aids. For example, for a Father's Day promotion the layout for a full-color magazine ad employed an open design. This provided a suitable window display background through the blowup of the conversions of the magazine color plates, saving $1000 in plate costs.

A standard application is the dealer window and counter display ("As advertised in" followed by a list of publications) which reproduces the whole full-color ad.

Spreading the Cost of Process Plates

We can't remind the reader too often that process color work is expensive. When it is used by many accounts, you should plan to spread the cost over several jobs. The use of conversions, including changes in size, serves this objective.

CAMERA COPY FOR FOLDING CARTONS IS A TECHNICAL FORM OF PASTE-UP

When you study the copy of Fig. 10-19, it is obvious that much of the work to complete the positives for the colors (Nabisco red and process colors) was handled by the platemaker. By stripping contact prints, the platemaker handles reverses, backgrounds, and so on, according to the tissue overlay or mockup of the carton. The one-piece–copy method is used for accuracy.

The lineup to the folds, determining the principal folds, proper bleeds, and glue pattern areas, makes the preparation of folding-carton art one of the most specialized fields. The necessity for perfect register to the cutting and scoring operations makes accuracy in dimensions on the black-and-white mechanical mandatory.

Packaging, particularly folding cartons, makes use of the lithographic process because of its ability to put fine process printing on boxboard. The paste-up copy by an art studio is frequently equivalent to a comprehensive

layout, and from this and the technical specifications of the customer the final copy for the camera is made. The cost is apt to be about $500.

Color register is specified in thousandths of an inch. Colors must be adjusted to the lighting of retail outlets. The kind of board has much to do with the halftone pattern used for tone copy, screens as fine as 200-line being used. Print orders may total 50 million pieces.

ADDING COLOR TO BLACK-AND-WHITE PHOTOGRAPHS

Duotone Process

To add a second color and get greater tonal range in detail, the offset producer makes two halftone negatives. For the black the producer shoots to get details in the shadow areas, and for the color, usually a light blue or tan, to hold details in the highlight areas. Thus a superior halftone in two colors is produced. A modified duotone has just a part of the subject, such as a fashion model's dress, in color.

This two-negative method is also used for halftones in black when full tonal range is required. The conventional halftone is a compromise since it is not possible to get full details at both ends of the gray scale.

Flexichrome Process

The special film for the original Flexichrome (Kodak) process is no longer available, but color photo studios can produce the same results by adding color to a black-and-white photo. The materials they use, however, are much more critical than the original film.

A standard device with two colors is the use of reddish yellow and greenish blue inks, which are particularly good for drinks in bottles. A color photo studio can produce the camera copy by the Flexichrome process: a 50 percent screen of each color gives a gray for the glass and surprinting for type results in black. Hairline register is required.

Velox Prints in Two Colors

For a low-cost budget job, two-color process art can be sent to a Velox printmaker, who can make the screen prints properly angled and scaled for the paste-up. Cost is figured by the square inch, but $40 or $50 will cover most of the smaller illustrations.

Watercolors Keyed to Process Inks

Greeting card publishers sometimes use these colors on thin, clear film, with each color on a separate overlay. When the overlays are placed together in a sandwich, the resulting secondary colors can be seen.

Most of the old methods for plate economies have been made obsolete by $75 process color separations.

PREPRESS PROOFING

For commercial-grade process printing by offset, various forms of photographic print proofs made from separation screened negatives or positives are used to convey an idea of the quality before the press plates are made. If further color correction is desirable, it can be done. This type of proofing is often used for the work of known producers, for it is fast and costs about 10 cents on the dollar compared with ink proofs from special offset proof plates.

For type matter on process color, this is the last thing handled by the platemaker, and it is not unusual to get a blueprint of the dominating color separation before deciding on the size and position of the headline. Type proof is then supplied with its position shown on the tissue overlay returned with the blueprint.

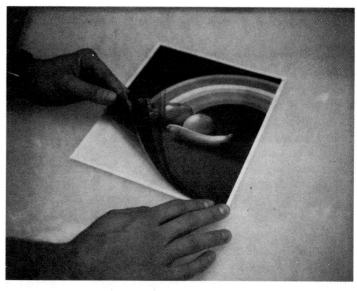

Fig. 10-20 Color proof made from Minnesota Mining and Manufacturing's Color Key sheets in the form of transparent sensitive material (one sheet for each color), placed on top of each other for final viewing of color break and register.

11

POSTER PRODUCTION

COMMERCIAL POSTERS ARE PRINTED IN standard sizes to fit posting boards or frames placed in transportation facilities or retail outlets. Car cards in various sizes are another form of display advertising. Used in conjunction with posters, they employ the same pictorial material, for which separations are already available.

The twenty-four-sheet posters seen on billboards along highways and in cities are so large that they are printed on ten sheets of paper, which are positioned by billboard posters. The lithographed press plates are produced by the photographic projection of fine halftone negatives; the halftone dot becomes the size of a BB shot. A three-sheet poster requires one and one-half sheets of paper; the one- and two-sheet sizes can fit on a single sheet in normal halftone screen.[1]

POSTER DESIGN

Since posters almost always are a form of collateral material in national advertising campaigns, they should be integrated and coordinated with campaign themes. The pictorial material is usually a key illustration from the magazine advertising, and the package or product is generally presented.

[1]Illustrations and data on twenty-four-sheet posters are presented courtesy of the Institute of Outdoor Advertising, New York; data on smaller posters, courtesy of Transportation Displays, Inc., New York.

According to the Institute of Outdoor Advertising, experience and research show that an outdoor advertising design should contain no more than three elements: identification, copy, and illustration. The effectiveness of the design will depend on the relationship of these elements to each other. The impact of the design can be increased by varying the size, color, type, background, and spacing of the basic elements.

For posters that are exposed to the weather for at least 30 days, colors should contrast boldly. Fugitive colors do not stand up in sunlight. Certain types of pinks, purples, blues, and greens tend to fade. Such shades should not be used for large areas of color unless the producer is allowed to approximate them with permanent inks. Shades that can be

Fig. 11-1 Twenty-four-sheet poster.

A one-unit design combines in a single unit the three basic elements: identification, copy, illustration. Usually this is possible only when all three are already combined, perhaps on the package or display. If you see that this situation exists, keep the design simple. Do not add another element.

Two units of design are most often practical when two of the basic elements are already united, possibly on the package itself. It is then a simple matter to relate the third element, probably copy, directly to the other two. When you exert creative discipline, you will not allow your design to become complicated.

Three units are the maximum number to be used if your design is to be effective. Each unit may well be one of the three basic elements. If they are properly related, the total impact will be much greater than the effect of the elements individually. However, if you complicate the background, it becomes a fourth unit; don't do it.

Fig. 11-2   Three units of design is the maximum.

guaranteed for 30 days require very expensive inks.

SKETCH RATIO

The sketch for a twenty-four-sheet poster must always be made in a ratio of 1 to 2¼. A popular size is 16 by 36 inches (406 by 914 millimeters), but if tone detail is desired, the finished art for camera should be even larger, measuring up to 20 by 45 inches (508 by 1143 millimeters). For the plain lettering and line copy designated as "flat treatment," the finished copy should measure at least 10 by 22½ inches (254 by 572 millimeters).

SHEET LAYOUT

An approved poster layout in rough form is usually the result of many preliminary sketches. Before any artwork is prepared, however, the sketch is submitted to several poster producers, who make color and composition sketches to show their sheet "layout," which may include slight adjustments to reduce the amount of printing and to avoid bad posting caused by a sheet edge running across a tone illustration. (A low quotation may be based on a risky layout of sheet position.) Alternatively, the approved poster sketch may be sent to a poster artist, who performs the same service and also produces the finished art and poster. The camera copy should be complete: lettering, illustration, background, and all other elements should be positioned. Color photography and some art are supplied separately, their position and size being shown by comprehensive color prints.

The average twenty-four-sheet poster requires forty-five press plates for the ten 44- by 60½-inch sheets (1118 by 1537 millimeters; work size, 42 by 58½ inches, or 1067 by 1486 millimeters) to provide a margin for lapping the sheets when they are posted. A three-sheet poster requires ten plates for the one and one-half sheets needed for process work. Every effort is made to reduce plate costs: a sheet may be laid out for cutting into two half sheets to provide parts of the design and thus save a set of plates.

One device of art production is to work on a plastic of some opacity. The camera operator places copy in the transparency holder of the copyboard, exposes it for reflective copy, and then backlights the copy, thus burning out

	24-sheet	30-sheet	Bleed
Copy area (length)	19′6″	21′7″	21′7″ Live area
Copy area (height)	8′8″	9′7″	9′7″ Live area
Top and bottom blanking	10½″ Top and bottom (21″ total)	5″ Top and bottom (10″ total)	5″ Top and bottom (10″ total)
End blanking	19″ (38″ total)	6½″ (13″ total)	6½″ (13″ total)
Frame width	11″	11″	11″

Total exposed area including bleed: 10′5″ by 22′8″

Courtesy Institute of Outdoor Advertising.

the highlights on the film. This method may save $500 in plate costs.

The minimum quantity required for twenty-four-sheet posters is 1000 (750, if separations or conversions are available).

MECHANICAL REQUIREMENTS

As shown in the accompanying table, there are three standard sizes of large posters that may be posted on regular billboards. Posters should be printed on 70-pound (31.8-kilogram) offset stock suitable for outdoor use. Allow a 1-inch (25.4-millimeter) free margin around all four sides of the poster to provide for overlap of the display frame. Uncoated paper is preferred; paper coated on one side is acceptable. Sizes are as follows:

	Overall size	Visible copy area
One-sheet posters	46″ high by 30″ wide	44″ high by 28″ wide
Two-sheet posters	46″ high by 60″ wide	44″ high by 58″ wide
Three-sheet posters	84″ high by 42″ wide	82″ high by 40″ wide

Car cards should be printed on 4-ply stock with a horizontal grain for side and overdoor spaces and 5-ply stock with a vertical grain for end spaces. Allow a ½-inch (12.7-millimeter) free margin around all four sides to provide for overlap of the display frame. Sizes are as follows:

	Overall size	Visible copy area
End spaces	33″ high by 21″ wide	32″ high by 20″ wide
End spaces	22″ high by 21″ wide	21″ high by 20″ wide
Overdoor spaces	16″ high by 38″ wide	15″ high by 37″ wide
Side spaces	11″ high by 21, 18, or 42″ wide	10″ high by 20, 27, or 41″ wide

Courtesy Transportation Displays, Inc., New York.

POSTERS AND SHEET LAYOUT

Fig. 11-3   Twenty-four-sheet poster. When printing presses were smaller, a poster panel required twenty-four sheets of paper. Today, with larger presses, fewer sheets are needed, but the original term is still used to describe the size. On the left is a typical paper pattern for a twenty-four-sheet poster. The area between the design and the frame is covered with white blanking paper.

Fig. 11-4   Thirty-sheet poster. The thirty-sheet poster provides approximately 25 percent more space for your design. The width of the blanking paper is considerably smaller. A typical paper pattern is shown, but considerable variation in the pattern is possible, often providing production economies when the design is reproduced.

Fig. 11-5   Bleed poster. The bleed poster carries the design out to the frame. This is achieved by printing the blanking paper, producing the bleed effect often used in magazine layouts. The frame crops the illustration rather than a band of white. A typical paper pattern for a bleed design is shown at the left. It offers 40 percent more design space than a twenty-four-sheet poster.

HAND POSTERS

Some poster producers have skilled lithographic artists who can take a rough color sketch and make all the necessary press plates by hand (the original lithographic method). This procedure is used for short runs, particularly for two- and three-sheet theatrical posters when only 400 or 500 posters are wanted. If the technique is suitable for the original design, the cost of both finished artwork and the photographic press plates is thereby avoided.

Hand methods are also employed for much large lettering, tints, and flat color backgrounds. A projector is frequently used to help the artist outline the work he or she is to put on the press plates.

SILK SCREEN AND COMMERCIAL COLLOTYPE

When fifty to a few hundred posters with a design in flat color and lettering are required, a silk screen is often used. If the screen stencil is made photographically, some tone work is possible.

Commercial collotype (gelatin printing) is used for short-run tone designs, particularly for two- and three-sheet theatrical posters. A screenless photographic printing process, it is usually handled on a direct litho press.

12

PLANNING FOR PRESS PRODUCTION

MANY BUYERS OF PRINTING HAVE at least five or six regular sources of supply for a range of press sizes as well as for the quality desired and for specialized production. The smaller producers may have only single-color equipment, and if they do have two-color equipment, it is not beyond a 28- by 42-inch (711- by 1067-millimeter) size. The larger color shops in major cities usually have no small or single-color offset presses. Long runs of single-color work will be handled on a two-color press.

The printing requirements of a large buyer are indicated by a report of Time, Inc.'s Central Printing Department for one year: more than thirty jobs a day, 15,000 purchases, and

Fig. 12-1 The printed web of this Hantscho Mark IV offset web press went to a sheeter. It could have gone to a folder for a thirty-two-page signature.

contracts with more than 150 printing firms. The department also has a small private plant for routine work.

User advertising departments keep records of press sizes and other facilities of selected producers, as well as of the quality of their work, the type of organization, their specialties, and so on. To meet cost and delivery demands, professional buyers determine *efficient press sizes* for the particular job, taking *quantity* into consideration, and the *bindery operations* required. Orders are placed, or bids obtained, only from producers having the needed press sizes.

BASIC OFFSET PRESS ADVANTAGES

In contrast to the preparatory costs for letterpress, an offset press plate is equivalent to a letterpress form *locked up and made ready*. Thus the basic offset plate cost includes the equivalent of letterpress preparatory costs except for press adjustments (feeder, side guides, ink distribution, and so on): the 8 percent of letterpress preparatory time referred to in Chapter 1.

Stripping the offset flat is form imposition, making the press plate is equivalent to form lockup, and the resilient rubber-covered offset cylinder provides for any difference in pressure, in the equivalent of form make-ready. Thus an offset press is ready to run as soon as press adjustments for the paper and job have been made; all else has been done previously. Even a large four-color offset press can be made ready in hours instead of days.

RATED PRESS SPEEDS ARE NOT PRODUCTION SPEEDS

You may recall that all offset presses are rotary, printing on every revolution. The stated "rated speed" of a sheet-fed press is its maximum capability, not the production speed used. A press rated for 10,000 impressions per hour (iph) will actually be run at about 6000 iph for single-color printing and at less than this rate for multicolor printing in order to hold the register of process color work. Because of plate changes, ink distribution for reverse areas, adjustments to retain hairline color register, washups, and other press problems, 30,000 acceptable sheets in a 7-hour shift is excellent for single-color printing, and a smaller figure for multicolor work.

OFFSET PRESS SIZES

There are about 150 press sizes and models larger than 17 by 22 inches (432 by 559 millimeters) and a dozen or so smaller ones. Instead of press sizes (maximum sheet sizes) being grouped for multiple impositions of the 17- by 22-inch unit, sizes now are governed largely by personnel schedules: the number of operators required for a given size and model of press. An example is the number of two-color presses which will come under the 42-inch (1067-millimeter) maximum sheet size requiring two persons. A sheet size just over 42 inches would require a third operator, adding about $20,000 a year to the printer's costs.

Most of the sheet-fed offset presses in use in the United States at present are imported, and odd fractional sizes result from the conversion of millimeters to inches. Most of these presses will handle a 9- by 12-inch (229- by 305-millimeter) page as well as the 8½- by 11-inch (216- by 279-millimeter) size.

Conclusions from two research studies on technological developments in the printing industry led Gilbert W. Bassett, executive director of the Graphic Arts Technical Foundation, to state in a published report: "The trends are to faster and smaller presses with more 38-inch (97-cm) sheet-fed lithographic presses becoming more popular for commercial printing. Presses as large as 60 inches (152 cm) will still be sold to package printers, but larger presses will slowly disappear."

USE OF NEW, FASTER PRESSES

Offset press production has been greatly changed by two developments: the use of new, fast small- and medium-size single-color and multicolor (even five- and six-color) presses; and the use of very fast web (roll)-fed perfecting presses, which have largely replaced sheet-fed two- and four-color presses larger than 60 inches (1524 millimeters). These web perfecting presses print on both sides of the paper web as it goes through the press in a desired arrangement, some webs handling up to five colors on each side. They also handle folding and some of the binding.

Quite a few of the new, fast two-color sheet-fed presses can be converted to "perfecting presses," printing one color on each side of the sheet instead of two colors on one side. Chart II (Fig. 12-5) shows that for more than about 20,000 units measuring 17 by 22 inches (432 by 559 millimeters) a two-unit converted perfecting offset press would be much more efficient than a straight work-and-turn offset press, particularly with a larger converted press printing the unit two on. In this case a two-unit straight press, work-and-turn, would be only a little more efficient than the one-unit press, printing on each side separately, because it would require two operators to run.

The major advantage, of course, of these small, fast offset presses is the extra production obtained with the same number of persons as compared with the slower offset presses.

COMMON UNIT USED IN COMPARING PRESS SIZE EFFICIENCY

In comparing press sizes and models to determine the most efficient press for a particular job, a common unit is used. We use a 17- by 22-inch (432- by 559-millimeter) unit, a multiple of the standard 8½- by 11-inch (216- by 279-millimeter) page generally used in offset. In general, offset presses will handle this unit one on, two on, and four on. Some smaller press sizes such as 24 by 30 inches (610 by 762 millimeters) and 23 by 31 inches (584 by 787 millimeters) will handle units one and one-half on for six-page folders and dust jackets for books (see Fig. 12-3). There are still a few large single-color presses which will handle an eight-unit sheet, but for multicolor printing such jobs are now done on offset web perfecting presses.

NECESSARY SHEET SIZE

As stated in Chapter 6, mechanicals should provide an extra ¼-inch (6.35-millimeter) space for fold trimming. Moreover, when designing for a specified sheet size, gripper and trim margins should be provided.

In Chapter 3 we discussed and listed the standard paper sizes for the different kinds of printing paper. In designing material to be printed, the user should consider these standard sizes to avoid unnecessary waste, but the mill brand and sheet size should be left to the printer. The printer is the one who figures the necessary fold and bleed trims and the space to be allowed between multiples of printed pieces on the sheet for binding trims. If the job is to be run work-and-turn, gripper margins may be needed on both long sides of the sheet. After the sheet has been printed and is ready to go to a bindery, the printer trims it down to allow an ⅛-inch (3.175-millimeter) bindery trim on all four sides because bindery equipment is set for this trim. Any difference adds to bindery costs.

Additional standard paper sizes for book papers were introduced in 1976, and size differences between offset and letterpress book papers were eliminated. Because of competition, paper merchants now generally stock any additional paper sizes needed by local printers.

Since paper is a major part of the cost of printed material, the choice is usually discussed with the printer's sales representative. Frequently the kind of paper is changed to get a standard size.

For smaller and medium-size presses, the designer is usually safe if an extra inch (25.4 millimeters) is allowed in both dimensions for gripper and trim margins.

MAXIMUM WORK AREA OF SHEET, MARGINS, AND TRIMS

As in letterpress production, jobs designed to be cut efficiently from a standard paper size must allow for the usual printing margins and for trims in the bindery. An extra inch (25.4 millimeters) for both dimensions is usually sufficient; however, inside bleed and fold trims may require slight adjustments in unit or page size to make it possible to use a standard paper size.

With offset, however, the extra variety of papers suitable for tone reproduction offers the additional standard sizes of uncoated offset and of the other types (text, cover, bristols, and so on) now surface-sized for offset.

OFFSET PRESS SIZES AND SCHEDULES

In the table "Sheet-Fed Offset Personnel Schedules," the user's press-time dollar rate shown is the mean rate of the group. Rates are

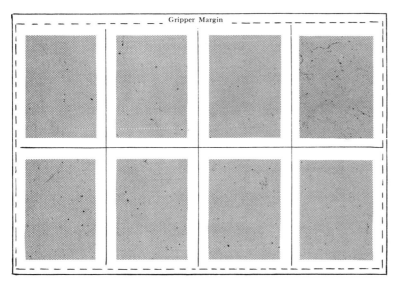

Fig. 12-2 The dotted lines indicate the maximum work area on the press sheet. A ¼-inch (12.7-millimeter) gripper margin on one long side and an ⅛-inch (3.175-millimeter) trim on other sides are required.

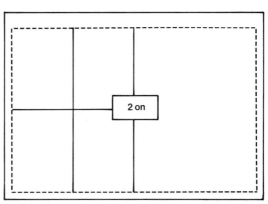

Fig. 12-3 A 17- by 22-inch (432- by 559-millimeter) copy unit with trim margins and common multiples on press sheets.

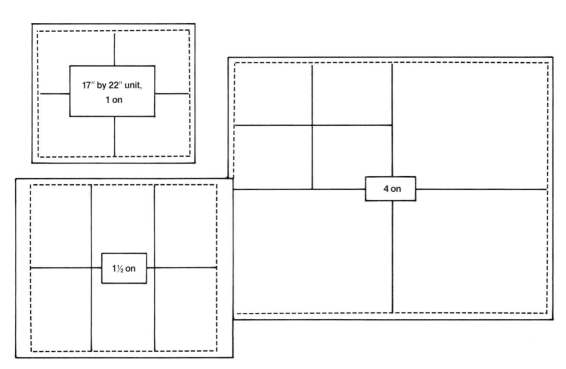

Sheet-Fed Offset Personnel Schedules (Sizes in inches)

	One person	Two persons	Three persons	Four persons	Five persons
One color	18⅛ by 22½ 18 by 25¼ 19 by 25 19 by 25¼ 19 by 25½ 18⅛ by 25¼ 19³/₃₂ by 26 18⅛ by 25¼ 19 by 26 20½ by 26 20½ by 28⅜ 20½ by 29⅛ 24 by 30 23 by 31 23⅛ by 32 24 by 32¼ 25 by 29	25½ by 36 24 by 36¼ 25 by 36 25¼ by 36¼ 25¾ by 38 26¾ by 39⅛ 28⅜ by 40³/₁₆ 28⅜ by 41 28 by 40⁵/₃₂ 28 by 40 28⅜ by 40⅛ 31½ by 44⅛ 41 by 56¾ 7000 iph 44 by 60 43 by 60	44 by 68¹³/₁₆ 7000 iph 54 by 77		
Two colors	11 by 17 15 by 18	18 by 25¼ 19 by 25½ 19³/₃₂ by 26P 19 by 26 20½ by 28⅜P 20½ by 29⅛ 23 by 31 24 by 30 24 by 30P 24 by 32¼ 25¼ by 36 25¾ by 38½ 26¾ by 39⅛ 26½ by 39½ 27½ by 39½ 28 by 40 28 by 40P 28 by 40⅛ 28 by 41 28⅜ by 41	38 by 50 38½ by 50½ 35¹/₃₂ by 51³/₁₆ 39 by 51 38⅜ by 52 41 by 54 41 by 55 41 by 55P 41 by 56 41 by 56¾ 42⁵/₁₆ by 63 44 by 64 44 by 65		
Four colors			12⅝ by 18 18 by 25¼ 19 by 26 20 by 28 20½ by 28⅛ 23 by 31 24 by 30P 25 by 36 25³/₁₆ by 38½ 28¾ by 39⅛ 28⅜ by 40 28 by 40 26½ by 39½ 27½ by 39½ 28 by 40 28 by 40P 28 by 41P 28⅜ by 41 28 by 40⁵/₃₂	28⅜ by 41 28⅜ by 42⅛ 32½ by 50½ 35¹/₃₂ by 51 41 by 54P 41 by 55P 41 by 56¾ 45¼ by 51⅝ 45⅛ by 56⅛	

Sheet-Fed Offset Personnel Schedules *(Continued)*

	One person	Two persons	Three persons	Four persons	Five persons
Five colors			24 by 30P 25¾ by 38½P 28 by 40P 28⅜ by 41 28⅜ by 41P	31½ by 44⅛	38⅜ by 52 41 by 55 41 by 55P 41¾ by 56 41 by 56¾ 44 by 60 43 by 60 7000 iph 43 by 60 44 by 60
Six colors				25¾ by 38½P 26½ by 39½ 28 by 40 28 by 40P 28¾ by 40 29⅜ by 41P	31½ by 44⅛ 38½ by 50½ 38⅜ by 52 41 by 55 41 by 55P 41 by 56¾

NOTE: All sizes shown are maximum sheet size; P = "perfecting." Five and six color presses usually are found only in metropolitan areas, and press costs to the user are apt to depend more on market conditions than on actual press-time costs.

those applying in a medium-size city, except for the five- and six-color presses, at 75 percent productivity. Single-color presses are figured on a one-shift basis, which is higher than a two-shift basis; multicolor presses are figured on a two-shift basis. Because of the high capital investment most multicolor equipment is operated in two shifts.

Two-color presses marked with a P for "perfecting" can be converted to print on both sides of the sheet as it goes through the press. Four-color perfecting (convertible) presses usually can print two colors on each side or three and one. Five- and six-color presses which can be converted to perfecting presses usually print one color on the backup; the six-color press can print two reds or two blues in addition to yellow and black on one side of sheet.

Personnel schedules apply in union shops. There are a few differences in metropolitan areas; in New York, for example, the one-person single-color schedule extends to the 30-inch (762-millimeter) sheet size inclusive, but elsewhere it generally extends to the 35-inch (889-millimeter) size inclusive.

DETERMINING EFFICIENT PRESS SIZE

Formerly all sheet-fed offset presses had a rated speed of about 6000 iph, with production averaging about 3000 iph for a 7-hour shift. As the size of print orders increased, larger presses became more efficient. The printing user's problem was to determine which press size would be most efficient for multiple impositions of the printing form. The bid list would include only producers who had the wanted press size.

User's Mean Hourly Press Time Costs for Sheet-Fed Offset Presses*

	One person	Two persons	Three persons	Four persons	Five persons
One color	$37	$75			
Two colors	25	62	$114		
Four colors			103	$163	
Five colors†			135		$248
Six colors†				198	233

*One color: single-shift rate; multicolor: two-shift rate.
†Rates for metropolitan areas.

To a limited extent this still holds true, but because of the use of smaller, faster sheet-fed presses press personnel schedules (the number of persons required to run the press) have become important, and the lower plate and makeready costs have also become important for smaller print orders.

The charts which follow show the relative efficiency of different press sizes, as affected by press speeds and hourly press running-time costs, in a medium-size city. Single-color press time is figured on a one-shift basis, and multicolor press time on a two-shift basis. The purpose of these charts is to show users how they can compile similar charts by obtaining base plate *selling* rates and hourly *selling* press time rates from the producers they use. These costs, of course, are only part of what a printer must charge a customer; we are merely trying to determine the efficient press size and model for a specified quantity: up to 100,000 units with Charts I, II, and III (Figs. 12-4, 12-5, and 12-6) and up to 250,000 with Chart IV (Fig. 12-7).

Chart I, which shows press time costs for four sizes of single-color presses printing on one side of the sheet, indicates the efficiency relationship of press personnel and multiple imposition for a 17- by 22-inch unit. The graph lines on each chart extend from the start of the pressrun to the chart's maximum. For intermediate quantities the height of the line indicates the press time cost; the point where graph lines cross is the "breaking point" between the efficiency of the two press sizes.

When preparing charts for a particular area, you should understand that any change in the preparatory cost (heavy line at the left edge of the chart) would move the whole line, not just the left end, up or down. In contrast, any change in the press time cost for a given quantity would move just the right end of the graph line up or down.

Chart II shows the comparative efficiency of a single-color press used to print on both sides of a sheet and that of a two-color press converted to a perfecting press that prints one color on both sides of the sheet, once through the press, and the efficiency of a larger (two-on) two-color press converted to a perfecting press.

Chart III reveals the comparative efficiency of different sizes of the new, fast two-color

presses with a 17- by 22-inch unit. Note that a two-on size is more efficient than a four-on size because the latter requires an extra operator.

Chart IV reveals the efficiency of the new, fast four-color offset presses for printing four colors on one side of sheet with a 17- by 22-inch unit. The four-on size, though requiring an extra person, becomes most efficient at 100,000 units. Color separation expense is not included in the preparatory costs because that cost is common to all the press sizes used.

Press time cost should not be confused with the total cost of the printing even though it includes plate and makeready preparatory costs. Paper alone averages 23 percent of the total cost, and ink, bindery or finishing expense, and profits have not been included.

COST FACTORS USED TO DETERMINE PRESS SIZE EFFICIENCY

The charts showing the relative press time cost for a 17- by 22-inch (432- by 559-millimeter) unit, one, two, and four on (with the number of operators), for single, two-color, and four-color offset presses give a general idea of press time costs in a medium-size city at 75 percent productivity, which is the average figure. Single-color costs are figured on a one-shift basis; multicolor, on a two-shift basis, because of the high capital investment.

In Chapter 1 we discussed the fact that each offset printer has a *base plate charge* for each press size. This charge includes the stripping of 8½- by 11-inch (216- by 279-millimeter) negatives to the flat, exposure on the press plate, and its development. The base charge must be adjusted if larger or smaller negatives are used. An exception to the base plate charge occurs when a step-and-repeat machine is used instead of a flat. In this case there are a setup charge and a charge for the time required for the number of images wanted on the plate. Also mentioned in Chapter 1 was the fact that the equivalent of letterpress lockup expense is included in the offset base plate charge and that press makeready in offset consists of press adjustments for the job and the paper.

Users who buy printing regularly generally do business with several printers as regular customers. As well as maintaining a list of the printers' press sizes, users should request the base plate charge sales rate and the average

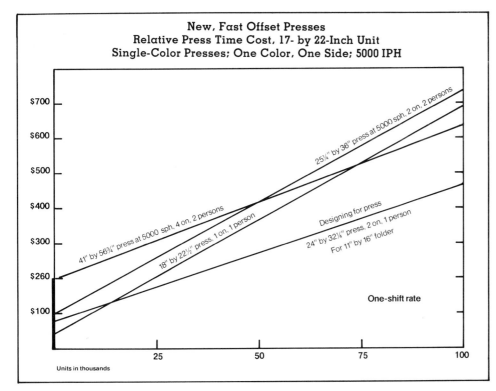

New, Fast Offset Presses
Relative Press Time Cost, 17- by 22-Inch Unit
Single-Color Presses; One Color, One Side; 5000 IPH

Chart I (Fig. 12-4) Heavy line, left edge, is preparatory cost. The graph shows that there is no advantage in using a two-on press as compared with a one-on size. The reason is that the former is a two-person press, while the one-unit size is a one-person press. The four-on press is still a two-person size, breaking with the two-on press just under 50,000 units and with the one-on press at about 70,000 units.

Designing for a press size can frequently save money by adjusting the size of the piece, as shown here with a 24- by 32¼-inch (610- by 819-millimeter) size. In this case, you get an 8- by 11-inch (203- by 279-millimeter) four-page folder instead of an 8½- by 11-inch (216- by 279-millimeter) one.

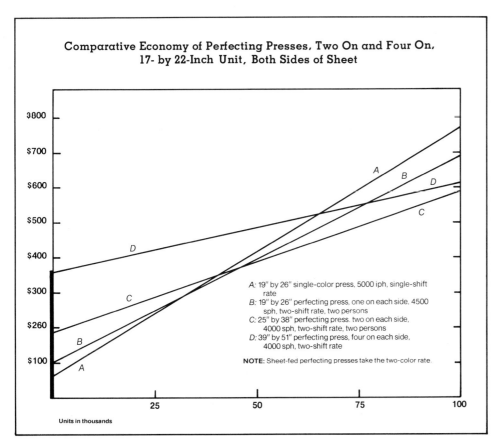

Comparative Economy of Perfecting Presses, Two On and Four On,
17- by 22-Inch Unit, Both Sides of Sheet

A: 19" by 26" single-color press, 5000 iph, single-shift rate
B: 19" by 26" perfecting press, one on each side, 4500 sph, two-shift rate, two persons
C: 25" by 38" perfecting press. two on each side, 4000 sph, two-shift rate, two persons
D: 39" by 51" perfecting press, four on each side, 4000 sph, two-shift rate

NOTE: Sheet-fed perfecting presses take the two-color rate.

Chart II (Fig. 12-5) Many of the new, small, fast two-color offset presses can be converted to perfecting presses, printing on both sides of the sheet as it goes through the press, or three colors on one side, one color on the other side, with two passes. Do they offer economy compared with two runs with a single-color press? The graph gives the answer. The single-color press has a slight advantage up to about 30,000 units, and the perfecting press a slight advantage when run on a two-shift cost basis; on a single-shift basis they are about the same. But the answer is different with a two-on perfecting size because only two operators are still required.

The efficiency of a 25¼- by 36-inch (641- by 914-millimeter) single-color press, work-and-turn, two on, would be almost identical to *B* (two-color perfecting press, one on) because it is a two-person size.

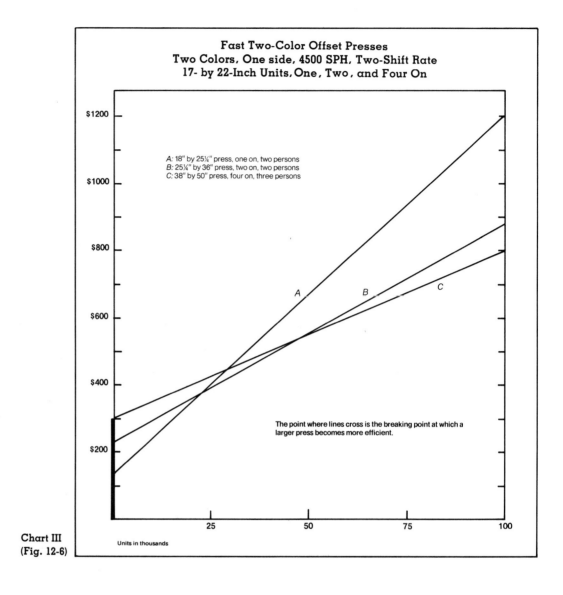

Fast Two-Color Offset Presses
Two Colors, One side, 4500 SPH, Two-Shift Rate
17- by 22-Inch Units, One, Two, and Four On

A: 18" by 25¼" press, one on, two persons
B: 25¼" by 36" press, two on, two persons
C: 38" by 50" press, four on, three persons

The point where lines cross is the breaking point at which a larger press becomes more efficient.

Units in thousands

Chart III
(Fig. 12-6)

makeready charge for each press size, as well as the hourly rate to the customer for each press size in the shop. These figures are needed to determine the efficient press size for a particular printing job.

THE THREE COST FACTORS

The efficiency of one press size as compared with another for the printing of a job is determined by these factors:

1. *Plate cost.* This is the base plate cost of the press size. The cost of halftones and color separations is not included because these are common to all plate sizes.

2. *Makeready.* The time required for press adjustments. This varies with different shops for different reasons, but for the newer fast presses it averages as shown in the accompanying table.

Time in Hours, 17- by 22-Inch Size*

Type of press	1 unit	2 units	4 units	8 units
One-color press	0.5	0.7	0.1	1.2
Two-color press	0.8	1.6	1.7	web press
Four-color press	1.3	1.7	2.3	web press

*Time in offset is figured in hours and tenths; the rate per hour for makeready is that of the press size and make used.

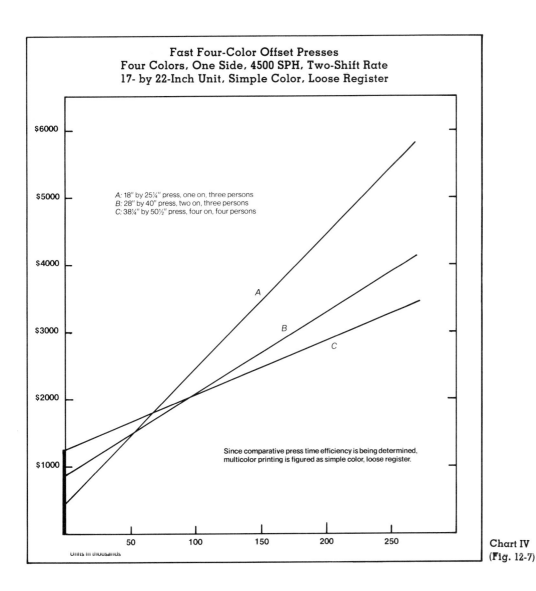

Fast Four-Color Offset Presses
Four Colors, One Side, 4500 SPH, Two-Shift Rate
17- by 22-Inch Unit, Simple Color, Loose Register

A: 18″ by 25¼″ press, one on, three persons
B: 28″ by 40″ press, two on, three persons
C: 38¼″ by 50½″ press, four on, four persons

Since comparative press time efficiency is being determined, multicolor printing is figured as simple color, loose register.

Units in thousands

Chart IV
(Fig. 12-7)

3. *Press time cost.* The number of hours required to run the necessary number of sheets at the hourly rate for the press figured. Production (iph) is estimated on the requirements of the job. Heavy solids or extra-light or extra-heavy stock will require slower speeds; average production for short runs tends to be less than for longer runs even with the same press speeds.

The cost of these three operations varies from city to city because of local labor rates and from plant to plant because of efficiency and craft skills.

DETERMINING THE BREAKING POINT OF TWO PRESSES

The quantity of units or pieces at which a larger press size becomes more efficient than a smaller size (or a perfecting type of press than a straight offset press) is termed the "breaking point." In Charts I, II, III, and IV this point is where two lines cross.

From your own experience or from these charts the relative efficiency of two selected presses can be determined by the following formula. To determine the breaking point of two press sizes, divide the difference in preparatory costs (plate and makeready) by the difference in the press time cost of 100 units or pieces. This gives the breaking point in thousands of units. For example, Chart IV (four-color presses) compares a 38¼- by 50½-inch press, four on, with a 28- by 40-inch press, two on (17- by 22-inch unit), for the breaking point in quantity:

Preparatory cost, four on	$730
Preparatory cost, two on	389
	$341
Cost of 1000 press time units, four on	$12.21 at 4000 sph
Cost of 1000 press time units, two on	9.00 at 4500 sph
	$ 3.21

$341 ÷ $3.21 = 106, or 106,000 units, the breaking point

Verification of Formula Result

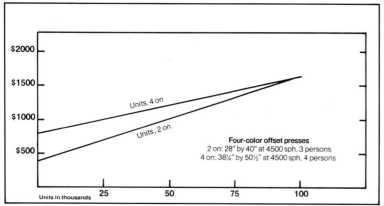

Fig. 12-8

Possible bindery economies should also be considered. In general, the larger the sheet and the longer the folded section, the greater the economy. With large quantities, the bindery economy may be worthwhile with the use of a larger sheet even though it is less efficient than a smaller sheet for quantity.

In compiling the charts, averages had to be used for the hours required for printing the number of sheets with a 17- by 22-inch unit, one on, two on, and four on, to show comparative efficiency. Single-color printing was figured at an average of 5000 sheets per hour (sph) in a 7-hour single shift. Multicolor press time was figured at 4500 sph (two-shift rate) for the smaller fast presses and at 4000 sph with the larger fast presses. Eight-unit multicolor printing is now done on web offset presses.

PREPARING CHARTS TO SHOW BREAKING POINTS

Since it is good production practice for the user to place printing orders with producers who have suitable press sizes, planning should use some method of determining the efficient press size. The method of using three cost factors to compare two press sizes can be employed for graphic presentation of press efficiency for any selected unit on a number of different press sizes in the user's area. The resulting graph will indicate which two presses should be figured in detail.

In the charts shown above, you will see that if a line is drawn from the sum of the base plate and makeready costs to a unit quantity for press time cost (100,000 used for Charts I, II, and III and 250,000 for Chart IV) for each press size selected, the graph lines cross at the breakeven point. These points are known as breaking points, at which a press becomes more efficient than a smaller size. A 17- by 22-inch unit has been used throughout because this is a multiple of the 8½- by 11-inch page and includes four-page folders, eight- and sixteen-page booklets, and so on.

Since a user's chart will be based on the producer's hourly selling rates, only shops of comparable quality should be employed for compiling the average figures with which to work. For some users charts for individual shops will be desirable. A user may find that a press speed average higher than that used here applies in the user's area.

There are books and services which give production standards, but usually a customer can obtain from regular printing sources the rates for basic plate, makeready, and hourly charges for their press sizes.

WORK-AND-TURN PRESS IMPOSITION

Not all printing is done "sheetwise," that is, by printing on one side and then turning the pile over and printing on the reverse side with a different form or plate and an additional makeready. If there are no suitable new sheet-fed perfecting offset presses in your area, you should consider planning to use a double-size press for work-and-turn imposition. Or since the efficiency of straight offset is close to that of a perfecting press for one on, both sides of sheet, the work-and-turn printing method should be figured for comparison. With offset, this method saves a plate and a makeready.

When the same color or colors are to go on both sides of the sheet, offset press imposition is usually work-and-turn. Using a press large enough to take the forms for both the front and the back of the sheet, the operator runs the sheets of paper through the press and then turns them over and runs them through the press again, producing two pieces of the printing to the sheet, which later is cut apart for the folding operation.

The important point is that the presswork is done with one plate and one makeready at quite a saving in cost. This method is practical with offset, particularly with color work, because the equivalent of letterpress lockup and makeready is absent.

The form layout for a work-and-turn four-page folder is the same as if you printed one side of the sheet for a french-fold piece head to head.

REDUCING THE CHOICE TO TWO PRESS SIZES

It is only in metropolitan marketing areas that you will have a wide choice of offset press sizes and models. The usual practice is to get the information you need from the printers in your area: press sizes and number of colors, sales rates for different sizes and types of press plates, makeready time for each press size, and the user's hourly press time cost for each press. In a city you get this information from just the shops with which you are going to do business. The four charts previously shown can be helpful:

Chart I. In printing single-color, on one side of the sheet, with a 17- by 22-inch unit, a one-on press is most efficient up to about 70,000 sheets, at which point a four-on press takes over.

Chart II. For the same-size copy unit, single-color on both sides of the sheet, a one-on single-color press would be best to 30,000 units, then a same-size two-color perfecting press to about 45,000 units (25,000 sheets on both sides), next a two-on two-color perfecting press until a little over 100,000 units, at which point a four-on two-color sheet-fed perfecting press would take over.

Chart III. For the copy unit in two colors, on one side of the sheet, a one-on press is best to almost 25,000 sheets and then a two-on press to 48,000 sheets, at which point a four-on two-color press would take over.

Chart IV. For the unit in four colors, on one side of sheet, a one-on press is most efficient to 51,000 sheets and a two-on press size to 100,000 copies, at which point a four-on press would take over.

In all printing, a two-shift hourly rate is lower than a one-shift hourly rate. Most multicolor printing is done on a two-shift rate. The exception would occur with a small shop using a one-on single-color press for multicolor work; such a shop would rarely operate on a two-shift basis.

QUOTATIONS ON LARGER QUANTITIES

Much printed material is used regularly by a particular company. Such printing, particularly multicolor work because of its high preparatory cost, calls for quotations on two- or three-quantity figures because the resulting savings will be far greater than storage costs. If this is not done, the customer should at least include in the order a specification that the printer save the flat for later reuse.

BLEED DESIGN

Bleed design is widely used in advertising material and usually requires extra paper for margin trims. With letterpress production, plates are fastened to a patent base or cylinders with hooks which require extra space, making a special paper size necessary with some standard page sizes as in this example:

Booklet with Bleed Design

Trimmed size	6	by 9	inches
Oversize plates	⅛ inch	¼ inch	
Hook room	¼ inch	½ inch	
Untrimmed size	6⅜	by 9¾	inches
Thirty-two pages	×8	×4	
Sheet size	51	by 39	inches

This would be a nonstandard paper size, and if less than 5000 pounds (2268 kilograms) of paper is required (about 17,000 sheets of 60-pound, or 27.2-kilogram, paper), it would

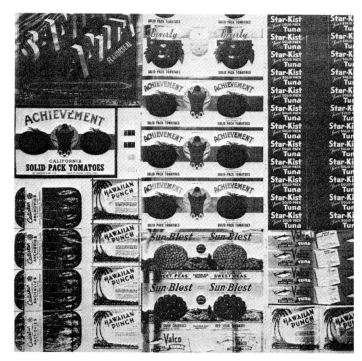

Fig. 12-9 This press sheet of labels illustrates how images can even be butted when a one-piece press plate is used. No alleys are necessary for hook room as with a patent base. Only the corner of the sheet is shown.

be an important point in paper cost: the 2000-pound (907-kilogram) price, plus a 10 percent penalty.

Since offset with its one-piece plate need not allow for hook room and the bleed borders of page units can even touch, this job can be run on a 38- by 50-inch (965- by 1270-millimeter) standard sheet, saving stock and penalties. Offset would also print with one form with less than 1 ton of stock.

PRODUCTION PLANNING OF RELATED JOBS

Consumer advertising campaigns in national magazines require a wide variety of collateral printed material for distributors and dealers as well as for the interested consumer. Since the campaign in all media is usually integrated by means of one or two dominant illustrations which carry the theme, this artwork in many different plate sizes will be required for the various collateral jobs before the publication ads appear.

Also, before this printing is produced, the campaign itself, the deals, and the promotions backing up the advertising must be merchandised—sold to the whole distributing organization so that the publication advertising will pay off. This procedure frequently involves process color in quantities as small as 500 sales portfolio pages, blowups, and so on. Folders for dealers must show the publication ads scheduled, the magazines used, the display material, and the special deals offered. Enlargement and reduction are involved in addition to short-run color methods.

Using the Same Producer for Related Jobs

The producer who makes the color separations should be awarded all such jobs, with advance notice of reproduction sizes required of subjects for different pieces and of publication color plates available for conversions if these are to be used. Thus color separation screened positives will be ready when layouts appear with the order. The 500 preprints will be made from proof plates. Frequently the producer takes care of such specialty work as twenty-four-sheet posters, for example. The producer will job out the order and supply the color separations to the poster specialist and can also arrange for 500 sales portfolio pages with a short-run color specialist or for the 500 blowups. By trade custom, negatives and plates are the property of the producer if the producer makes them and are not billed separately to the user.

When quantities are large and the initial producer does not handle the specialized production, users sometimes make an arrangement that duplicates of the color separations will be supplied to another producer. In one case, an automobile account placed a catalog with one producer, and duplicate separations were supplied to a display specialist for the dealer material. Such arrangements should be in writing if they are not included in the specifications of the initial order.

SHEET SIZE AND MILL BRAND SELECTED BY PRODUCER

In Chapter 3, "Offset Paper," we gave the technical reasons that lead to the producer's handling of paper selection and size decisions. Here, it is well to mention that frequently paper sizes in addition to standard sizes are available if there is sufficient demand. For example, though 35 by 45 inches (889 by 1143 millimeters) is a standard size, some mills also supply 35 by 46 inches (1168 millimeters) as a standard uncoated offset to allow an extra inch for bleed trim between impositions. Some merchants stock 36 by 46 inches (914 by 1168 millimeters) to allow an extra inch for work-and-tumble runs (a gripper margin is required on both of the long sides of the sheet).

Mill brands are important to producers for uniformity of the paper, since they must rely on the paper to meet their estimates of press production. There is also the matter of color tones of white paper (some are bluish, some pinkish, and so on); the mill brand determines process ink hues to some extent. Paper, inks, and dot structure are a team: each depends on the others.

ALLOWANCE FOR PAPER SPOILAGE

The quantity ordered must provide for paper spoilage. Including color proving, press, and bindery spoilage, total spoilage may amount to 6 or 7 percent with a medium run of process color but much less for longer runs.

It is hardly possible to estimate to 100 percent accuracy, and sometimes more or less than the quantity ordered is delivered. By trade custom, 10 percent over or under an order constitutes delivery; the invoice price makes an allowance either way. Usually delivery is a little over the quantity ordered.

SPECIFYING INK COLORS

For flat colors, the best method is to attach a small ink swatch from an ink maker's catalog. Swatches are printed on both coated and uncoated stock and are identified by make and number for shade. If a satisfactory color shade cannot be found from several ink catalogs and an artist's watercolor swatch is supplied, the colors used should be identified or shown. A pastel swatch sprayed with fixative is unreliable because it is apt to have more than one tone—which one is wanted? Color swatches should be made on the paper to be used or on a similar surface. A sample of ink on coated paper should not be offered for a job to be printed on uncoated paper. The same ink will look different because of light reflection.

Fig. 12-10 The Pantone ® Color Specifier for specifying ink colors is now widely used. The user, producer, and ink companies all have matching swatch books with color and shade identified by number on both coated and uncoated paper. The art director's copy ($24) contains small numbered ink swatches for pasting to camera copy. The producer orders the necessary ink from any ink company, for all have the formula filed by number. In quoting a price, the printer may specify, for example, black and one Pantone ® color.

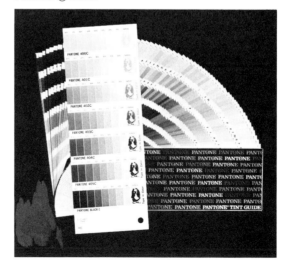

Fig. 12-11 Pantone ® Tint Guide, companion to the Color Specifier, a book of all Pantone colors extended in eight specific screened tints from 8 to 10 percent increments. Artists' materials in the same colors are available at art supply stores.

**Hantscho Mark IV
Perfecting Web
Offset Press**

Fig. 12-12 Shown are the four double printing units, the dryer, and the console from which the press is operated. This press can handle paper roll widths to 38 inches (965 millimeters) and has a rated speed of 35,000 iph. Auxiliary equipment determines just what such a web press can do in folding and bindery operations.

Many catalogs and folders show equipment or products in their actual colors but under a halftone. A sample of the color of paint used should be provided for matching. For matching hair tints in the maker's literature, one producer insisted on specimens of human hair with the tint applied. With eight-color work, the producer was taking no chances with color swatches.

Color matching is more satisfactory if variables are eliminated. The kind of light in which color is viewed is very important, the background against which color is seen influences the human eye, and all but the wanted color should be masked. Two persons rarely have identical color perception. A color match which is perfect according to instrument measurement may not appear so to an art director when he or she sees proof for approval.

REPLACEMENT OF LARGE SHEET-FED MULTICOLOR PRESSES BY WEB PRESSES

Several years ago the Printing Industries of America predicted that 60 percent of all commercial printing would be done on web presses by 1980. Sheet-fed offset presses larger than 60 inches (1524 millimeters) are disappearing, and all but the smaller orders of multicolor printing have been shifted to offset web presses. Not only are the rated speeds of these presses now 25,000 and 30,000 iph, but the web of paper is split and the sections fed into various types of bindery equipment for folded signatures or for a whole publication bound in a cover. The economy is so great that the printer avoids the usual bindery expense.

All the operations other than the printing are handled with auxiliary equipment, which governs just what a web press can do and its actual running speed. The simplest form of web production is to a sheeter, whose maximum speed may be 22,000 cuts an hour. Obviously the press speed must be reduced to that of the sheeter. But with this limitation the presswork is far faster than that of sheet-fed presses, both sides of the web are printed, and the printer has the layout flexibility of sheet-fed production.

TYPES OF WEB PRESSES

Most web presses are custom-made for size and kind of production. We are concerned mostly with commercial webs, but there are web offset presses for newspapers and other kinds of publications, as well as for books and special forms of production.

Web presses are available in different widths, usually up to 38 inches (965 millimeters). Cylinder circumferences of the 36- and 38-inch (914- and 965-millimeter) widths range from 22¾ inches (578 millimeters) to 23⁹/₁₆ inches (598 millimeters) or 24¹³/₁₆ inches (630 millimeters). This usually determines the cutoff size, but the use of auxiliary equipment makes variable cutoff sizes possible. The narrower web sizes have 11-, 17-, and 22-inch (279-, 432-, and 559-millimeter) cutoffs. An offset web press can use rolls of paper narrower than its maximum size. Roll width and cutoff size determine the size of the sheet before it is folded.

Commercial offset web presses compete with sheet-fed presses 38 inches and larger. The size for an 8½- by 11-inch (216- by 279-millimeter) page is a 26½- by 17⅜-inch (673- by 441-millimeter) cutoff; for a 9- by 12-inch (229 by 305-millimeter) page a roll 31 inches (787 millimeters) wide is used with a 19⅜-inch (492-millimeter) cutoff. There are also wide commercial web offset presses which can handle a 50-inch (1270-millimeter) web.

Web presses offer an additional economy with paper in rolls, averaging a saving of 15 to 20 percent. Moreover, thinner paper feeds better than on a sheet-fed press.

A basic advantage of web offset production, like that of sheet-fed production, is the low makeready expense. A producer with both letterpress and offset equipment for publications had this to say: "If the publications job were four-color, letterpress makeready would take from 24 to 48 hours. The same job run web-offset would be on the press and running in less than eight hours. At printing speeds of 20,000 impressions per hour, the minimum savings of 16 hours on web-offset makeready would produce 320,000 copies by the time the letterpress would be ready to start—enough copies to be important even on a two-million run."

Weekly news magazines are turning in whole or in part to web offset because of fast

M-80 Harris Eight-Page Web Press

Fig. 12-13 This is a four-color perfecting press designed to bring the productivity of web printing to the 38- to 40-inch (965- to 1016-millimeter) sheet-fed market. Using rolls of paper up to a width of 18½ inches (470 millimeters), it has a rated speed of 31,000 iph. It can be used profitably on run lengths as low as 10,000 signatures or sheets.

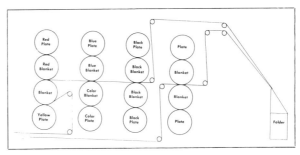

Fig. 12-14 Arrangement of cylinders for printing two colors and black on each side of one web and combining it with a second web, one color on each side. [*Courtesy Inland Printer*]

Fig. 12-15 A wide web, after being printed, is slit into narrower webs. With angle bars all three webs are combined for a multiple folded signature.

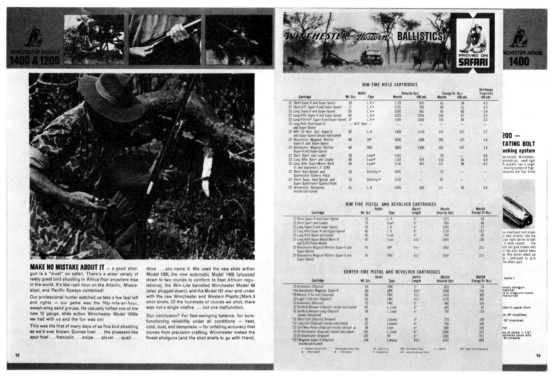

Fig. 12-16   This catalog of thirty-six pages in full color required a four-page center-fold insert on different stock with a narrower page width for the ammunition list. The web offset press handled both stocks with one pass for 3 million copies.

closing, faster and cheaper preparatory operations, and lower production costs to the advertiser for full-color pages. Work from transparencies to press is being handled overnight. *Electrical World* in a promotion to agencies showed that production costs for a full-color page in its offset section were less than $300. *Newsweek* magazine took a color picture in Texas and had it on its cover in 19 hours and 20 minutes by the use of web offset.

The odds are now about 50-50 whether negatives or relief plates will be shipped by advertisers to publications. Weekly newspapers are now printed predominantly by web offset. The American Newspaper Publishers Association (ANPA) estimates from its research that fewer than 200 dailies are printed on letterpress equipment. *The New York Times* and other large newspapers are now printed by offset. Book printing is now predominantly offset because of the efficiency of the web offset press and the economy in the use of halftones and process color illustrations.

In general, the minimum run with a web offset press is reported to be 10,000 impres-

sions or folded pieces. This figure is governed by the setup time required: if a job can use the setup on the press, the minimum may be lower. The long-life offset press plates now available can handle runs in the millions without the use of duplicate sets of plates.

The paper used for web offset ranges from regular newsprint, employed widely for newsstand illustrated periodicals, to machine-coated stock. A number of paper mills now feature O grade newsprint as a whiter sheet with a little more finish but still with greater bulk and opacity than the calendered or machine-coated stocks. Paper in rolls costs less than in sheets (20 percent differential), but web producers claim that the paper economy is less than this figure because of broken webs and paper spoilage at high speeds.

A CONTINUOUS OPERATION FROM PAPER ROLLS TO FINISHED PRODUCT

The folding and binding operations are the major bonus operations in web production. What a web press can do besides single-color or multicolor printing on both sides of the

Fig. 12-17

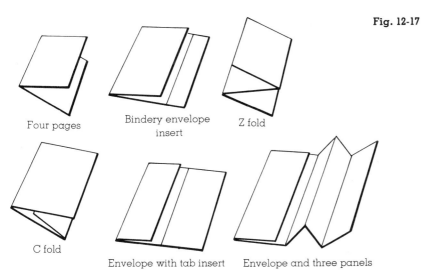

Four pages

Bindery envelope insert

Z fold

C fold

Envelope with tab insert

Envelope and three panels

Fig. 12-18 Offset web presses are custom-made for the great majority of orders, being designed for the type of printing production wanted. There can be a choice in one width by the roll width, or a wide roll can be slit and the other width depends on the cutoff of the press or on the use of supplementary equipment. Eight printing units provide a thirty-two-page signature for a magazine or catalog in full color. Four units may print two on two or three on one.

sheet depends on auxiliary equipment. The web itself, after being printed, can be slit (plow-cut), and with the use of angle bars sections can be combined for folding or diverted to folding equipment and trimming. Or the paper from two webs can be combined after folding to put a cover on a booklet or to handle a center-fold insert on different stock.

The Winchester catalog shown in Fig. 12-16 (full color; 3 million copies) is an example of the latter. Without the ammunition list on a different stock and in a narrower page width, this would be considered a rotogravure job, but with the web offset presses running more than one web of paper and being able to combine the webs as wanted, the job was naturally done by offset.

Examples of finished products printed on a web press and completed with an auxiliary finishing system are shown in Fig. 12-17.

Auxiliary Equipment Does the Folding and Bindery Operations

Copies of the revised Specifications for Web Offset Publications are available from the American Association of Advertising Agencies, 200 Park Ave., New York, N.Y. 10017; American Business Press, Inc., 205 E. 42nd St., New York, N.Y. 10017; and Magazine Publishers Association, Inc., 575 Lexington Ave., New York, N.Y. 10022.

Fig. 12-19

13

BINDERY ECONOMIES

PLANNING FOR PRESS PRODUCTION TAKES into consideration possible economies in the bindery and finishing operations which follow printing. When possible with multiple imposition, such economies may indicate the use of a larger press size even though such a size is less efficient for quantity alone: the bindery economy is greater than the higher press cost.

The user's production person should consult two or three of the producers with the larger presses for their recommendations as to whether or not worthwhile bindery economies would be practical with a larger form. In fact, it is not unusual for the user planning a large job to go directly to one or more binders for their recommendations on impositions; the selected producer is then referred to the binder for imposition layout. The producer's planning works backward from the binder's instructions.

PHASING OUT OF LARGE SHEET SIZES

With the wide use of offset web perfecting presses for multicolor printing except for small orders, sheet sizes larger than 60 inches (1524 millimeters), which were formerly used for multiple impositions to achieve bindery economies, are obsolete if folding is required. Since bindery cost is an important factor, imposition for the new smaller fast sheet-fed offset presses, now often converted to perfecting (printing on both sides) and sometimes in line with the roll sheeter, receives first consideration by the user in production planning. The press personnel schedules shown in Chapter 12 also are considered. Maximum sheet sizes for press staffing are shown in the accompanying table.

Number of colors	1 person	2 persons	3 persons	4 persons	5 persons
1 color	25″ × 29″	41″ × 56″			
2 colors	15″ × 18″	28″ × 41″	44″ × 65″		
4 colors			28″ × 40″	45″ × 56″	
5 colors			28″ × 40″	31½″ × 44″	44″ × 60″
6 colors				29″ × 41″	41″ × 56¾″

The number of persons required to run a press obviously has much to do with its hourly cost. The 25- by 38-inch (635- by 965-millimeter) offset press (maximum paper size) is very widely used because it is practical for various forms of automation with other operations and requires only two operators for two colors and three for four colors.

The new sizes of Baum folders should reflect the present requirements of the commercial printing industry:

400 series (commercial):	11½ by 18 inches
	18 by 25 inches
	20 by 32 inches
Registers for slitting, scoring, and perforating.	
600 series (professional):	20½ by 32 inches
	23½ by 46 inches
	26½ by 50 inches
Mark III (large production needs):	36 by 48 inches
	39 by 52 inches
	44 by 58 inches

SMALLER SHEET SIZES FIT AUTOMATIC EQUIPMENT

Some types of folding, particularly with heavier stock, are too slow with large sheets. For example, a four-page, 8½- by 11-inch (216- by 279-millimeter) folder on cover stock might be printed twelve up. For binding, three accordion folds could handle a section of six folders; however, this folding would be too slow to match the efficiency of one fold of a three-deep section on automatic equipment. In such a case, there would be no bindery efficiency with a form larger than three multiples. If the folder were printed in multiples of 4, in most cases the folding would be done in 2s.

When only cutting or trimming is required, as for return cards, coupons, square-cut labels, and the like, the smaller press sheets are suitable for fast, automatic equipment in the bindery.

Catalogs and booklets with a larger page size usually require right-angle folding with a large sheet. For economy, thirty-two- and sixteen-page signatures are best, preferably in even forms, all thirty-two-page or all sixteen-page signatures.

Stock for thirty-two-page signatures should not be more than 60 pounds (27.2 kil-

ograms) for antique, English-finish, machine-finish, or offset paper or 70 pounds (31.8 kilograms) for coated paper. Heavier stock is bound in sixteen-page signatures. Only the thinner book papers are bound as sixty-four-page signatures because of the danger of wrinkling or creasing with several right-angle folds.

VARIED BINDER'S IMPOSITION

Imposition not only varies according to the bindery equipment used but also according to the requirements of the job. The layout of color pages may make it desirable to put these near the gripper or guide edges of the sheet, or the lineup of rules or design on facing pages may make it desirable to place these pages on opposite sides of a fold. A cheaper imposition might result in a poor lineup.

In planning press production, it is important that bindery economies be considered and that these as well as press efficiency be figured in determining efficient press sizes for the job.

Work-and-Turn Press Imposition

For short and medium runs work-and-turn imposition is apt to be used, with the cut sheet folded as shown in Fig. 6-22. This job could also be planned for binding two deep.

Both front and back are printed on one side of sheet, and the sheet is then turned over and run through the press again. The sheet is cut in half, giving two signatures for binding. A plate and a makeready are saved. The cost of two pieces on a larger press is less than one piece on a smaller press.

Four-page folders are usually produced this way except in long runs. For booklets of eight pages, the cut sheet would be bound with two right-angle folds. Planning could provide for four on the press plate with the cut sheet bound two deep.

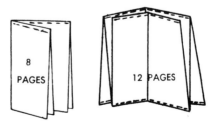

Fig. 13-1 Folded signature ready for binding and trimming.

Most Folding Can Be Done with a Long Section

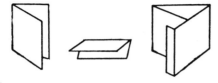

Fig. 13-2

Four pages (left and center) result from one upright fold. Six pages and a flap (right) are made with three parallel folds.

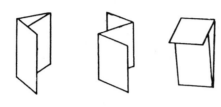

Six pages made from two parallel folds (left) and two accordion folds (center). Two parallel folds make four pages and a flap (right).

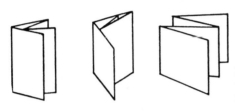

Eight pages made with two parallel folds (left), three parallel folds (center), and three accordion folds (right).

Bindery Economy Goes with a Large Sheet and a Long Folded Section

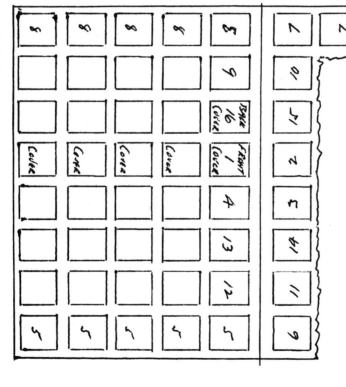

Fig. 13-3 Ten sixteen-page booklets were printed on the sheet work-and-turn. The sheet was cut, and the two signatures were folded five deep ready for stitching, the front being trimmed and cut apart in lifts. Folding, stitching, and trimming in multiples lower bindery expense. This job illustrates the bindery economy with a long folded section.

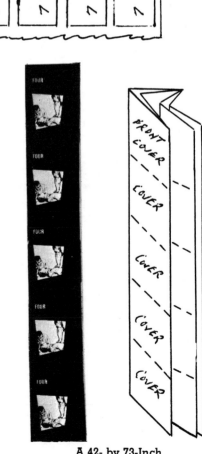

A 42- by 73-Inch (1067- by 1854-Millimeter) Press Sheet and Folded Section Five Deep

When considering bindery economies, we must remember from Chapter 12 that use of offset web presses, particularly for two- and four-color printing, has largely replaced use of sheet-fed presses larger than 60 inches (1524 millimeters). A major advantage in addition to greater press speeds is that the web is usually folded and bound; a booklet can even be inserted and bound with its cover and delivered trimmed. The capability of these presses depends on auxiliary equipment. For details, refer to Chapter 12.

The Number of Signatures as a Cost Factor in Binding Booklets

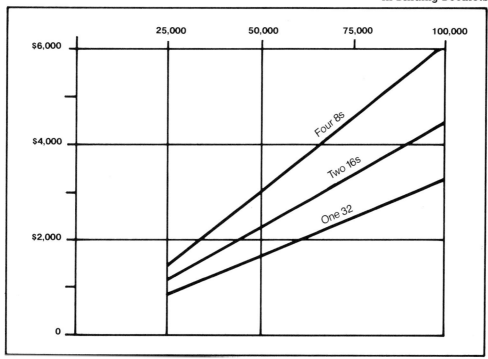

Fig. 13-4 This graph illustrates the economy of larger signatures for bound booklets. Figures used are from an estimating service. They cover thirty-two-page booklets, saddle-stitched, without cover, and with a page size of 8½ by 11 inches (216 by 279 millimeters).

14

SELECTING THE PRODUCER AND ORDERING

IN SELECTING THE PRINTING PRODUCER for a specific job, you are buying the necessary facilities and skills. In smaller cities producers handle the needs of the community. In larger cities they tend to be more selective in soliciting business because of their equipment and the quality of their workmanship, some of them specializing in particular types of production or service. Reliability and organization are important.

KNOWLEDGE OF FACILITIES AND SERVICE

Large users of a variety of printing requirements, such as advertising agencies and national accounts, do business regularly with many different printing organizations. Their lists range from A (top-quality) and B (commercial-quality) process color producers, through specialists in posters, dealer displays, and labels, and producers geared for simple color and single-color printing, to letter shops and contract "production" printers, who handle fast ordinary-quality work.

In addition to a printer's facilities, reliability and quality standards are very important. Before large users put a printing producer on a list for bids, they generally inspect the printer's shop, check its organization, and list the press sizes, process, and other facilities of interest. It may be obvious that the quality of the shop's work is not up to the standard wanted or that the organization consists of one key person. If that person is absent, questions will not be answered or instructions taken by telephone.

SEASONAL VARIATION AND PRINTING VOLUME

As in most industries, the supply and demand for printing varies seasonally, ranging from 50 percent below to 50 percent above the annual average. Demand is low from April to July and high in early spring and in autumn. To retain their organizations printers must keep their presses busy. This necessity influences their prices, and in extreme situations a volume job quotation may be very low.

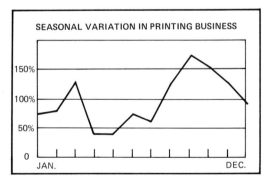

Fig. 14-1 The graph shows the number of orders received monthly in a major printing center and indicates the monthly variation in the area. It is a coincidence that the variation closely checks with the sale of consumer goods.

Pricing policies may change. For example, a producer's quotation may be cushioned for such customer's errors as inaccurate or incomplete camera copy or a greater number of focuses than were specified. If the cushion is removed from the quotation, extra charges are added because copy has not been supplied as specified.

GETTING BIDS

The purpose of getting bids from several producers on a sizable job is to determine the going market rate on printing and the current situation with the producers selected. A low bid does not always secure the order; usually the order is given to the most suitable producer for the job if the price is in line with the market.

Bids should be obtained only from shops of comparable quality and service. Quality printers usually insist on knowing which shops have been asked to bid; if what they consider to be a lower-grade shop is included, they will refuse to bid. Estimates cost money. It is meaningless to get bids from unknown printers. Their conception of quality work varies widely, and there will be a correspondingly wide variation in quotations, particularly if few specifications have been supplied.

Very large multicolor printing jobs, such as an annual calendar, are frequently placed in a slack season regardless of the date when they are needed. In a slack season a printer with large four-color offset presses will usually offer a very low bid for work that will keep such a press running for a week or two.

Industrial advertisers generally do all their ordering through a purchasing director, who bases the choice on price. In such a case the advertising department generally provides a bid list, which does not include printing producers who are unqualified for the quality and service wanted.

The delivery date frequently is more important to the user than price, and it always has a bearing on the producer's price. When the user eliminates rush work by planning, overtime costs are avoided.

PLACING AN ORDER WITHOUT A QUOTATION

Most small orders are placed without getting bids because of lack of time and the small cost

involved. Sufficient work of such a nature should be placed with two or three producers to warrant the special attention given a regular account. This policy also affords a method of checking prices.

Among the specialists in various types of production are contract shops that want a steady volume from a limited number of accounts. Costs are usually determined on a price-list basis, under a contractual arrangement that provides the producer with a volume of a particular type of production without the usual sales expense. This arrangement is common with small orders for ordinary-quality black-and-white printing for delivery in a day or two: bulletins, notices to salesmen or distributors, and so on.

COMPLETE INFORMATION FOR ACCURATE ESTIMATE

As camera-ready copy nears completion, job specifications should be prepared, and the sales representatives of selected producers should be shown the layout and camera copy (at least the roughs). The producers' estimators will want to see the color art or at least pencil tracings with notations. Polaroid cameras are sometimes used if the artwork cannot be taken to the printer's shop. Sales representatives usually make out a standard form, "Request for Estimate," which should contain all the data necessary for an accurate estimate. This producer's estimate should be in written form for the customer. A delivery date earlier than conditions require should be avoided because such a date may necessitate overtime and raise the price.

The winning producing organization is usually advised as early as possible so that it can order the paper and schedule the job in its production department. The formal purchase order is accompanied by the job specifications and dummy, together with all camera copy except process copy, which should be sent earlier because it requires more time. A list of what is being sent helps the producer check to make certain that nothing is missing and that specifications do not differ from the data on which the quotation and delivery date are based.

Jobs using the same process art in different plate sizes should always be placed with the same producer, the producer who makes the color separations. If copies of the separations are to be supplied to another producer (for posters, displays, and so on), this proviso should be included in the specifications. However, quotations frequently include all work even though some pieces are jobbed out to specialists (canvas banners, wall hangings, and so on).

For a firm quotation, complete specifications are usually necessary, and the form of the copy and the delivery schedule should be as originally specified to the producer's sales representative. Quoted prices are usually based on "copy ready for the camera" and are "subject to inspection of artwork."

A producer schedules work for various departments, and if artwork is not ready as specified, the resulting delay will remove the job from the schedule. Overtime may be required to adhere to the original delivery date. If the budget requires a low price, extra time is a factor. Not only will overtime be avoided, but the job may be scheduled, at least in part, as a filler. The user should have an understanding from each producer of the length of time in which a quotation and delivery date will remain firm.

By trade custom, negatives and plates supplied by a producer remain the property of the producer, and any other arrangement should be in writing. Moreover, 10 percent over or under the quantity ordered constitutes delivery unless the user specifies otherwise in writing.

IMPORTANT: Never give a job without a written order, and never take a job without a written order.

Appendix

1

CHECKLIST: PREPARATION OF ART AND TYPE FOR THE CAMERA

1. Know exactly what you want to do and be able to explain your job to the producer clearly.

2. Consult with the producer during the preparation of the copy, and accept the producer's advice.

3. Provide a complete dummy with specifications for the job.

4. Submit all the copy for the job complete before shooting, neatly prepared, clean, and clearly marked with all instructions.

5. Don't request changes while the job is in progress.

6. Provide with the job samples of the paper and the colors to be used.

Preparing Mechanicals

Here are some helpful hints to be kept in mind when preparing mechanicals:

1. Prepare mechanicals for the same size.

2. Be sure that they are accurately squared.

3. Be sure that the type lines up.

4. Be sure that your Photostats or vandykes are accurately pasted down.

5. Key mechanicals with page and code numbers.

6. Identify all marks for corners, trim, folds, and bleeds in red ink.

7. Indicate reverses on an overlay. Circle reverses in red ink or, better still, paste in reverse Photostats.

8. Indicate tint areas with a solid black panel or a red outline, and provide a sample of the precise tint wanted.

9. Indicate the breakdown of color on an overlay as solids, if possible, or outlined in red ink. Be sure to provide samples of colors.

10. Prepare spreads in imposed form if possible.

11. Paste up mechanicals on clean white heavy board.

12. Erase all pencil guidelines, and remove all rubber cement.

Preparing Type and Proofs

The following are pointers for preparing and organizing type:

1. Pull type proofs in the same size.

2. When possible, set type areas in the exact position.

3. Select typefaces with strong serifs and body, especially when you know that they will be used as a reverse area (white on black).

4. Check for clean, even reproduction proofs on white coated stock. Desirable papers are Lusterkote, Kromekote, and Relyon reproduction paper.

5. Examine type for worn and broken letters and missing serifs.

6. Avoid smearing.

7. Supply extra proofs.

Line Copy

Here's a checklist to be used when preparing line copy:

1. Be sure that all line copy is drawn in solid, dull black on white paper.

2. Be sure that outlines are sharp and free from smears.

3. Be sure that all copy is clearly marked for size.

4. Check vertical and horizontal proportions against each other.

5. Prepare as much copy as possible for the same proportionate reduction or enlargement to permit money-saving grouping.

6. Prepare overlays on clear acetate, Vinylite, or white tracing paper, in black ink or dull black color for large areas.

7. When converting from letterpress proofs, be sure that proofs show unsmeared solid-dot reproductions.

8. Be sure that drawings on Ross board are jet black and clean.

9. Be sure that Craftint copy and Zip-a-Tone tints are clean and smooth.

10. Examine the completed copy for dirt, smudges, extraneous pencil lines, and so on.

Tone

Keep in mind these pointers when planning pictures for halftone reproduction:

1. Mark photos for their correct size and precise proportions.

2. Indicate crop and bleed positions.

3. Outline silhouettes in Chinese white.

4. Prepare pictures for the same proportionate enlargement or reduction.

5. Avoid excessive enlargement or reduction.

6. Mount photos on smooth white board. Avoid ferrotyping, which can cause trouble.

7. Don't write on the backs of prints; don't stamp prints with rubber stamps.

8. Be sure that photos are rich in detail and have good-quality highlights and shadows. Be sure that middle tones are clearly defined.

9. Indicate dropouts when you want them; use Chinese white.

10. Retouch with grays of the same cast throughout a job.

11. Avoid delicate vignettes in pencil or wash drawings. Be sure that the board is white and that there is a definite step between background and art.

12. Maintain scrupulous cleanliness.

Art for Color Reproduction Transparencies

These ideas may be of help in preparing art for color reproduction with transparencies (Kodachromes, Ektachromes):

1. Use a standard viewing light.

2. Maintain the balance of color.

3. Avoid excessive contrast, dark shadows, and burned-out highlights.

4. Prepare for some compromise because the range of color and tone in transparencies is twice that of a printed sheet.

5. Use a color photo laboratory to enlarge small transparencies for color correction or to produce larger prints. Scale or proportion tone for same-focus economies. Color-correct a duplicate instead of using an expensive transparency. Convert a single opaque subject to a transparency if other subjects are transparencies, or vice versa. Prepare an assembly for electronic scanning machine separations.

6. Keep the copy clean. Protect it with a cellophane envelope.

Opaque Process Copy (Paintings, Color Photoprints, and So On)

1. Keep the copy clean.

2. Scale and position with color photoprints or proportion subjects in one or more groups for a reduction in size.

3. Convert a transparency to a color print if the group for same-focus reproduction is opaque.

4. Use clean colors in the same brand for a group. Don't overpaint, but remove old work.

5. Accept a compromise when particular colors are unobtainable with the four-color process.

6. Use overlays for knockouts or for overprinting type, or prepare overlays on Photostats.

7. Avoid knockouts when printing several colors within an area, for the register is difficult.

Appendix
2

CHECKLIST: OFFSET SPECIFICATIONS

General

Customer's name; brand name
Present or last supplier
Address
Credit rating (source)
Sales representative
Date when estimate is wanted
Approximate date on which order is to be placed
Quality required:
 Equal to sample
 Regular commercial
 Best
Have we printed or figured this or a similar job before?
Approximate unit price or total price customer wants to pay (arrived at from best sources available at the time estimate was requested)
Subject (kind of job and description)
Quantity
Size:
 Page size; flat size; sheet size; folded size
 Size of backs
 Gang size
 Size of pad
 Trimmed or untrimmed
 Can dimensions be altered slightly for economy purposes?
Layout:
 Number on; allowances between subjects; printing allowance
 Sheet size
 Number of pages
 Number of leaves if calendar pad
Margins (white; bleed; even color; number of sides)
Cover (self or separate; flush or extended)

Glue laps (size—left or right; free from color; varnish)
Form number or imprint:
 Litho; printed or made in the United States; company imprint
 Union label
 Copyright notice
Instruction sheets:
 Furnished by us?
 Specifications
Number of samples (for customer; for sales representative's file)
End use:
 Customer intends to use subjects as giveaway, at point of purchase for resale, in packaging product
 Will be packed by hand or by machine; will be applied by machine
 Will be in contact with food products; should be resistant to finger marks and soiling; will be exposed to weather or bright sun; other uses

Artwork

Please furnish pencil tracing, rough sketch, printed sample to show nature of job
When will art be ready? (Size of art or reduction)
Condition of art:
 Completely assembled—ready for camera
 Complete black-and-white paste-up; full-color art separate but properly assembled
 Other (Describe fully number of scales in black and white and in color)
Type of art:
 Full-color (transparency; oil painting; watercolor; pastel; color print; other)

Black-and-white (photos retouched; photos not retouched; airbrush; other)

What lettering can be set in type?

Composition and reproduction proofs furnished; number of pages

If by us, what size and face, page size, number of pages?

What special colors must be matched in printing?

On completion, return artwork to:

Nature of art:

    Are illustrations still lifes or figures? (Give description of illustrations, including size, nature, number, and so on)

    Does the customer's production of the package reproduce in the illustration?

    How much of design consists of lettering?

Printing

Method of printing (process); sheet-fed; web; other

Number of printings

Print from deep-etch, albumen, other

Special operations:

    Imprint (number of colors; number of imprints; number of lines per imprint)

    Number

    Press perforation

    Press score

    Pen rule; sides; ways

    Bronze (area)

    Emboss (number of subjects)

    Is enclosure material printed? (Envelopes, containers)

Rerun possibility (assured; possibly; no)

Grind off plates

Wash off glass

Kill standing type

Ink and Varnish

Ink coverage percentage area (submit sample, tracing, description)

Regular, gloss, or metallic inks

Special requirements (permanent or fadeproof; odorless; acid-resistant; nontoxic)

Varnish (printed; spirit; lacquer; other)

Gum (spot; strip; solid)

Positives and Negatives

Plates, positives, or negatives:

    On hand; furnished by customer

    If furnished

        Negatives (glass or film)

        Positives (glass or film)

        Will negatives or positives fit our step-and-repeat machine?

Type of reproduction:

    Process halftone

    Special colors

    Benday; strip tints

    Duotone

    Line only; flat colors

    Fake

Proofs:

    Quantity required

    Full-color

    Partial (Which part?)

    Blueprint; ozalid; salt print

    Press

    None

    Proof date necessary

Stock

We to supply

Customer to furnish (If furnished, will moisture content be in balance with our requirements, or will conditioning be necessary?)

Grain of printing sheet if furnished

Weight basis (paper); thickness (board)

Texture and finish (CW1S; CW2S; super; offset MF; bond; other)

Color of stock

Grain of subject on sheet

Specific brand of stock if required

Finishing Operations

Emboss

Gum (spot, strip; solid; which dimension?)

Varnish; lacquer; other

Mount (number of points finished thickness; kind of board liner)

Die cut (irregular; square)

Score (one side; two sides)

Guillotine cut; corner cut

Easel (kind and size; stock)

Drill and punch (size; rounds or slot or Kalamazoo)

Eyelet (size; kind)

String (kind; length)

Fold (number of folds)

Insert

Stitch (saddle; side; number)

Sewing

Pad (number up; edge)

Hinge (cloth or invisible; top or bottom cover)

Enclose (in envelopes, containers, bags, tubes; stiffener; seal; tuck-in flap; clasp; paper ends)

Tipping

Collate (How many signatures?)

Round corners (How many?)

Perforate (pin or slot; Damon one or two ways)

Glue (pasting)

Slip sheet; tissue; wax

Machine or print ruling

Binding (manila top; strawboard back; cloth strip; full duck tight back; single thread; double thread; quarter bind; green edge)

Laminating bind (size of comb; color)

Plastic

Crimp

Packing

Band (paper or rubber)

String tie

Completely wrapped

Chipboard

Bundle

Individual folders; bulk corrugated; wooden cases; skids or pallets

Special copy for stenciling or printing of containers

Size or weight limit

How many in?

Zoning; addressing; typing labels; attaching labels and postage; bundle; handling; stamps (regular; precanceled; furnished with order)

Delivery

Hold (How long?); deferred billing (Give details)

When? (partial; complete) Where?

Method of shipment; transportation charges (prepaid or collect); advance copies

Amount of overrun

Drop shipments (How many? Will labels be furnished?)

Invoicing Instructions

Mail to attention of:

Transportation prepaid? Collect?

How many copies?

Appendix
3

TRADE CUSTOMS

Alterations Proposals are only for work according to original specifications. If through the customer's error or change of mind work must be done a second or additional times, such extra work will carry an additional charge at prevailing rates for the work performed.

Approval of proofs If proofs are submitted to the customer, corrections, if any, must be made thereon and the proofs returned to the producer marked "OK" or "OK with corrections" and signed with the name or initials of the person duly authorized to pass on the proofs. If revised proofs are desired, the request must be made when proof is returned. The producer is not responsible for errors if work is completed per the customer's OK.

Color proofing Because of the difference in equipment and conditions between the color proofing and the pressroom operations, a reasonable variation in color between color proofs and the completed job shall constitute an acceptable delivery.

Customer's property The producer shall charge the customer at prevailing rates for handling and storing the customer's paper stock or printed matter held more than 30 days. All the customer's property that is stored with a printer is at the customer's risk, and the printer is not liable for any loss or damage thereto caused by fire, water, leakage, breakage, theft, negligence, insects, rodents, or any other cause beyond the printer's control. It is understood that the gratuitous storage of the customer's property is solely for the benefit of the customer.

Delays in delivery All agreements are made and all orders accepted contingent upon strikes, fires, accidents, wars, flood, or other causes beyond the printer's control.

Delivery Unless otherwise specified, the price quoted is for a single shipment, FOB the customer's local place of business. All estimates are based on continuous and uninterrupted delivery of the complete order unless specifications distinctly state otherwise.

Drawings, negatives, and plates Artwork, drawings, negatives, positives, plates, and other items supplied by the producer shall remain the producer's exclusive property unless otherwise agreed in writing.

Experimental work Experimental work, such as sketches, drawings, composition, plates, presswork, and materials, performed at the customer's request, will be charged for.

Orders Regularly entered orders cannot be canceled except under terms that will compensate the producer or printer for loss.

Paper stock furnished by customer Paper stock furnished by the customer shall be properly packed, free from dirt, grit, torn sheets, bad splices, and so on, and of proper quality and specifications for the printer's requirements. Additional cost due to delays or impaired production because of improper packing or quality shall be charged to the customer.

Press proofs An extra charge will be made for press proofs unless the customer is present when the plate is made ready on the press so that no press time is lost. Presses standing awaiting the OK of the customer will be charged for at current rates for the time so consumed.

Quantities delivered Overruns or underruns not to exceed 10 percent of the amount ordered shall constitute an acceptable delivery, and the excess or deficiency shall be charged or credited to the customer proportionately.

Sketches and dummies Sketches, copy, dummies, and all preparatory work created or furnished by the producer shall remain producer's exclusive property, and no use of this material shall be made, or any ideas obtained therefrom be used, except upon compensation to be determined by the owner.

Terms Terms are net cash, 30 days, unless otherwise provided in writing. All claims must be made within 5 days of receipt of goods.

Appendix
4
GLOSSARY[1]

Burn *See* PLATE BURN.

Camera-ready art Typical black-and-white or color art and illustration assemblies suitable for photographing in a process camera.

Contact-printing frame Glass-topped frame used to bring a film into contact with another film or plate for the purpose of perfect emulsion-to-emulsion contact. It is usually vacuum-operated.

Cropping Trimming an illustration of "excess" or nonimportant details so that it better suits the purpose of the page design.

Density On film negatives, the greatest density area is the area that is blackest or most developed.

Emulsion Usually a thin, membranelike surface that is the working surface of photographic films as well as of Ulano Rubylith and Amberlith. The emulsion is coated on a support base to facilitate stripping, processing, and handling.

Fatty Designating a photographic internegative mask which slightly enlarges copy. This technique, performed in a contact printer, makes possible precision butting and kissing of tints, screens, colors, and halftones. Its most common use is for the accurate overlap of two stripped elements.

Flat Assembly of various film negatives or positives attached in register to a piece of film, goldenrod, or suitable masking material; an assembly of film elements ready to be exposed to a plate; all elements on the flat exposed on one plate.

Floating Technique of attaching peeled Rubylith and Amberlith to another film support base. The peeled Ulano emulsion is laid sticky side up on a flat surface, and the other film is dropped carefully on top of it. This procedure eliminates the chance of wrinkles or bubbles forming.

Highlight In a photograph the highlight area is the lightest area. Often it is as bright as the paper

on which the photoprint or artwork was prepared. It is represented by the densest portion of a continuous-tone negative and the smallest dot formation in a halftone negative and printing plate.

Key (key negative) Most paste-up art has key lines, indications from the artist of where a panel, color tint, or halftone is to be positioned. The term "key negative" or "key plate" usually refers to a negative or plate that carries most or all of these indications as a guide for the stripper.

Mask Hand-cut or photographically prepared cell that effectively blocks out light in areas where light is not wanted. Ulano Rubylith and Amberlith are hand-cut masking films.

Moiré pattern Undesirable pattern occurring when reproductions are made from halftone proofs, caused by conflict between the ruling of the halftone screen and the dots or lines of the original; a similar pattern occurring in multicolor halftone reproductions, usually due either to incorrect screen angles or to misregister of the color impressions during printing.

Opaque Designating a substance and technique for applying light-obstructing paint to negatives in order to eliminate unwanted areas or imperfections from the negative.

Overlay cell Element of clear material with mask areas or artwork intended for masking negatives or preparing camera-ready copy. *See also* MASK.

Pin register Method of getting fast and efficient register by using a punch not unlike a three-hole binder punch. Copy, film, masks, internegatives, and plates can all be punched identically. Punched material is then put on register pins to achieve fast register.

Plate burn Exposing a plate.

Register pins Stubby pins usually attached to a small metal base. They correspond to the size of register punch holes. *See also* PIN REGISTER.

Screen angles Screens and tint screen lines should run at predetermined angles when they overprint. Incorrect angles can result in moiré ef-

[1]Courtesy Ulano Graphic Arts, 210 East 86th Street, New York, N.Y. 10028.

fects. Check the manufacturer's specifications for exact angles.

Shadow area   Darkest area in a photograph. Control of the values of this area in halftone preparation is accomplished by a supplemental "flashing" of the film to a filtered light. This reinforces the dot exposure in the dark areas only.

Staging   Chemical alteration and controlled deletion of developed silver deposits from film.

Stripper's blotter   Usually several stiff yet pliable cuts of cardboard or bristol board for making an effective burnishing instrument to rub out air bubbles or apply smoothly adhesive-backed film to another support base. The term originates from the technique photoengravers use to squeeze moisture from under stripping film as it is applied to the glass plate.

Stripping tweezers   Sharply pointed pair of tweezers. Its fine points allow stripper to slip the tip under the Ulano emulsion and peel it back.

Support base   Usually a stable and manageable cell of material upon which film emulsions are coated. Ulano Rubylith and Amberlith support bases are 0.003, 0.005, and 0.007 inch (0.076, 0.127, and 0.178 millimeter) in polyester and 0.005 inch (0.127 millimeter) in vinyl.

Tint (tint screen)   Various tones (strengths) of a solid color used for rough work. Sometimes a piece of stock shading sheet is pasted down on the copy, which is handled as line copy. Photographic (halftone) tints are stock developed film (negative and positive) in various strengths of tone (25 percent, 50 percent, and so on) and usually 133-line screen that are prepared by the camera department and inserted by the stripper as indicated on copy.

Window   Clear, usually rectangular or square panel in a litho negative. Halftone negatives are positioned in this window, usually with tape or rubber cement.

Index